NEW PATHWAYS TO APPROVALS

Developing Better Communities Together

Michael A. von Hausen

Advance Praise for
New Pathways to Approvals

Michael is a pro's pro, whether working inside City Hall, trying to open up City Hall, or having the community say 'yes'. His advice is wise, and seasoned with years of superb education, training, and experience.

– **Mike Harcourt**, *Former Premier of British Columbia; former Mayor of Vancouver*

This thoughtful and comprehensive text unpacks how projects get stuck and plots a new course through one of the world's most complex and challenging development ecosystems. For developers, regulators, or students; everyone needs *New Pathways to Approvals.*

– **Gordon Harris**, *President and CEO, Simon Fraser University Community Trust*

This is a seminal read and resource for cross-discipline professionals and engaged citizenry on the 'sweet spot' between planning, development, community-building and the critical roles and relationships needed for success. Michael's renaissance-like experience in all of these arenas, and strategic style, prove a great recipe.

– **Susan Haid**, *Deputy Director of Planning, Long Range and Strategic Planning, City of Vancouver*

While this book has all you will ever need to know about the mechanics and legalities of development approvals, its real value is in the lessons it provides on development as a human process driven by trust, relationships, and perceptions. It should be on the desk of anyone who wants to help build better communities in the post COVID-19 era.

– **Ken Cameron**, *Former Manager, Metro Vancouver Regional Planning; former CEO, British Columbia Homeowner Protection Office; Adjunct Professor, Urban Studies, Simon Fraser University*

This is one of Michael's very best books! Michael imparts much knowledge in this book from his experiences being creatively artful in applying a hard to define science, while never forgetting that what we do in our work is *all about people.*

– **Bob Ransford**, *Vice President, Development, The Century Group*; *Former Chair of the Board, Smart Growth BC; Columnist, Vancouver Sun*

I am very impressed with this work. It's a rich composition of wisdom, insights and coaching that is unparalleled among the resources available to all community builders—be they developers, planners and policy makers, councils, designers or community advocates—who wish to better understand the unique context they are working in and deliver more success in their projects.

– **Deana Grinnell**, *Vice President, Real Estate (BC and Ontario), Canada Lands Company; President, Vancouver Chapter, LAI Land Economics Society*

Once again, Michael von Hausen has packed an enormous amount of wisdom and experience into an easy-to-read book. His unique combination of technical skills and personal charisma are clear in this book, and he provides a great guide in how to think about, and act effectively, through the difficult approvals processes that characterize nearly every development project in our urban centres. A great contribution to the industry.

– **Mark Holland**, *President, Holland Planning Innovations; Professor, Master of Community Planning Program, Vancouver Island University*

It is often said that you can't judge a book by its cover, and this seems most apt for Michael von Hausen's latest book. While it may appear to be about obtaining building approvals, it is much more since it offers valuable lessons for property developers, planners, government officials, politicians and private citizens wanting to create better neighbourhoods and cities.

– **Michael Geller**, *President, The Geller Group; Adjunct Professor, SFU Centre for Sustainable Development, Resource and Environmental Management; Columnist, The Vancouver Courier*

Through his decades of professional practice and teaching, Michael von Hausen offers a constellation for readers to navigate the waters of real estate development. An undiscovered country for many, he layouts the terrain of a project approval process approach from concept to completion. Readers, from newcomers to practicing professionals in urban development, will find this book a great addition to their toolkits.

– **Andy Yan**, *Director of the City Program, Simon Fraser University; former member of the City of Vancouver City Planning Commission; former member of the Development Permit Board Advisory Panel*

This is a book that sets out, for all those involved in the important work of placemaking, a well-conceived, clear, articulate analysis of 'the how' for improving the development approval process. In so doing, it lays out a critical foundation for the delivery of enhanced, higher quality development that addresses the needs of both the development industry and affected community.

– **David R. Witty**, *Senior Fellow, Urban Design, Master of Community Planning Program, Vancouver Island University; former Dean of Architecture, University of Manitoba*

Michael is a gifted planner, teacher, and negotiator. His personal charm and wisdom are apparent in his latest book, drawing upon decades inside and outside city hall. Michael unpacks a tangled, mangled, and bungled spool of civic barbwire. This is a must-read for all students and urban planners who want to stay relevant in the 21st century.

– **Gary Pooni,** *President, Pooni Group Inc.; Member, Urban Development Institute Board of Directors; former Chair, Downtown Vancouver Business Improvement Association*

This book addresses a series of critical disconnects among the approaches, practicalities and politics of application, review, and approval processes. Ideally, all parties can find ways to work together to build better communities, places that elevate the lived experiences for all. The text provides a roadmap for navigating this terrain and creating places we are proud to call home, and should be required reading for students, politicians, planners, and all who inhabit our shared spaces.

– **Pamela Shaw**, *Director, Master of Community Planning Program, Vancouver Island University; Research Director, Mount Arrowsmith Biosphere Region Research Institute; Member, College of the Royal Society of Canada*

One of my favourite Zen quotes is, "It takes a wise man to learn from his mistakes, but an even wiser man to learn from others." Michael has captured decades of invaluable knowledge within a well-written, interesting, and easy-to-understand book. An incredible effort and a must-read for all involved, or even interested in, real estate. Well done!

– **David Eger**, *Vice President, Western Canada, Research, Valuation & Advisory, Altus Expert Services, Altus Group*

This is the book that every student and professional in architecture and urban design, development and real estate, planning and approvals, local politics and community involvement—yes, all of them, not just the developers—needs, whether they know it or not. While Vancouver-specific, the lessons, insights and instructions are generally applicable. It's a book that will make even seasoned veterans of the development game stop and say, "Oh, if only I knew that, not just when I started my career but yesterday when I was starting a new project."

– **Gordon Price**, *Fellow at the SFU Centre for Dialogue; former Director, SFU City Program; former Councillor, City of Vancouver*

Michael is a thoughtful and excellent communicator with fascinating insights. He brings a unique perspective with decades of experience which allows him to demonstrate how to navigate what, at times, can be a very daunting and complicated process to find common ground. In so doing, he brings opposing positions to the same side of the table and reaches a results-oriented conclusion. The process is a journey and Michael's book provides facts, figures and, most importantly, real stories to learn from. An industry 'must read' and a long-term resource!

– **David R. Bouskill**, *Vice President, Realtech Capital Group Inc.*

As our world changes and we enter a 'new normal', this book offers a timely analysis and hope for the future based on Michael's nine characteristics of the *Approvals+* process. Although twists and turns in approving developments in communities large and small are part of the real estate development process, this book offers insights, lessons, strategies, and touchstones for all parties. Michael candidly challenges readers engaged in different aspects of real estate development to thoughtfully consider multiple viewpoints. Michael's '*Rule One: Be nimble and adjust*' has a whole new meaning today.

– **Judy Oberlander**, *Former director, City Program, Simon Fraser University; former member of the Development Permit Board Advisory Panel, City of Vancouver*

Michael has provided a very comprehensive review of the development approvals process from the perspective of all stakeholders, public and private. This book highlights the multi-faceted, strategic balancing needed to secure approvals acceptable to all parties, while also meeting the critical test of project economic viability. A must-read for newcomers to the development process, as well as a refresher for seasoned professionals.

– **Hugh W. Carter**, *General Manager, Pollyco Group of Companies*

NEW PATHWAYS TO APPROVALS

DEVELOPING BETTER COMMUNITIES TOGETHER

Michael A. von Hausen
vhausen@telus.net or www.mvhinc.com

President, MVH Urban Planning & Design Inc.
Adjunct Professor, Simon Fraser University
and Vancouver Island University

With support from the
Urban Development Institute Pacific Region,
FortisBC, and Simon Fraser University City Program

New Pathways To Approvals

Tellwell Talent
www.tellwell.ca

ISBN
978-0-2288-4196-8 (Hardcover)
978-0-2288-4195-1 (Paperback)
978-0-2288-4197-5 (eBook)

This book is for the developers, builders, municipalities, regional districts, provincial and federal governments, First Nations, and community members who are charged with the awesome task of helping review, approve, and build our next generation of Canadian communities.

Thanks to FortisBC, the Urban Development Institute Pacific Region, and Simon Fraser University's City Program for their support over the past 20 years in helping train the next generation of real estate development professionals and urban designers.

This book is dedicated to the memory of my dear friends and colleagues Don Wuori, Randy Fasan, and Paul Rollo who were committed to planning, designing, and building great places.

And finally, thanks to my family, Laura, Athena, and Jackson, who support me with unconditional love and devotion.

Table of Contents

PART 3: TRANSFORMATIONS

PREFACE

I have been on three sides of the application and approvals process over the past 40 years. First, I was on the development side, then I was on the City of Vancouver side, and now for the past 20 years I've been on the private consulting, financing, and teaching side.

During the scope of my career, I've worked across Canada, the United States, and internationally, and I've seen much development, and I know what works and doesn't work. Today, because I have both private and public clients, I still see both sides of the coin. I even facilitate strategic workshop sessions with governing councils and so am able to observe processes that occur at the highest level of approvals.

I have also had the privilege of developing and facilitating the sought-after FortisBC School of Development courses for the Urban Development Institute (UDI) Pacific Region over the last 20 years. The support and generosity of UDI, FortisBC, and the development community for this program have been outstanding. Without them, and our team approach, the UDI FortisBC School of Development would not continue to grow and prosper. We strive to make content rich, progressive, and relevant by bringing in new faculty and current projects in rotation. One example is a course we developed in the early 2000s called *The Art of Approvals*. This course emphasizes the importance of the technical and process side of development applications and approvals. Many students still come to me after the course and tell me the course was amazing, and then they ask, "But how can I learn more?"

In 2019, the Province of British Columbia stepped up and completed a *Development Approvals Process Review* that reinforced my observations. This study exemplifies a concerted effort to highlight the challenges and opportunities affecting development approvals today.

This book takes the provincial study a few steps further. It not only explains the *why* and the *what* of approvals, but it offers ideas on *how* to improve this challenged and conflicted landscape. However, we need the cooperation and support of all those involved in approvals processes to make improvement happen. Ultimately, improved approvals are really about building mutually beneficial, trusting relationships with a common end goal of creating great communities. This book is hopefully part of shaping those *New Pathways to Approvals*.

Michael von Hausen, January 2021

INTRODUCTION

Unfortunately, all too often, what occurs is a free-for-all between competing self-interests, and the city becomes a chaos, resulting in the lowest common denominator—the collective interest suffers but so do many individual interests.

—*Larry Beasley, Vancouverism (2019)*

Same Processes, Same Results

It happens more frequently now; it is bad news, but not to my surprise. I get a phone call, or a person approaches me after a seminar at Simon Fraser University or the Urban Development Institute, and they say almost desperately, "We have a problem and think we need your help." Often, I sit down over tea or coffee to chat with this person to discuss the challenges with their development, and usually they wonder if it may be too late to save their project. By the time they talk to me, their project is already dead or nearly dead. The damage has been done and the question now is, is the prognosis terminal or can it be saved?

Normally, the same themes emerge—the project has been turned down by the municipality or the regional district, or a perceived insurmountable issue is stopping it from progressing. In some cases, the project is in a never-ending game of what seems like amusement park bumper cars bumping into each other and getting nowhere, with constant and never-ending meetings being held that result in no substantial progress. Eventually, trust evaporates between parties, and the relationships dissolve. In extreme cases, after significant expenditure of funds on site plans, architectural drawings, and other professional assistance, the project is barely alive. By this time, not only has it little or no support from municipal staff and council, but often the surrounding community is also against it. The developer has spent most, if not all, of their money and are not sure if they can keep going. They are facing a dead end or, as I refer to it, 'dead patient' syndrome.

These extreme situations are what I specialize in; there are other, more talented, larger consultancies that can ably assist with more standard, *technical* approvals processes ... but what is to be done with a project like this one? I specialize in approvals processes for these 'last chance' patients, processes that aren't just technical but involve relationship-building and establishing trust.

A common first reaction when a project hits a dead end is for the developer to silently say, "Let the patient rest in peace." Case closed; the land will be sold (possibly at a discounted price) and the next owner will reinvent or reposition the project for potential success. But the analytic sage in me always first asks, "How dead is this patient? Are there any vital signs? Has someone missed something important? Can this patient be brought back to life?" Typically, I take a contrarian approach and, before declaring defeat, I assess the situation from many dimensions to avoid making what could be a premature conclusion.

I examine the project, like any physician examines their patient. I visit people and ask questions to find out what is fundamentally wrong so that I can determine if the patient can be healed and brought to new life. Questions in the examination may include the following and many others:

- What are the merits and detractors of the property's location?
- Is there a market for what is proposed?
- Are there competitive projects in the area and how could these affect the development?
- Is the project viable from a financial perspective, considering time delays and potential changes in density and land use?
- What are the municipal and regional policies that apply to this location?
- How does the municipal staff view this development?
- What does the community think about this project?
- How does the local municipal council and mayor see the situation?

It is often the case that the project has failed due to misunderstandings, lack of technical due diligence, and maybe most importantly, loss of trust and support across the *politics* of the project. Once enthusiasm has been lost, the death knell for the project is inevitable. In the Canadian context, the signs of a project's terminal condition are not always obvious, as it is not what is *said* but what is *not* said that is most important. Relationships matter.

These elements of misunderstanding and 'trust lost' will be discussed in greater detail in this book. Approvals are only one piece of the development puzzle, but without them the project isn't complete and does not proceed. Similarly, reviving potential 'dead patients' is just part of this story; making sure patients are properly cared for from the start—preventive real estate development practice—is more important, as you will see.

One thing we can agree on from the outset is that a sound *project approvals process approach* is needed, otherwise vital signs indicating either success or the early demise of a promising project might be missed.

Why this Book?

Success in real estate development is tied in a large part to real estate approvals. Without the approvals, nothing happens. Simple. In fact, the approvals process—though underrated and misunderstood—may be the most important part of the real estate value-building process.

Real estate development approvals demand rigour, inclusion, and collective support to obtain consistent success. It is fundamentally important to realize that approvals aren't the municipalities' or the regional districts' responsibility alone but are a challenge for all parties involved. Many municipalities and regional districts constantly renew, review, and refine their processes, but it takes support from all parties involved in the process to create healthier, more efficient processes that benefit all parties. Granted, each party involved—developer, municipality, regional district, and community, among others—have their own interests and positions that influence outcomes.

This book is meant to help improve understanding and relationships in the real estate development approvals processes in British Columbia and elsewhere in Canada. It builds on a 2019 Province of British Columbia study, *Development Approvals Process Review*, that advocates and supports further education, training, and knowledge development.[1] It is designed for developers and other professionals wanting to clearly understand and improve their approvals processes, as well as municipal and district staff, mayors, and city councillors, and their communities. My hope is that this book will help empower them to ensure the right development is in the right place. It is about building better communities together.

New Pathways is meant to build bridges and mutual, respectful understanding within entire communities, including among city administration, regional districts, other approving authorities, concerned citizens and, of course, developers. We have a common interest in building a place called 'home' together, in a cooperative, collaborative fashion where mutual public and private interests blend for better results, saving time and money while creating great communities. I refer to this fundamental concept, where we all benefit, as 'net community gain'.

This book unpacks the real estate approvals 'riddle' by:

1. Examining the existing *people, policy, and economy* as the shapers of approvals and future trends;
2. Describing the *past* and *present* state of approvals, and some of the reasons why the approvals process has frequently undermined projects;

---

1 Ministry of Municipal Affairs and Housing, 2019.

3. Explaining *what* the applications and approvals requirements are (focusing on British Columbia, but including examples from elsewhere in Canada and the United States);
4. Understanding *who* has the *power* and how to work with it, or redirect it, for better results;
5. Expanding knowledge about *evaluating risk* by project type, financial analysis, and associated due diligence to improve the 'approvability' of a project from all lenses;
6. Introducing an *enlightened approach to approvals (Approvals+)* for real estate developers and communities so they can help lead change and improve results; and
7. Providing case studies of *strategy drivers* that shift all the players to a winning hand in the development approvals process game.

New Pathways provides a 'how to' guide, from the inception of a project (due diligence) through to final approvals. As you will learn, seeing a project through inception to creation is as much, or more, about building trust relationships and conducting equitable negotiations (based on measured principles and criteria) as it is about technical precision.

My hope is that the discussions and ideas presented in this book will render better results for my readers which will build value into their projects and ultimately build better communities.

Scope and Limitations

Not much has been written on the theory and practice of obtaining approvals in real estate development. This concept is normally part of a larger text and in the past it has been relegated to a more technical 'check the boxes' role in the development process. This needs to change; in these complex and ever-changing times, the approach to obtaining approvals needs to be more sophisticated, agile and interactive.

As with any text on real estate development, data becomes dated the moment a book is released. With this in mind, I have made every effort to make sure the data is relevant and current, and I have ground-proofed it with references and colleague verification. Undoubtably, there will be errors or oversights; I apologize in advance for this. However, the most beneficial aspect of this book is the universal *Approvals+* framework that will continue to be relevant and inspirational over time. This framework and its preconditions have worked for me and I want to share them with you. Hopefully, the refreshed approach of the *Approvals+* framework will be enlightening and help you to shape your own approach. The stories on lessons, rules, and takeaways are my own, as are other stories throughout the book, and are based on events from my own life.

Most of the examples described in the text of this book are focused on the Vancouver region of British Columbia, though case studies from elsewhere are used to provide illustrative examples for the discussion, or ideas for innovation. Although the content is Vancouver region-centric, it is meant to have application throughout the province, and throughout Canada as well. The term 'approvals' within the context of this book is meant to be synonymous with 'applications and approvals', as both are intricately intertwined, although they follow in sequence. The use of the terms 'jurisdiction' and 'municipality' include by implication the term 'regional district', to cover both urban and rural areas of British Columbia.

These lessons, rules, and my 'new approach' treat approvals as an 'equal partner' in the real estate development process. The business success of each project depends on a smooth approvals process, and getting these approvals is imperative if your project is to succeed. This book's intention is to provide a comprehensive but concise progressive approach to the approvals process.

In sum, real estate developers have an incredible responsibility to build the communities of the future, yet their world is full of risk and exposure in uncertain times. They are expected to build dream communities but are faced with all kinds of barriers. As part of a collective partnership of public, private, and community interests, some of those barriers I am convinced can be transformed into bridges. With clarity, managed expectations, and measured results, many new breakthroughs in community planning and design will be made.

This book is a training guide and resource for the next generation of real estate developers, approval authorities, and communities. It goes beyond the 'what' and moves toward the 'how' of improving approvals processes, considering alternative ways of doing business that will increase speed of approvals and, by decreasing associated costs and conflicts, improving quality as well.

Book Guide

For convenience, and to find specifics quickly, the following is a summary book guide you can use continually as a reference and project resource:

Chapter 1 – Process Shapers: In this chapter I discuss people, policy, and economy as the three principle shapers for approvals. This chapter ends with a discussion of future trends responding to changing demographics, employment, immigration, and associated supply and demand of different types of real estate, which seed opportunities.

Chapter 2 – Lessons, Take-aways, Realities: In this chapter I share my experiences inside and outside city hall, as a staff person (inside) and developer and consultant (outside) in the development process.

Chapter 3 – Rules of the Game: In this chapter I describe the legislation that shapes British Columbia real estate industry, from the *Local Government Act* (LGA) to official community plans (OCPs) and zoning bylaws, as well as regulations, studies, processes, and permits that govern the planning, design, and construction of a project.

Chapter 4 – Variables in the Game: In this chapter I dig into the unique aspects of application and approval processes across British Columbia, beginning with Vancouver's unique model and its specific approach to approvals. I further go on to discuss funding growth tools; municipal and community perspectives; and approval controllers and influencers.

Chapter 5 – Risk and Assessment: In this chapter I outline the fundamental diagnostics and due diligence required to proceed with a project, including risk factors associated with specific real estate types, preliminary financial analysis, the concept of leverage, and residual land value analysis.

Chapter 6 – Changing Approach: In this chapter I explain the need for innovation, the nine distinct characteristics leading to a changed process, working with multiple interests, and shifting paradigms.

Chapter 7 – New Pathways Framework: In this chapter I detail the recommended *Approvals+* process including the preconditions for success, systemic operating elements, and the specific phases.

Chapter 8 – Successful Strategy Drivers: In this chapter I profile nine case studies of innovative projects that have four common elements—leadership, drivers, unique emphasis, and sensitivity.

Chapter 9 – Re-visions: I conclude the book with a reflection back to former ways of doing business and then look forward into the future at what the *Approvals+* framework approach could do to inform and enlighten decision-makers during the next generation of approvals, creating less conflict and greater communities. This chapter ends with 10 overall touchstones for improving the approvals process, a reminder that we have to change our processes to change our results.

PART 1: BACKGROUND

1. SHAPERS OF APPROVALS

> *Few real estate projects are approved without elaboration of the plan concept, evidence of public need, and a convincing argument that the benefits of the project accrue to the community and are greater than the cost.*
>
> —*Jim Whitehead, Real Estate Development (2008)*

Shapers Pyramid

Think of the COVID-19 crisis as an opportunity to reconsider, change our paradigm and pivot in a fundamentally new direction. This is a special time for us to pause and take stock. It may be hard to imagine the current pandemic in this way, but let's explore the possibilities before we dismiss the idea prematurely.

Delays in development approvals affect project costs, economic viability, and delivery of necessary housing. On the ground, it means that the housing affordability crisis, particularly in the lower mainland of British Columbia, continues to not be solved. Further, as real estate development and construction make up 40 to 50 percent of British Columbia's economy, keeping this engine moving and healthy is of utmost importance for keeping people employed. But delay continues to be part of the game. In some respects, we are in a state of 'approvals emergency', but it appears that the development industry is locked in a never-ending dance of development review without much significant change. The dance partners change, but the dance remains the same.

Our timing for approvals continues to erode. According to the Organization for Economic Cooperation and Development (OECD), Canada ranks 34 out of 35 in the length of time it takes to obtain a building permit. It takes nearly 250 days to get a permit in Canada—three times (168 days) longer than it takes in the United States. Only the Slovak Republic takes longer to have a construction permit approved.[2] So why are we facing this dichotomy of good intentions and less than acceptable results when many municipalities work hard to streamline processes and requirements where possible? This is a complex question, demanding a complex answer.

One answer to this question is that many real estate development projects have to go through a complex rezoning process, with construction only following after protracted community engagement and design review processes. It can take up to five years to rezone a property in the Vancouver region and take it from acquisition to construction.

---

2 Gardner, *Closing Shot,* ReNew Canada, March/April 2020, 42.

Many of you may say that this length of time must be wrong, but I say, "Do the math and monitor the projects." The answer is the same. It's unfortunate, but real.

Further adding to these challenges are misunderstanding, confusion, and compromise, all of which are part of the real estate development approvals processes. When there are multiple interests involved, the misunderstandings become even more distorted and confusing. Further, employment cycles, migration, costs, revenue, supply and demand patterns have changed character in the last several decades and are, at least now, unpredictable based on the previous ten-year cycles. We live in a time of disruption and erratic change, and the unpredictable is the new normal. We have to be able to adapt, be flexible, and plan for the unexpected; only then will we be prepared for the unexpected.

However, while it is difficult to consider that these systemic, seismic changes offer us an opportunity, they do; today's unprecedented times actually allow us time for reflection and reinvention. This is good because, if we continue using the same processes that we have been, we will predictably (and probably) end up in the same places, and with the same problems, we have had before. If we change our ways and pathways, though, chances are we will arrive at a different place—a more successful place for all. Just imagine what we can create if we start working together rather than against each other! My belief is that we have no choice, as many aspects of the current approvals crisis are not necessarily temporary and will command change. In the context of this discussion, we will reflect on the situation. This is a chance to modify our behaviours and approaches in order to get better results for the future.

This foundational chapter will attempt to unpack the macro and micro components that shape and influence the approvals process. In so doing, we will begin to understand the complexities and intricacies of approvals process, sometimes separately and sometimes together.

These components are divided into three main themes, represented below in the 'Shapers Pyramid' (Figure 1.1), which fits within the greater context of 'society' and 'environment', both of which influence the three micro themes of people, policy and economy:

1. *People:* Developers, community, staff, council, provincial and federal government decision-makers (value-makers).
2. *Policy:* Planning, bylaws, and regulations (rules).
3. *Economy:* Immigration, employment, and supply and demand (business).

Each of these thematic groups are inter-related, but let's first review them separately and then repack them at the end of the chapter.

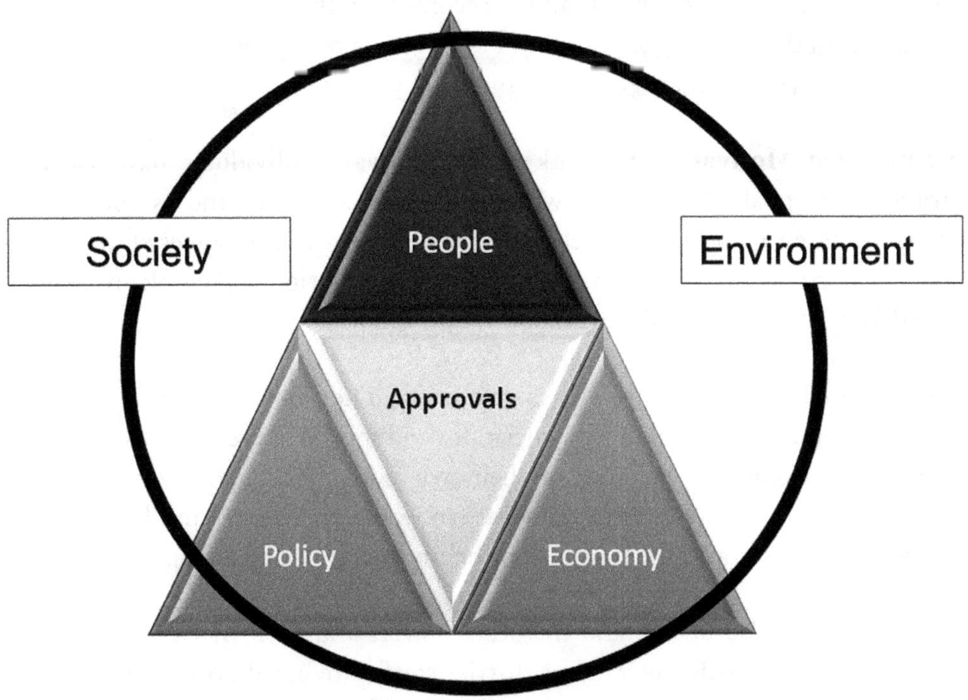

Figure 1.1: Shapers Pyramid
People should be at the top of the pyramid, supported by policy and the economy in the approvals system.

These themes will continue to emerge throughout the book as we further analyze the overall approvals system and its related parts, including the regulatory environment, risk assessment, a new pathways framework, and innovative strategies. By first discussing people, policy, and economy separately, we will find intricate, related components and we can work them together to our mutual advantage.

People

People are at the top of the Shapers Pyramid. Why do we begin with people? Is it not the economy that drives real estate development? Is it not policy that shapes development?

Yes, maybe from fundamental economic viability or bylaw perspectives, but not from an overall approvals viewpoint. If we change our view (the 'people' component), maybe then we can change results, as our values should shape our laws and policies.

If we think of the three shapers together—people, policy, and economy—it is easy to conclude that people's interests are the core drivers of policy and, in part, economy, as I will explain in further detail. If you can get people pulling together and in the same direction, rather than in opposite directions, you can have momentous results. These results can push policy amendments and the economy in the same way that social capital drives success in the new digital economy. Hence this is why 'people' are more important in the Shapers Pyramid than 'economy' and 'policy'.

Self-Interested Motivations: Think of it this way: individuals have their own motivations and goals. It is people whose values direct policy and essentially create direction for the economy. Collectively, they manage the scarce resources of the economy. Economies don't act on their own. People drive immigration and employment, which in turn drives our growth and wealth.

Likewise, people drive approvals in many ways. They may be self-interested, but community members in community associations and special interest groups can expedite or stonewall development depending on their own motivations. Politicians have to listen to these groups, otherwise their positions are in jeopardy. Votes count. Understanding these special interests, and the motivations behind them, is key to approvals success.

Next, you need to also understand the other players and their motivations. Examine the motivations of boards, regional or district staff, provincial government concerns, and the interests of the federal government, and you find a game of competing interests that are frequently not aligned, and usually not pulling in one direction. Acrimony and misunderstandings are common, which leads to divisiveness and indecision. A history of different agendas rotating every few years at the provincial and federal government levels doesn't help with certainty and consistency—two key ingredients to successful processes—when making multi-million-dollar decisions.

Further, when there are multiple interests, another challenge is that there appears to be constant imbalance between development rights, community expectations, staff requirements, and the approvals processes. The result is longer, increasingly complex, more uncertain, inflexible approvals processes. These factors (among others) can mean higher risk to investors, extended development timeframes, or infinitely stalled projects.

This situation is unsatisfactory, yet everyone points to one another as the culprit, or simply shrugs their shoulders, saying, "It's not my fault, that's just the way it is." Having been on both sides of the blame game—both municipal and development—I find this ironic. We have to understand everyone's particular motivations, to somehow walk in their shoes and see through their lenses if we are to get the full picture.

To help us with this sensitized understanding, let's first look at the dysfunctions of the current approvals structure to bring awareness to its weaknesses. If we can transform each weakness into a strength, we will be able to strengthen the process one step at a time.

As illustrated below in Figure 1.2, I have portrayed the approvals process as circular and called it the 'Cycle of Municipal Disapprovals'. Why is this? There are a number of reasons that create a mood of disapproval from the moment a project is launched.

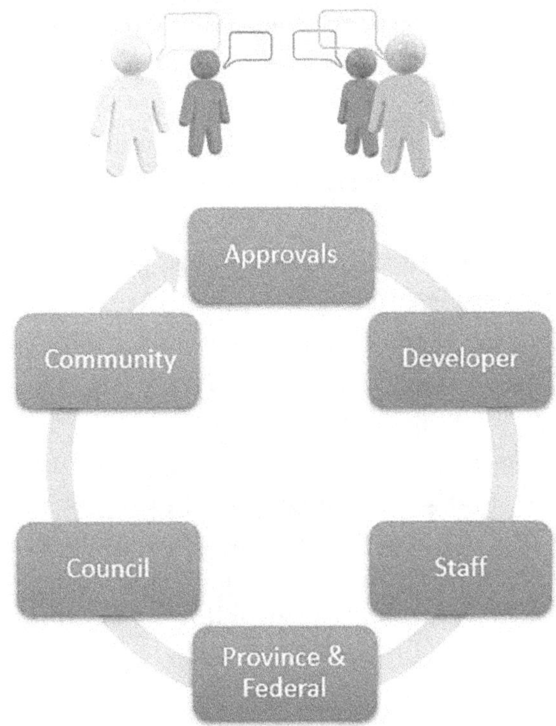

Figure 1.2: Cycle of Municipal Disapprovals
Existing separated interests in a risk-prone process

In a situation where the process is not meeting expectations, it's important to understand that its shortcomings are not necessarily the result of anyone's ill intentions, but are instead the result of design, evolution, risk, and self-interest.

1. **Design:** Figure 1.2 illustrates a municipal application and approvals process that has three characteristics: separated steps, sequential in nature, and the process arrives back at the same place it started. This circular characterization most richly reveals its current weaknesses:
    a. The sequential process separates each participant, which is logical but often isolates important components of the process, either by function or priority.
    b. Consultation with the community is left to the end in many cases, resulting in frustration and reconsideration—hence the inclination to start over. But starting over is not a good solution and often results in proponents landing in a renewed dysfunctional cycle. I note here, however, that this is changing;

now in many processes, engagement with the neighbours and community is required or encouraged earlier in the process.

c. Technical staff reviews take sequential priority over council review, and these should work hand-in-hand—otherwise, insurmountable political issues can derail an application after significant investment in detailed drawings has been made.

2. **Evolution:** I've watched many well-intended municipal development evaluation processes morph into elongated processes, despite good intentions. Most cities periodically instruct development approval officers and directors to evaluate the efficiency and expediency of their approvals processes. Often this is prompted when a council or a chief administrative officer changes. The incoming person responsible for the approvals process generally makes an effort to remedy past faults and incorporate a better, more inclusive way of doing things as well as create a transparent organization.

   These are the storylines, well-crafted and method-driven, of organizational change agents. What evolves is often less than inspired. Leadership wanes, staff are reassigned, enthusiasm softens, and the front-line development planners revert back to policy, risk aversion, and tried and true methods in their own minds that end in the same, equal, or lesser results.

   As many municipal approval officers can attest to, although there is much motivation for change and improvement, there are valid reasons why habitual reversion to the status quo is tough to break. Staff positions depend largely on a routine that creates a consistent, systematic review of development applications. This system is rigorous in its own way, and it can be taught to others systematically. It is a good fallback system, especially when there is an overwhelming backlog of applications and ever-more developers knocking on the door. Change could cause further, significant delay as it might create misunderstanding, and will inevitably add more stress to the system. Further, if the change doesn't work, or has been attempted before, you will hear, "I told you so," or, "We tried that before and it didn't work!"

3. **Risk:** Risk is something that makes people not do things. 'Fight, flight or freeze' are primal reactions to stressful or threatening situations. If you are fearful of an outcome, and have a choice not to take the path that leads to that outcome, why would you take a risk if you don't have to or are not motivated to?

   Picture a city engineer reviewing a development application proposing a different roadway right-of-way dimension than the norm. The Transportation

Association of Canada (TAC) standard dictates one standard, and his proposal suggests another. The fire chief weighs into the conversation and indicates an 18-metre right-of-way minimum is his/her bottom line. The developer illustrates a 16-metre right-of-way with a sidewalk on one side, not both sides, and makes the case that it is a local road and so the standards applicable to a more major thoroughfare do not apply. The city says 'no', as the engineer's idea deviates from *their* standard—dual sidewalks are their policy.

By not even entertaining the ideas of the engineer, and adhering strictly to policy, no risk is taken. Everyone agrees that the safe route is to stick to the standard. Why change? The engineer could argue that there is not much risk inherent in this alternative development standard, especially as there are precedents throughout British Columbia and Canada that support this alternative, but there has to be a *reason* to change.

I remember looking directly at a city engineer and a developer who were sitting at the front of class at Simon Fraser University and saying to them, "You are partners in development," to see if I would get a reaction. To my surprise, they almost immediately recoiled in denial away from each other. But once I explained that each had a role in approving and building development and community infrastructure, they calmed down and acknowledged their dual roles. But it was still a hesitant acquiescence.

Fear of risk generally makes people say 'no' more than 'yes'. If there is no encouragement to change the status quo, and if there are potential legal or career ramifications, then you will hear a definite 'no'; on the other hand, if there is broad support, and risk is mitigated, if not eliminated, then—to paraphrase an old Chinese proverb—you 'build them a golden bridge' to cross and, in so doing, give them the ability to say 'yes' without risk of recourse. If you don't give them a valid reason to say 'yes', why should they?

4. **Self-Interest:** Self-motivation always drives individuals. People need to be recognized and needed; this gives them self-worth and purpose. Understanding this fundamental aspect of human nature, especially in a splintered, sensitive development application process, is crucial to creating a successful turnaround strategy. But you have to be careful to differentiate genuine self-interest from self-interest represented as community or municipal interest. Many participants can be guilty of both, sometimes without really being aware of it, and sometimes because they just ignore it. People believe they are right based on *their* value system, not yours. Misrepresenting or exaggerating the facts, which can be done

by organizations as well as by individuals, can be a real project threat, especially at a public hearing.

Again, let's reflect back for a moment on Figure 1.2, a project in a constant cycle of municipal disapproval between developer, staff, provincial and federal governments, council, and community players. Then consider Figure 1.3 below where all participants are active and interactive systemically throughout the process. The redesign portrayed in Figure 1.3 requires a fundamental paradigm shift to enable it to happen. I will discuss this in more detail in chapters 6 and 7.

Figure 1.3: Cycle of Municipal Approvals Reloaded
Working together from the beginning for mutual benefits

Policy

Policy is the rock, or the malleable piece of clay, in the development process. It can be inflexible like a rock, or can mold to the needs of the project. Policy directions are the touchstones by which staff and council measure applications. Good policy should reflect the social norms and values in the community. Good policy should also be flexible so it can respond to change and, as part of its core structure, even anticipate it.

Policy can either be an unreasonable burden or a gateway to innovative and progressive development. Overall policy for a municipality in British Columbia is enabled by the provincial *Local Government Act* (LGA) and directed by a hierarchy of plans that start with a high-level regional growth strategy and move down to official community plans, zoning bylaws, and subdivision bylaws, among other plans and regulations that give further dimension and detail.

Statutory plans, or required plans, are approved by bylaw; other non-statutory plans, like transportation plans and housing plans, may be adopted by council resolution to provide guidance. Provincial regulations such as the B.C. Building Code (BCBC) provide further details for building design and construction. Other provincial and federal regulations inform the development detail, from riparian area treatment along streams to final flood construction grades. These are generally inflexible and require conformance. In any case, these plans and regulations go through periodic review, and are amended concurrent with other policy changes. Examples of this are alterations to fit new conditions, such as climate change or energy conservation measures like the Provincial Energy Step Code (an optional compliance path of the BCBC).

The challenge with policy is that it can be inflexible, and changes can add a risk dimension to the approvals process. In some instances, this inflexible response is understandable and arguably defensible. Sometimes policy for the urban areas has been extensively reviewed by the community and is part of an official community plan with reinforced land use designations and associated zoning. In rural situations, a growth study could have determined that regional growth should be focused in specifically designated areas to limit sprawl and concentrate development.

For example, in Metro Vancouver, high density residential development is normally focused in designated regional growth centres near transit nodes, which is a good strategy and unlikely to change. Similarly, in the Regional District of Nanaimo, urban residential development is directed to designated village centres to preserve rural elements of the area. In both cases, policy is clear and a regional growth plan amendment is required if a developer seeks to work outside these specified areas.

In other cases, as in Vancouver's 'discretionary zoning' or 'bonus zoning' areas, rules are flexible but discretionary, and therefore there is uncertainty as to what is required for development to proceed. Emerging affordable housing requirement policies, community amenity contributions and development cost charges can be volatile topics. These discretionary elements can take considerable time to negotiate reasonable terms for all parties. This is especially concerning in protracted rezoning processes.

There are four elements that shape development policy: Provincial legislation, the hierarchy of plans, local policy, and political forces.

British Columbia and City of Vancouver Planning Legislation: The *Local Government Act* (LGA) governs legislation that provides tools for municipalities and regional districts to shape their policies. There are limits to the powers and tools each municipality and regional district has available to it for implementing its policy framework. For example, with regard to development, under the LGA all charges collected from developers can only be used on specific, off-site improvements. The City of Vancouver is unique in that it has its own *Vancouver Charter,* which enables it to craft its own framework. This charter grants the city different powers than other communities in the province, which are governed by the LGA. In either case, there are distinct boundaries, but the framework may be amended from time to time.

Hierarchy of Plans: The hierarchy of plans is particularly important from a 'difficulty to change' standpoint (Figure 1.4 below), as anything to do with governance requires stringent review, both internally and publicly. The regional growth strategy is especially difficult to modify, as it is the bedrock of regional growth policies and to change it involves input from all the regional directors. Official community plans and zoning bylaws are less difficult to change, as such change only requires approval from local council and directors after public review. However, changing planning documents can pose significant challenges, usually related to entrenched views and bias. It is wise to never presume a policy change, especially under this kind of scrutiny, will help your project move ahead. In contrast to attempting to change policy, the development permit, building permit, and subdivision plans are technical processes and require no public review.

Figure 1.4: Generalized Policy Hierarchy

Local Policy: Be aware that local policy, from the official community plan to the zoning bylaw applications and approvals processes, have their own nuances in each municipality and regional district. Pay attention to all the requirements at the local level, especially permit fees and associated requirements. Ensure that you double-check timing of payments and any proposed changes that do not have grandfather clauses or stepped implementation tied to them (which we will discuss further in Chapter 3).

Although certain aspects of the development process are regulated at the provincial government level, for instance public hearing requirements, the actual application and study requirements may vary due to specific site conditions or approval variations that have evolved over time. Feasibility and assessment studies, as well as selecting the right, qualified consultant, are especially important to gain support for your application. These are further described in Chapter 5, as part of a discussion about diagnostics and due diligence.

Political Forces: Policy is often shaped by the motivations and biases of participants in the development process, especially in sensitive neighbourhood situations. Ultimately, the decision to develop or not can rest in councils' hands, as council members represent their communities. As discussed earlier, these are largely self-interested participants who vary in influence.

Just think back to the sensitivity and stigma associated with secondary suites, scorned as 'illegal suites' at one time. Residents of some areas of the lower mainland were branded almost as outlaws if they had a secondary suite in their house. In the City of Surrey, for example, secondary suites required a neighbourhood referendum before they were permitted. Now, only a couple of decades later, secondary suites are not only governed by permit and building code requirements only, but are seen as an essential element of affordability, both as a mortgage-helper for the owner and as a valued facet of affordable housing rental supply. They are built into many single-family homes now as part of the builder package. Similarly, lane homes are an additional method to create what Vancouver calls 'eco-density' or gentle densification.

It is important to note here, however, that when designing your project, you must be careful about the difference between the 'leading edge' and the 'bleeding edge' of politically motivated policy changes, especially when the local community is not supportive, and the innovation has not been tested. Sometimes government takes steps that are not popular. In Ontario, for example, the Progressive Conservative Government issued a series of what are known as 'Minister's Zoning Orders' (MZO). They allowed the province's Municipal Affairs and Housing Minister, Steve Clark, to make a final ruling on how a piece of land would be used, with no appeals permitted. In 2019 and 2020, the conservative government issued eight new zoning orders, more than their liberal predecessors did over their entire last decade in office. Although each of these cases had local council approval, the province had the final say in expediting plans for final approval, which is a slippery slope when it comes to development plans.[3]

Policy is definitely the bedrock of development and growth planning, and it enables consistent and coherent community planning. The detailed structure and rules governing policy in British Columbia are detailed in Chapter 3.

Economy

The year 2020 will never be forgotten. Catastrophic changes of many natures took place around the world and across Canada. The intersect between the pandemic, the plunge of oil prices and the deep dive of the stock market left world economics in tatters. The International Monetary Fund (IMF) declared the economic downturn the worst since the Great Depression. The broadly-based U.S. S&P 500 Index experienced a 35 percent decline in 33 days—the fastest and steepest drop in its history. The Canadian and American governments reacted immediately with an insertion of trillions of dollars into the economy, an unprecedented move, and the S&P recovered to within 13 percent of its earlier benchmark.[4]

The world as we know it will never be the same. The foundation of our financial system and the robust economies of first world nations such as Canada and the U.S.A. were ravaged by the shockwave of a global pandemic as people were forced indoors and isolated and 'non-essential' businesses were closed. It was a death knell for many small businesses; one estimate is that one-third of Canadian businesses will never open their doors again.[5] This time in history could very well be the tipping point for many Canadians who are too debt-rich and savings-poor. Even with temporary governmental subsidies, grants, loans, and deferral of taxes, many are scrambling to figure out what 'ever after' looks like.

Random Cycle and Development Cycle: Where does this shockwave leave us British Columbians? We appear to be climbing out of an economic bomb-shelter, not really realizing the magnitude of the devastation. Like the rest of the world, we are in a business and development cycle, with the latter normally lagging behind the former. Where we *actually* are is hard to determine but we are somewhere in the stagnation/ recovery cycle. We were hit with what is referred to as a 'random cycle'[6] and were arguably already in a stagnation/recovery 'development cycle'.

---

3 Globe and Mail, Toronto, May 26, 2020, n.p.

4 Murray Leith, Odlum Brown Newsletter, May 2020.

5 Canadian Broadcasting Corporation, *As It Happens*, April 18, 2020.

6 Jim Whitehead, *Real Estate Development*, 2.14.

Let's now look briefly at the contrarian side of recent events. With interest rates at near zero percent, there is no place for money to go except back into the stock market, as other investment options will gain practically nothing when you take into consideration taxes and inflation. There are trillions of dollars worldwide looking for a relatively safe haven to make money, which will, of course, contribute in part to economic recovery.

Also take into consideration, as eminent Nobel Prize–winning economist Paul Krugman points out, that this was not an *economic* collapse but an *external factor* collapse, so the fundamental strengths of the world economy have stayed the same, although workforce and employment have been significantly affected and buoyed only by government subsidy.[7]

With the cost of borrowing money at almost zero, mortgage rates are at an all-time low, helping fuel a buyer's market. For example, a five-year fixed or variable mortgage of $500,000, amortized over 25 years at 3.5 percent interest, results in payments of $2,500 per month. The same mortgage, at 2.5 percent interest, requires a payment of $2,240 per month, a savings of $260 per month or $3,120 in after-tax dollars per year.

From a development perspective, as one senior developer shared with me, even before the pandemic, the Vancouver market normally followed a seven-year cycle of four years up and three to recover—but with the previous ten-year up cycle, it may take seven years to recover. So, simply put, what goes up eventually comes down and then recovers. The question is: How long will the recovery take? If there is really nothing preventing a steep rebound (once social distancing is relaxed), then the recovery cycle could, in fact, be condensed—assuming migration continues and the economy rebounds.

Sound Fundamentals but Affordability Challenged: It's important to keep in mind that the City of Vancouver and region has evolved from a provincial city to an international destination of capital on the Pacific Rim. Add to that a superior education system, a safe and secure location, a super-natural setting, a temperate climate, an immigrant-friendly community, and you achieve a unique alchemy rarely found in the world today. Vancouver is an attractive city, and so is the province of British Columbia; in fact, the City of Vancouver has consistently ranked as one of the world's top ten most livable cities for the past decade based on The Economist Intelligence Unit's (EIU) annual Global Liveability Ranking, which ranks 140 cities for their urban quality of life based on assessments of stability, health care, culture and environment, education, and infrastructure.[8]

---

7 Paul Krugman, Economist, April 2020.

8 Economist Magazine, Economic Intelligence Unit, *Most Livable World Cities*, 2019.

At the same time, as the epicenter of British Columbia, Vancouver is colliding with a housing affordability crisis that is eroding its shine. Along with its wonderful liveabilty rating, it is also ranked as the second most unaffordable city in the world behind Hong Kong, out of 309 world cities. The comparative ratio between median housing price and household income is a halting 11.9.[9] A healthy price-to-income ratio is 2.6 (i.e., it would take 2.6 years of median household income to purchase the median home).

Further, Vancouver is ranked number two out of the 20 largest cities in Canada for its residents spending more than 30 percent of income on housing, yet it ranks one of the lowest (at number 16) for median income (as of 2016).[10] This lack of affordable housing, and Vancouver's expensive lifestyle, is a definite detractor for professionals considering building lives and careers in British Columbia, as wages are definitely not competitive with housing price demands.

If there is any good news from this scenario, it's that growth in other parts of British Columbia may take off as a result of the Vancouver unaffordability factor, which could provide a healthy boost to the 'gig economy' (short-term contracts or freelance work) outside Vancouver. People are realizing they can live anywhere to do business, whether in British Columbia or world-wide—as I have discovered in my own office, located 10 minutes from the US border and 29 minutes from the Vancouver International Airport. This phenomenon is called 'outmigration', and I will further discuss it in the 'future trends' section of this chapter.

Now let's look briefly at the fundamental economic shapers of the approval process: employment and immigration, demographics, preferences and, finally, resulting supply and demand. Each one of these groups affects the others and ultimately shapes the state of the market and its dynamics. 'Market dynamics' is how the market responds to the forces around it. Figure 1.5 below illustrates these interrelated economic forces as they relate to real estate development, from the macro employment and immigration force to the micro real estate supply and demand forces that shape local markets throughout British Columbia.

---

9 Demographia International Housing Affordability Survey, January 2020

10 City of Vancouver, *Vancouver Social Indicators Profile* 2019, 40.

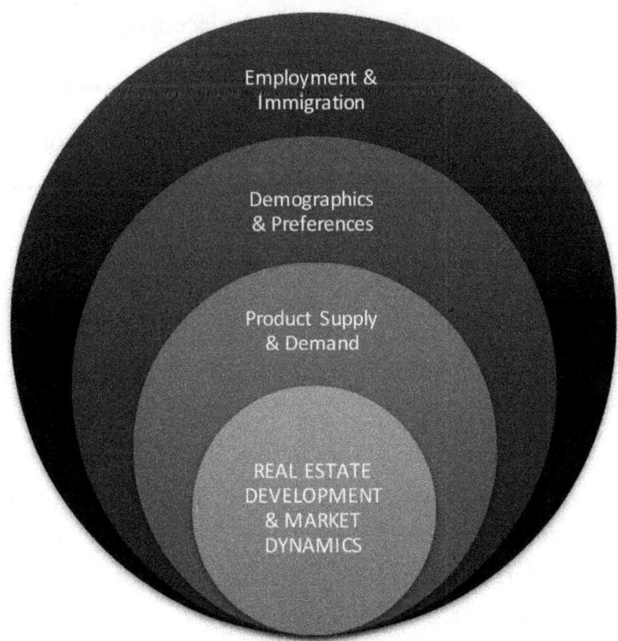

Figure 1.5: Economic Factors
Macro and micro economic factors affecting real estate development approvals

Employment and Immigration: When the British Columbia economy expands, there is a demand for labour in various industries including tourism, technology, services, and the resource sector. If local residents cannot fulfill the demand, these industries become catalysts for employment of immigrants, and increased immigration. Employment expands, participation in the labour force increases, and so does income and wealth.

Related spin-offs and service demands expand the economy further. Development and construction follow, first with demand for commercial office and industrial spaces, then residential and institutional housing to meet expanding employee living demands. Disposable family income also increases as a function of rising demand for skilled labour and associated increased labour rates.

Demographics and Preferences: Richard Florida, an American urban studies theorist focusing on social and economic theory, notes that the importance of 'place' trumps even income when it comes to choosing a city to live in.[11] John Helliwell, University of British Columbia economics professor emeritus, believes the same thing and has verified this theory through statistical research across Canada. He claims that, in addition, in places where there is a high trust factor, there is higher happiness, which makes such places

[11] Richard Florida, *Who's Your City,* 2008, 157.

more attractive to younger generations. Sense of place matters, and often it is 'people relationships' that help shape the nature of a place.[12]

In the new digital economy, attractive places have become even more important, because people can largely do work online instead of in traditional on-site locations. They can choose where they want to live and build the job around the location instead of the other way around. As you can see, there is a growing trend against the job-first/lifestyle-second tradition, and this is something that very much informs the building industry.

The rise of millennials mixed with an aging baby boomer population has created different demands on the marketplace. Baby boomers are often in enviable positions, having invested in real estate before the astronomical rise in the lower mainland/Vancouver area. But millennials are just getting their start, and the affordability crisis is pushing them, and people of lesser means, out of Vancouver to suburban locations, or elsewhere in British Columbia where they can raise families in what are largely perceived as safer communities. Most of the younger generation get their real estate start in townhouses or single-family homes if they leave the high-density areas and settle in smaller, outlying towns. In urban areas, such as in Metro Vancouver, single-family starter homes have largely been replaced by apartments, and even those are out of reach for many, if not most.

Purpose-built rentals are one technique for filling the void in housing affordability, but rents in the $2,000 to $3,000 per month range are not exactly affordable, even to the budding professional. Some people try to get around this by choosing to live out of town in Kelowna, parts of Vancouver Island, or in the interior, commuting into Vancouver a few days per week.

Product Supply and Demand: As price goes up, demand normally goes down but externalities from overseas influences, particularly Asian ones, in the past decades have created additional demand in the Vancouver area. Bidding wars for houses have forced prices to exceed initial asking prices, which is disturbing for people trying to enter the market. This trend has waned as China has tightened laws on exporting capital to other countries, and B.C. has implemented a speculation and vacancy home tax.[13] However, at the same time, instability in Hong Kong might bring some of the estimated 300,000 residents with Canadian passports home, which could create a further demand in British Columbia, especially in the Vancouver region.

---

[12] Charles Montgomery, *Happy City*, 2014, 38.

[13] Annual BC Provincial tax based on how owners use residential properties in major urban areas. This tax does not apply to principal residences and homes that are rented six months of the year. It differs from the City of Vancouver Empty Homes Tax – Bylaw No.11674.

The Province of British Columbia introduced their 30-Point Plan for Housing Affordability in February 2018. With a budget of $6.6 billion, it included plans to build 114,000 affordable housing units over 10 years, and 14,000 rental units for middle income people and families. The province also created a 'HousingHub' to build partnerships with other levels of government, non-profit groups and for-profit builders and developers to deliver affordable housing. As Selina Robinson, Minister of Municipal Affairs and Housing, said, "It takes years of sustained action to bring housing affordability home."[14]

We are constantly supply-challenged in the urban markets of British Columbia, where demand exceeds supply. When supply is less than demand, housing cost is pressured upward. Affordability is the intersection of housing cost, location, and transportation cost. To illustrate, as of April 2020, as a result of the pandemic the number of sales shrunk predictably, but housing prices remained relatively stable.[15] This situation could simply be an interim condition, as time will force prices down if demand declines. However, if surplus demand comes into play, it could cause prices to go up even higher in the short term. This appears to be the case, which parallels Canada Mortgage and Housing Corporation predictions for the immediate term and into 2021.[16]

Meanwhile, the systemic affordability crisis is making home ownership in the City of Vancouver almost an impossibility for most people, considering a minimum 20 percent down payment is required if a house price exceeds $1 million. A $200,000 down payment can't go on a credit card, and so many young people have to resort to the bank of 'Mom and Dad'. Typically, parents cash out of their own homes for suburban townhouses in the Fraser Valley or Squamish, or move to small towns in the Okanagan Valley for retirement (or 'refirement' as some boomers refer to their new, energized lifestyle). They sell, give some money to the children, buy a smaller home, and invest what's left.

Since the coronavirus disease outbreak, the search for more rural properties has skyrocketed, affecting small towns in the southern interior, such as Castlegar, heavily and driving real estate prices up. This could be a macro trend of safe distancing, literally, from bigger cities, more urban areas and more potential disease associated with concentrated populations.

Another reason for this trend is simply how unaffordable Vancouver is. Only 47 percent of Vancouver residents own their houses, and of that, 53 percent have mortgages. Of the

---

14 Ministry of Municipal Affairs and Housing, *Homes for B.C.: A 30-Point for Housing Affordability in British Columbia*, February 2018, 3,18.

15 Frontline Real Estate, *Market Report,* April 2020.

16 CMHC Special Edition: *Housing Market Outlook,* May 27, 2020.

53 percent of Vancouver residents who rent, 14 percent are subsidized.[17] For mortgage holders, mortgage payments eat up to 50 percent of their income—not the 30 percent considered the historic benchmark. In the demographic of 'less than 35 years of age', only 20 percent own their own homes and 80 percent rent. So, what about this 80 percent?

With almost no vacancy (at 0.8 percent—normal is 3.0 percent), rents continue to push upward, even with new construction and a boom in purpose-built rentals. Renters are protected by a two percent Consumer Price Index (CPI) limit, but only until they move. Given such limitations, shared accommodation and cramped quarters are becoming more common and renters are moving further out of the Vancouver core so they can afford accommodation.[18]

So, one of the biggest questions we face in urban planning is, how do we meet the demand with housing that is affordable?

---

17 City of Vancouver, *Vancouver Social Indicators Profile 2019*, 17.

18 City of Vancouver, *Housing Vancouver Strategy*, 2019, 3,4.

Future Trends

The *Metro Vancouver 2040* Plan (2011) projects the region will grow from 2.4 to 3.4 million people, adding a million new residents in the next 20 years to become the third-largest metropolitan area in Canada. This is expected to add an estimated 600,000 jobs and 575,000 homes. Together, these numbers equate to approximately 35,000 new residents and 20,000 new jobs each year (Figure 1.6 below).[19] The diversity and tenure of home demand will also be affected, as illustrated in Figure 1.7 on the following page, which demonstrates regional demand from 2016 to 2026.[20]

TABLE 2
Metro Vancouver Dwelling Unit and Employment Growth Targets for Urban Centres and Frequent Transit Development Areas

DWELLING UNITS			TARGET		TARGET		TARGET		GROWTH	
	2006		2021		2031		2041		2006-2041	
	#	%	#	%	#	%	#	%	#	%
Metropolitan Core	88,000	10%	110,000	10%	116,000	9%	119,000	8%	31,000	5%
Surrey Metro Centre	8,300	1%	27,000	2%	36,000	3%	43,000	3%	34,700	6%
Regional City Centres	71,000	8%	110,000	10%	142,000	11%	162,000	11%	91,000	16%
Municipal Town Centres	49,000	6%	82,000	7%	106,000	8%	123,000	9%	74,000	13%
Urban Centres Total	**216,300**	**26%**	**329,000**	**29%**	**400,000**	**31%**	**447,000**	**31%**	**230,700**	**40%**
Frequent Transit Development Areas	**217,000**	**26%**	**281,000**	**25%**	**337,000**	**26%**	**378,000**	**27%**	**161,000**	**28%**
General Urban Area	382,000	45%	486,000	43%	535,000	41%	561,000	39%	179,000	31%
Rural, Agricultural, Conservation and Recreation	33,000	4%	34,000	3%	35,000	3%	36,000	3%	3,000	1%
Metro Vancouver Total	**848,000**	**100%**	**1,130,000**	**100%**	**1,307,000**	**100%**	**1,422,000**	**100%**	**574,000**	**100%**

EMPLOYMENT			TARGET		TARGET		TARGET		GROWTH	
	2006		2021		2031		2041		2006-2041	
	#	%	#	%	#	%	#	%	#	%
Metropolitan Core	256,000	22%	286,000	20%	302,000	19%	313,000	18%	57,000	10%
Surrey Metro Centre	18,000	2%	31,000	2%	40,000	2%	49,000	3%	31,000	5%
Regional City Centres	124,000	11%	177,000	12%	208,000	13%	237,000	14%	113,000	19%
Municipal Town Centres	69,000	6%	107,000	7%	135,000	8%	163,000	9%	94,000	16%
Urban Centres Total	**467,000**	**40%**	**601,000**	**42%**	**685,000**	**42%**	**762,000**	**43%**	**295,000**	**50%**
Frequent Transit Development Areas	**254,000**	**22%**	**323,000**	**22%**	**370,000**	**23%**	**412,000**	**24%**	**158,000**	**27%**
All Other Areas	437,000	38%	524,000	36%	567,000	35%	579,000	33%	142,000	24%
Metro Vancouver Total	**1,158,000**	**100%**	**1,448,000**	**100%**	**1,622,000**	**100%**	**1,753,000**	**100%**	**595,000**	**100%**

Notes:

1. This table provides guidance to assist in regional and local planning.
2. Frequent Transit Development Area targets are conceptual and subject to future municipal and transit planning processes.
3. "All Other Areas" refers to areas outside of Urban Centres and Frequent Transit Development Areas.

Figure 1.6: Metro Vancouver Growth Targets
Metro Vancouver Dwelling Unit and Employment Growth Targets
(Source: Metro 2040, p.68)

---

19 Metro Vancouver, *Regional Growth Plan 2040*, 18 and 68 (Currently being updated to Metro 2050).

20 Metro Vancovuer, *Regional Growth Plan 2040*, 69.

TABLE A.2

Housing Demand Estimates by Tenure and Household Income for Metro Vancouver Subregions and Municipalities (2016-2026 Estimates)

SUBREGIONS AND MUNICIPAL ESTIMATES	HOUSING DEMAND BY TENURE			HOUSING RENTAL DEMAND BY HOUSEHOLD INCOME				
	Total Demand	Ownership Demand	Rental Demand	Very Low	Low Income	Moderate Income	Above Moderate	High Income
Metro Vancouver	**182,000**	**128,000**	**54,000**	**23,500**	**11,200**	**8,700**	**4,800**	**5,800**
Burnaby, New Westminster	24,000	15,900	8,100	3,740	1,760	1,280	630	690
Burnaby	19,000	13,100	5,900	2,520	1,260	1,010	510	600
New Westminster	5,000	2,800	2,200	1,220	500	270	120	90
Langley City, Langley Township	19,000	15,400	3,600	1,380	850	540	360	470
Langley City	2,000	1,300	700	420	130	70	40	50
Langley Township	17,000	14,100	2,900	960	720	470	320	420
Maple Ridge, Pitt Meadows	6,000	4,600	1,400	780	250	220	120	20
Maple Ridge	5,000	3,800	1,200	730	210	190	80	10
Pitt Meadows	1,000	800	200	50	40	30	40	10
Northeast Sector	22,000	15,700	6,300	2,770	1,430	990	470	580
Coquitlam	17,000	12,000	5,000	2,140	1,180	840	350	480
Port Coquitlam	3,000	2,200	800	470	160	70	50	30
Port Moody	2,000	1,500	500	160	90	80	70	70
North Shore	7,000	4,800	2,200	1,150	430	250	150	190
North Vancouver City	2,000	1,000	1,000	580	240	70	30	50
North Vancouver District	3,000	2,300	700	360	80	120	60	70
West Vancouver	2,000	1,500	500	210	110	60	60	70
Delta, Richmond, Tsawwassen	18,000	13,600	4,400	1,890	980	750	350	350
Delta	3,000	2,200	800	430	210	90	20	10
Richmond	14,000	10,800	3,200	1,300	700	600	300	300
Tsawwassen First Nation	1,000	600	400	160	70	60	30	40
Surrey, White Rock	48,100	36,320	11,780	4,510	2,660	2,200	1,230	1,070
Surrey	47,000	35,500	11,500	4,290	2,600	2,200	1,200	1,100
White Rock	1,100	820	280	220	60	-	30	(30)
Vancouver, Electoral Area A	32,000	19,200	12,800	5,910	2,340	1,930	1,120	1,450
Vancouver	32,000	19,200	12,800	5,910	2,340	1,930	1,120	1,450

Notes:

1. To meet this estimated demand, funding from other levels of government is required.
2. Increase in total households over 10 years based on regional population and household projections. Regional total exceeds municipal aggregate totals due to municipal variance.
3. Very Low Income <$30,000/year, Low Income <$30,000-50,000/year, Moderate Income $50,000-75,000/year, Above Moderate Income $75,000-$100,000/year, High Income $100,000/year plus.
4. Household maintainer rates and cohort projection method using census/NHS based household maintainer rates and projected demographic, characteristics (age, births, deaths, immigration, Canadian migration, intra-regional migration). Assumes that household income and household type ratios remain constant over the projection period. See Metro Vancouver Regional Planning, Metro Vancouver Housing Demand Projections – Overview of Assumptions and Methodology, Dec 2015.
5. The Housing Demand Estimates are not targets. These estimates are provided only as reference to assist in long range planning and represent a mid-range/ average trend projection based on the existing rental households in that municipality.
6. The housing demand estimates set out in Table A.2 are net additional units based on the population and household projections set out in Table A.1.
7. Anmore, Belcarra, and Lions Bay are not included in the table above given the modest levels of growth anticipated in these communities.
8. Bowen Island is not included in the table above as it does not fall under the jurisdiction of the regional growth strategy.

Figure 1.7: Metro Vancouver Growth Targets

Metro Vancouver Dwelling Unit and Employment Growth Targets

(Source: Metro 2040, p.69)

Unaffordability Continues: The disparity between income and affordability is concerning and ever-widening, as per the following graph depicting the City of Vancouver's East Side, which is typically seen as one of the most affordable areas in Vancouver. This graph could also indicate a trend across the lower mainland and some other cities in British Columbia (Figure 1.8 below) toward gentrification of previously undesirable areas, which drives prices up in those areas.[21]

In the East Vancouver area, between 2009 and 2017, median household income increased approximately 20 percent, while detached housing prices rose an average of nearly 150 percent; apartment sales prices rose more than 90 percent; and apartment rents increased by 40 percent. In simple terms, rents rose twice as fast as income; sales prices rose more than four times as fast as income for apartments; and sales prices rose over seven times as much as income for detached home sales.

Percentage change in housing costs and median household income from 2009-2019

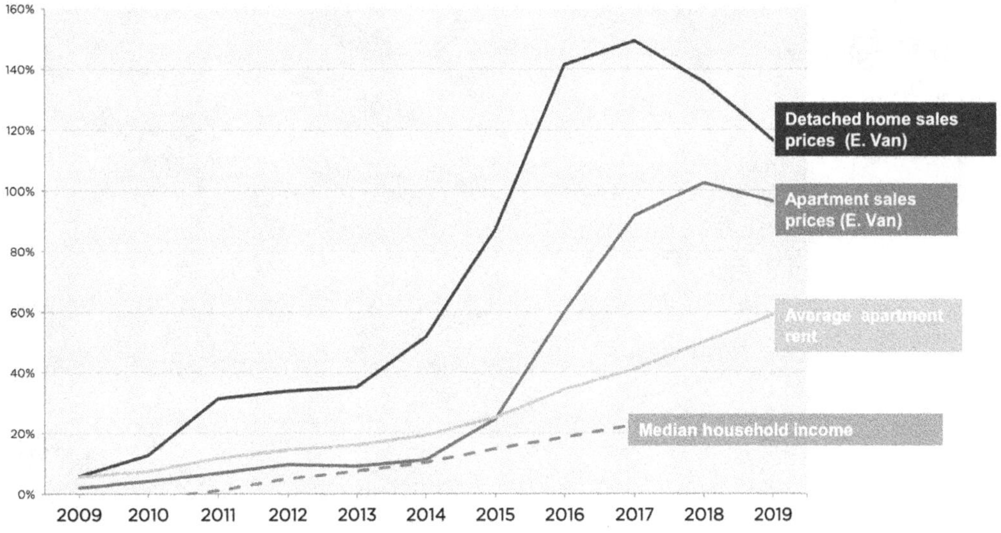

** Source: Benchmark prices from MLS Home Price Index. All data for Vancouver East in October of each respective year.*
*** Source: CMHC 2018 Rental Market Report.*
**** Source: Statistics Canada Income Statistics Division, 2016. Median Income is shown for all family units*

Figure 1.8: City of Vancouver Housing Costs versus Median Income
(Source: City of Vancouver)

21 City of Vancouver, Housing Vancouver Strategy 2019 Update, May 2020.

Density and Rentals at the Centre with Outmigration: In many neighbourhoods across Canada, lower density areas are losing population and more central areas are *adding* population, as higher density areas have proximity to rapid transit, as illustrated in the City of Vancouver (Figure 1.9 below). Meanwhile, the growth of purpose-built rentals continues—as detached home purchase is out of reach of many buyers—causing rental prices to go up, with near-zero vacancy rates as illustrated in Figure 1.10. With the Canada Housing and Mortgage Corporation's (CHMC) special rental housing financing program, development is further spurred on. A record number of laneway house permits (1,300 in 2017 and 2018) also partially helped affordability and provided further diversity of housing types and tenures. Laneway houses, detached suites typically built in backyards, and opening onto the back lane, are an emerging trend across the lower mainland, as are secondary suites (Figure 1.11). Rising housing costs, and growing families, could account for the outmigration from the City of Vancouver to other municipalities between 2011 and 2016 (Figure 1.12).

Vancouver neighborhoods are changing – population growth in transit-rich neighborhoods, loss in single-family zones away from transit

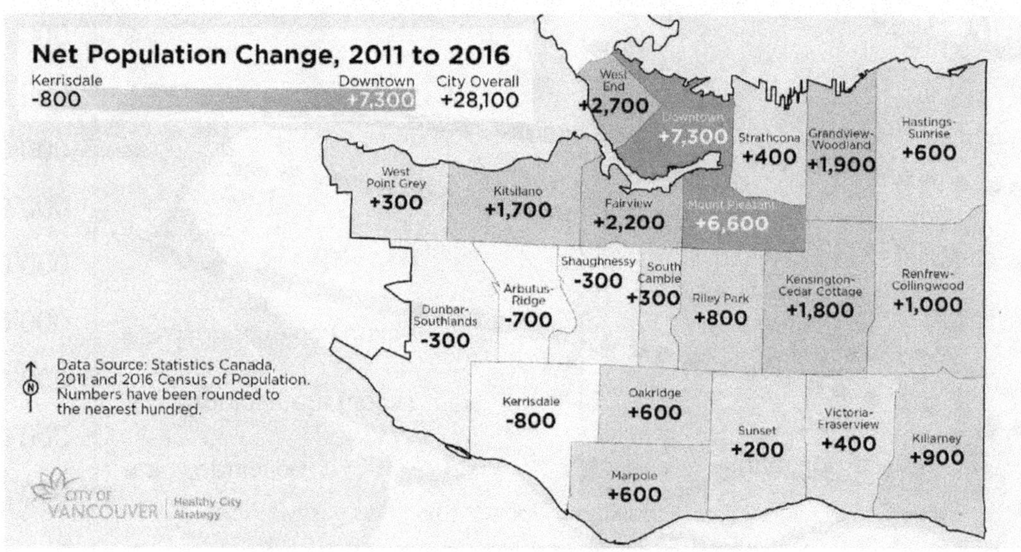

Figure 1.9: Population Growth and Location
(Source: City of Vancouver)

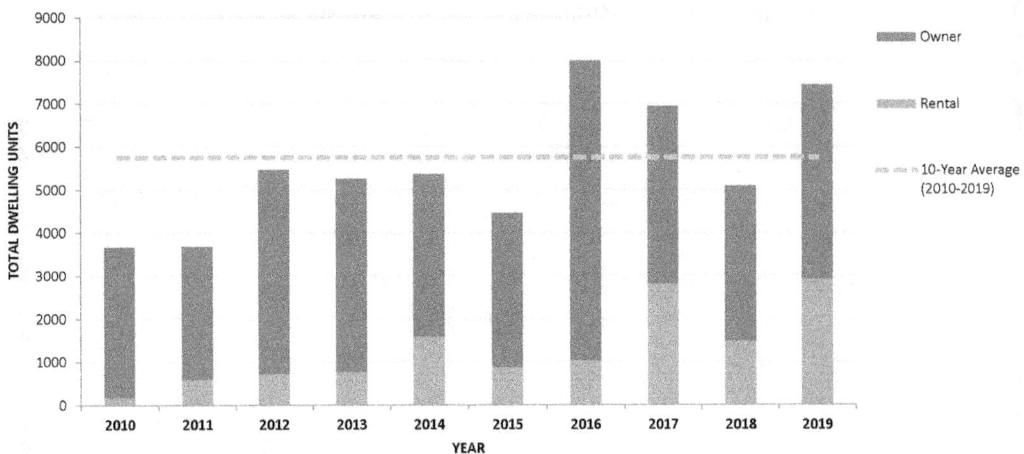

Source: CMHC (Starts and Completions Survey)
Effective January 2013, single-detached houses with an attached accessory suite are recorded as one unit "Ownership, Single" and the accessory suite as one unit "Rental, Apt + Other". In 2012 and prior years, these structures were recorded as two units, "Ownership, Freehold, Apt + Other" in some markets, including the Vancouver CMA and

<u>Figure 1.10: Annual Housing Starts and Growth of Rental Stock</u>

(Source: City of Vancouver)

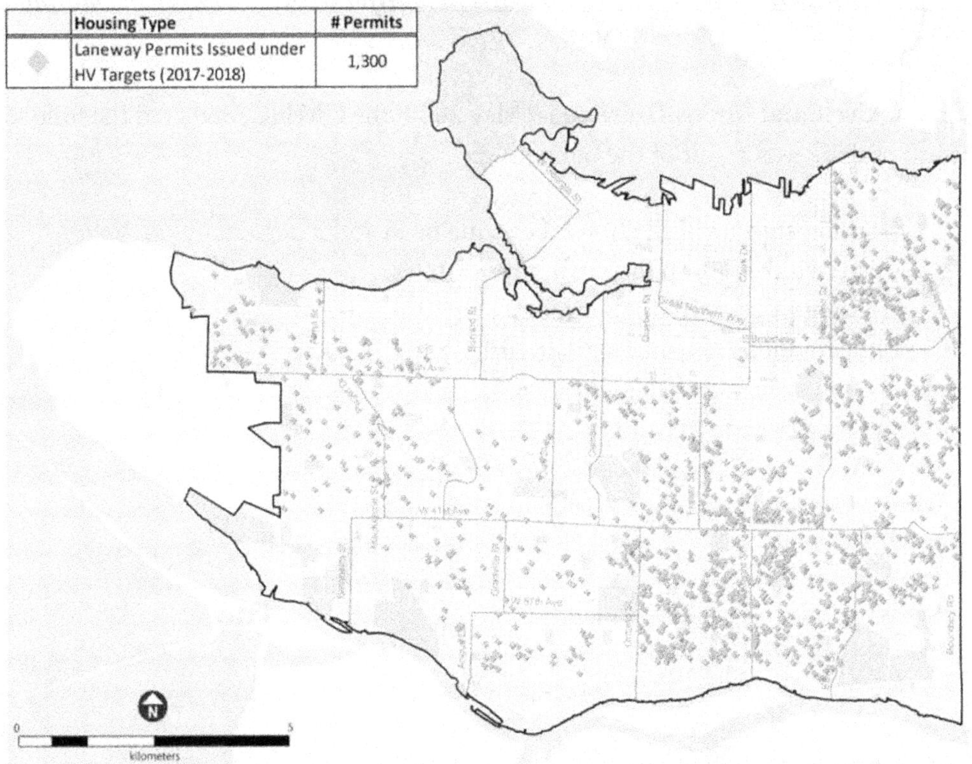

<u>Figure 1.11: Record Laneway House Permit Trend</u>

(Source: City of Vancouver)

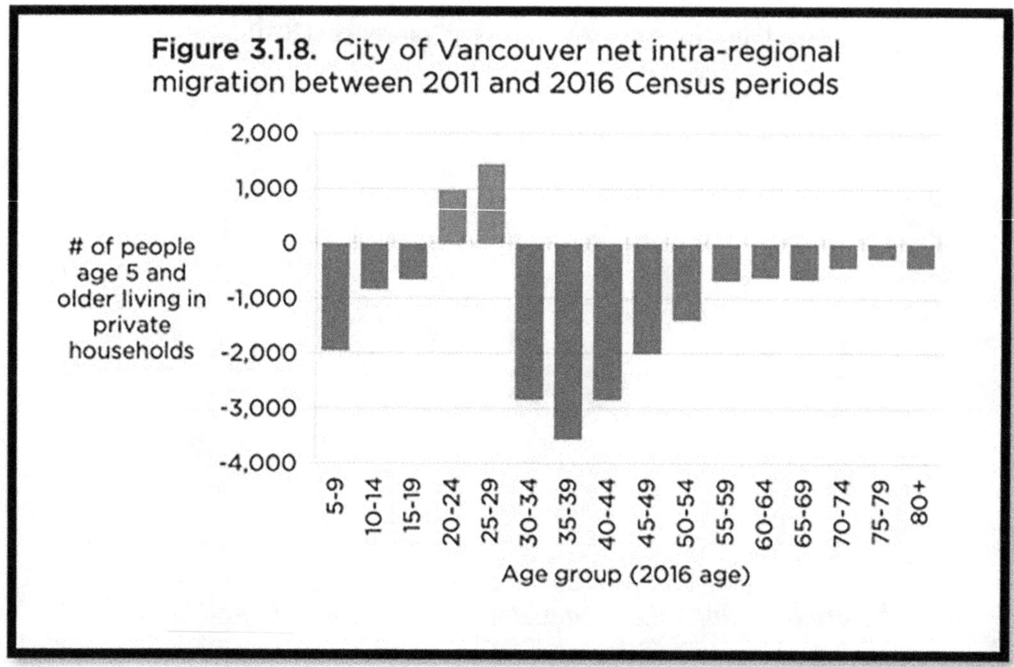

Figure 1.12: Outmigration and Connection to Affordability/Family Formation
(Source: City of Vancouver)

Regional Cycle and Intensification: In May 2020, the CMHC predicted the following housing outlook as a result of the pandemic:[22]

- Housing starts will likely see a decline of 51 to 75 percent.
- There will be a drop in existing home sales.
- Housing prices will dip but recover in 2021.
- The provincial housing market outlook will decline.

[22] Central Mortgage and Housing Corporation, Special Edition: Housing Market Outlook, May 27, 2020.

Figure 1.13 graphs the existing decline, potential stagnation, and recovery in 2021. The real question is when, and how, will the development market recover?

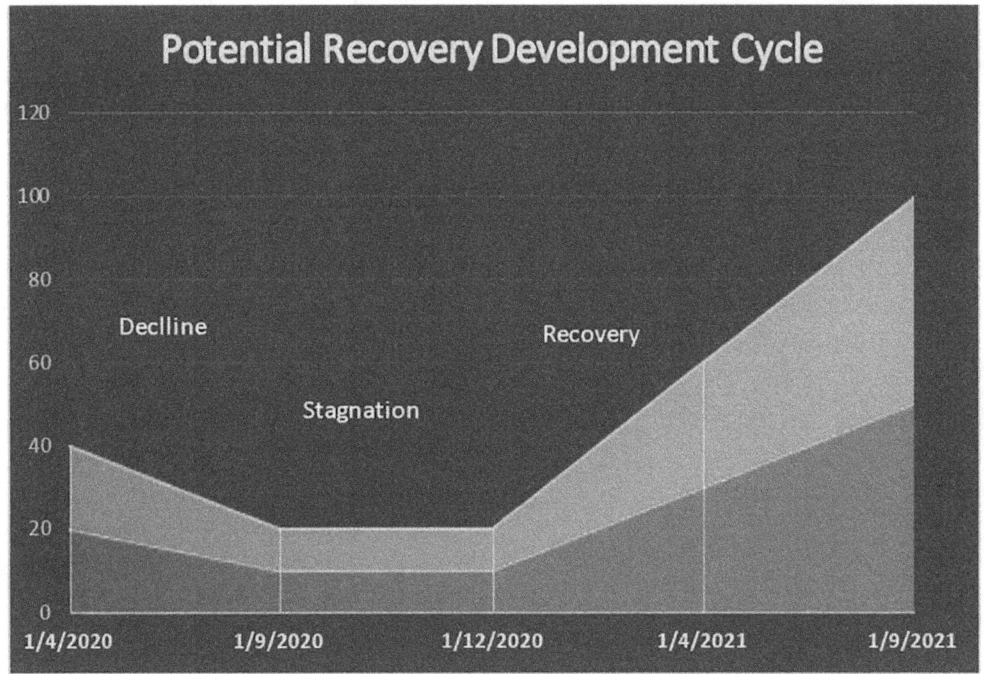

Figure 1.13: Conceptual Decline, Stagnation, and Recovery Cycle in Development (by author)

Factors such as population growth, an aging demographic, smaller households, smart transportation, and higher environmental priorities are important economic and social drivers that will further change the face of the region. Interestingly, in the first quarter of 2020, the ratio of population to housing starts was 2.8, the highest since 2015, and 61 percent above the five-year average for first quarters. This anomaly should mean further pressure on housing prices as demand exceeds supply.[23] Maintaining a critical balance of managing growth, retaining neighbourhood character, and establishing new neighbourhoods through insightful community development will be central to the quality of the emerging growth in the lower mainland region of British Columbia and the cities within it.

The Vancouver region's form is shifting to higher intensification of urban land use. The president of one of the region's largest housing development companies recently commented, "We don't build single-family housing anymore," referring to the radical transformation of building type and consumer demand that has evolved over the past 20 years in Metro Vancouver. Limited land, escalation in prices, and changing consumer preferences are some of the factors making higher density 'cool' in the region. The

23 Urban Development Institute, *State of the Market Quarterly Research Report*, May 2020, 4.

massive influx of immigrants over the past 25 years, a high proportion of who are from Asian countries, has especially fed the high-rise markets, as the original 'office boom' transitioned to the creative economy and a tourism emphasis.

However, there is a 'missing middle' layer of housing in the Vancouver area, homes that are somewhere in-between single-family housing and tall apartment buildings. Intermediate forms of density make neighbourhoods more neighbourly and human-scaled and include townhomes and other single-family dwellings that are not large single-family lots. Some suburbanites see such dwellings as intrusive and totally unacceptable, but the irony is that these same people will want to downsize in a few years and their children won't be able to afford to live in the same neighbourhood because of the lack of diversity and choice of housing.

Major transformations are happening in the Vancouver area. Transit use is on the rise, and the city has set a target of 50 percent of all regional travel being made by sustainable modes (walking, cycling, and transit) by 2040. Existing patterns are 49 percent for Vancouver and 29 percent for the overall region.

Vancouver's housing density is the highest in Canada at 54 units/hectare (22 units/acre), even compared to Toronto's 47 units/hectare (19 units/acre) and Montreal's 43 units/hectare (17 units/acre). Vancouver's density is six times that of the overall region.[24] Considering that the region is approximately 50 percent Agriculture Land Reserve (ALR) and open space, that number may be skewed somewhat to be actually three times the density at approximately 18 units/hectare (7 units/acre) depending on what assumptions are driving the density.

Following current trends, new clean employment areas can live harmoniously adjacent to, or within, new residential development. Mixed use, telecommuting, coworking space, live/work options, compact living, transit focused, and high amenity are core attributes—especially when gig economy startups are the incubators of the future, with solopreneurs leading the way. These employees want to be where the action is, and they want that action to be reachable by bike or foot. They don't necessarily need or want to own a car (there are car-sharing services for that), and so proximity to transit is a must. Single is cool, and small is big for housing. Townhome and apartment living are the new single-family housing, as prices continue to escalate, and density (done well) comes into vogue. Who wants to mow grass when they can do things that are more worthwhile, like roller-skate on the seawall?

[24] City of Vancouver, *Social Indicators Profile 2019*, 10, 50.

Single-Family No More and the New Urban Alchemy: In 2020, according to CMHC data, approximately one of every four housing starts was a single-family home. This translates to 25 percent across Canada and approximately one in five in British Columbia, or 20 percent. British Columbia averaged 20 to 25 percent of the approximate 210,000 housing starts across Canada over 2018 and 2019; therefore, 75 to 80 percent were not single-family homes.[25] This trend reflects the continuing squeeze to multiple-family housing, as affordability continues to erode. Formerly, especially in suburban locations, this proportion was reversed in that the majority of housing starts were single-family homes.

I am currently working for Langley City, and we are finding that the community's tolerance and preference for higher density housing options over the traditional single-family home is changing significantly compared to a few years ago. Done well, even low- and mid-rise apartments and condominiums can fit into a neighbourhood, if they respect the necessary physical transitions to adjoining properties. A duplex (two attached units), triplex (three attached units) or quadruplex (four attached units) can fit seamlessly into an existing neighbourhood, if it reflects in material, scale, and design details the style of the neighbourhood's single-family homes. Such structures present affordable buying options, aging in place opportunities, and alternatives for emerging smaller families and singles.

Townhomes or rowhomes, part of the 'missing middle' (between single-family homes and high-rises) can also be integrated into existing communities without detrimental effects. There is a perception that densifying neighbourhoods will cause real estate value to fall, but this is not necessarily true, not when demand for housing exceeds supply. In fact, these options create a more diverse neighbourhood and can provide housing for residents who want to age in their home community but downsize from the responsibilities of a detached, single-family home. Such options can also provide opportunities for adult children to stay close to home, especially where lane housing and coach houses provide affordable, compact options. Supplemental suites, lock-off suites in condominiums, and small housing on the same lot also provide mortgage helpers for the primary resident.

---

[25] Canada Mortgage and Housing Corporation, *Preliminary Housing Starts Data*, Ottawa, April 2020.

Climate Transformations and Responsive Green Design

> *We already value buildings and spaces that connect us to nature, as we demonstrate to pay a premium for such buildings … Buildings created in harmony with nature are valued by people because they allow us to be happier and healthier.*
>
> —*Amanda Sturgeon, Creating Biophilic Buildings (2017)*

Building in a manner that respects nature creates value through health and productivity, among other benefits. At the same time, climate change—drastic changes in our weather patterns—is bringing with it impending sea level rise, air pollution and related illness. Predictably, this has prompted most municipalities and regional districts to change their development and approval standards. The B.C. Building Code, and other provincial and federal regulations, have been modified to reflect this pattern of increased standards and regulations.

As one builder lamented, these new regulations collectively have added at least $10,000 if not more to the cost of a townhome. Counter to this argument is that the increase in quality, and associated resilience of the unit, make it worthwhile. Still, if additional costs can't be integrated into a redesign as part of a value-engineering exercise, they are normally handed down to the buyer as a premium. Affordability, at least in part, then becomes the victim because this change is not normally a small, incremental cost; if it was, it could be absorbed into the next generation of design efficiencies and construction. More significant increases, without question, will affect the sales price to the consumer in the end.

You may disagree with the whole idea of climate change, or perhaps you are simply numb to the idea due to an overload of information and fearmongering. Whatever your stance, you still may agree that designing to work with nature and our natural ecosystems instead of against it makes sense, especially if it contributes to healthier, more productive workplaces or homes. These days, home buyers and office renters look for healthy home and working environments and building with this in mind can give a developer an edge in the marketplace, especially when given comparative prices.

Eminent scientist Hope Jahren, when looking at the possibilities of the future in 2020, said it will take a transformative approach rather than the incremental approach supplicated in the Kyoto Protocol and the Paris Agreement. In other words, we have to change our fundamental ways of being to make effective and enduring environmental change.[26] Likewise, American author James Howard Kunstler, building on his books *Geography of Nowhere* (1991) and *The Long Emergency* (2005), tells stories of new ways

26 Hope Jahren. *The Story of More*, 136.

to thrive as we navigate the discontinuities facing us in the wake of the pandemic, in *Living the Long Emergency* (2020).

The difference between climate change and any other threat we face is that, like the pandemic, climate change can affect us personally. Thermometers don't lie, and 2016 was the hottest year on record. The previous environmental watchword 'sustainability' has lost momentum in the face of this, possibly because of its abstract, conceptual nature. Climate change brings the aspect of drastic and possibly life-threatening environmental change to our living rooms.

Whether you believe in climate change or not, you can't escape the fact that we are living through unprecedented physical, social, cultural, and economic change, and it is creating constant challenges and disruptions, some of which, like the recent pandemic, require adaptation or isolation. I choose the former: to adapt. It is not the talent of learning one thing really well that is the secret to success, but the talent of learning new things all the time, and adapting to constant, disruptive changes. This ability to adapt is part of the proposed *Approvals+* framework that I will discuss later in this book.

In Vancouver, aggressive moves to 'green site design' and improved building standards are in progress. The City of Vancouver aspired to be the greenest city in the world in 2020. The national and provincial building codes are both moving to Energy Step Code 3, the third step in the BC Energy Code system, as a requirement. To comply with Step 3, builders will need to create and adhere to a whole-building energy model, then test the building enclosure on the ground for air tightness. Minimum green building requirements are not options anymore; what once was viewed as innovative and progressive 'green design' is now the new standard. These green design features include rainwater management, tree retention and replacement, passive solar orientation, electric car readiness, non-toxic material standards, proximity to natural light, ventilation and heat recovery systems, and reduced parking standards, among others. In encouraging recycling and site construction management, as well as green building envelope construction, we are intentionally creating more resilient buildings, healthier living environments, added value, and more enduring communities.

Let's now look at one community that is leading the Vancouver region in innovation: UniverCity.

UniverCity Innovations: UniverCity is a sustainable community located on top of Burnaby Mountain, adjacent to Simon Fraser University (SFU) in the City of Burnaby. UniverCity has won several awards for sustainable planning and development and is currently home to over 4,000 residents. The UniverCity project demonstrates the importance of melding together appropriate housing type, form, tenure, accessible transit, and local services to create a complete, resilient, sustainable community. UniverCity is a case study in what we should look to for future planning. It is a high-intensity, high-amenity development that is also green, sustainable, and resilient.

At UniverCity, density, housing diversity, walking distances of only five to ten minutes to get to essential services, and effective public transit options all contribute to a highly liveable community. The master developer is a leading innovator: This was the first place in the region to offer lock-off suites (rental suites within condominium and townhouse units that can be locked off from the main suite). The first 'living building' in Western Canada (a living building mimics nature in processes such as generating its own energy and capturing and treating its own water) was developed at UniverCity and it currently serves as a home for the UniverCity Daycare (Figures 1.14, 1.15, 1.16, 1.17, and 1.18 below).

Even with no traditional stand-alone single-family housing units, UniverCity provides flexible living and convenient services. There is even a public transit gondola that has been proposed and is being considered. One might look at the place, and the politics behind it, and suggest that UniverCity was a special project—and that's true. But UniverCity also illustrates some of the best trends in the marketplace. Let's examine it a bit closer.

This isolated, mountaintop site was always going to be a challenge for development. SFU, which owns the land, pondered development for decades before then-President John Stubbs initiated planning in 1995. SFU holds the land in trust from the provincial government, and was unable to sell it, so instead SFU established a master developer, SFU Community Trust, in 2000. Chair David Gillanders then hired developer and architect Michael Geller as the first President and CEO of the Trust.

Parcels of land were leased for 99 years, pre-zoned and subject to specific design guidelines, and Geller helped convince his colleagues in the development community to begin bidding and building on them. This was a successful approach: The Trust's Request for Proposal (RFP) process provided certainty for developers and ultimately the Trust earned a reasonable return, which SFU uses to support its core teaching and research mission. Individual developers enjoyed a healthy profit, while creating affordable housing in the country's most expensive market, and people were given the opportunity to live in a sustainable, well-thought-out community.

The Trust's Request for Proposal (RFP) process has provided certainty for developers and for community members, whom the Trust surveys regularly to ensure the development continues to deliver on homeowner expectations. UniverCity has won numerous awards as one of the greenest communities in the world. When Geller stepped down as CEO of the Trust, he was succeeded by Gordon Harris. Harris went on to negotiate the first comprehensive green zoning bylaw in Canada. We owe much to these visionaries who have set a new standard in resiliency and sustainability. In this challenging environment, they have created a rich, diverse community that complements and supports SFU while delivering the highest standard of livability. UniverCity is a healthy alternative to typical suburban developments that are still auto-dependent, unevenly serviced and overly expensive.

Figure 1.14: Townhomes within five-minute walk to elementary school at UniverCity, Burnaby, BC

Figure 1.15: Stacked townhomes with daycare at UniverCity, Burnaby, BC

Figure 1.16: Mixed-use on High Street at UniverCity, Burnaby, BC

Figure 1.17: Low-rise apartments at UniverCity, Burnaby, BC

Figure 1.18: High amenity streetscape at UniverCity, Burnaby, BC

Richard Florida, in his visionary book, *Who's Your City,* looks forward to the next generation of urban life, which will be driven by changing demographics, associated preferences and emerging economic forces. Says Florida:

> *The new spatial fix will take shape around humongous mega-regions, which blend city and suburb into denser and more extensive urban agglomerations with multiple city centres and business cores, greater clusters of workplaces, residences, and industry more than anything we've seen before.*[27]

Efficient approvals processes are critical to the success of existing and future local development, neighbourhoods and entire communities, as all are connected in planning, design, and implementation. The costs from lost time, consultants' fees, and burdensome development processes are becoming untenable and are threatening the viability of projects. This story is not new, but it is becoming more complex, and in some instances, incomprehensible.

So, it's positive that municipalities, regional districts, and other levels of government are now trying to unpack and repack regulations and processes to make them more efficient, even as standards and costs continue to rise.

With this background and foresight in mind, let's further examine lessons, take-aways, and realities from the past as a basis for planning a more effective and inspiring future.

---

[27] Richard Florida, *Who's Your City*, xvii.

2. LESSONS, TAKE-AWAYS, AND REALITIES

> *Another thing the people didn't seem to understand is that the developer doesn't really control the process: a community can approve or reject a plan; construction costs can go up or down; buyers are unpredictable.*
>
> —*Witold Rybczynki, Last Harvest (2008)*

The development process as a whole is unpredictable, but the more knowledge and ground-proofed project intelligence we have, the more we can reduce uncertainty and risk. This chapter provides context for understanding what the challenges are and how we got here. Without context, decisions are made in a vacuum and the chances of stimulating change are next to none.

The business of real estate is not the wild west anymore and, in many municipalities across Canada, it is a sophisticated game that requires more and more finesse to take a project through the gauntlet of approvals at the local, community, provincial, and sometimes federal levels. First Nations have also entered the game as legitimate stakeholders and active players in the development process, as we will see. They are also the biggest landowners in British Columbia.

All these stakeholders have layered the approvals game into a three-dimensional Rubik's Cube that seems to be constantly changing and, to be successful, negotiations require a more front-end loaded, agile approach. We will speak further about this in the next two parts of the book.

Right now, let's first discover some timeless lessons from the past and then examine emerging realities about approvals you may not want to hear about. But you must, as they are current blockers to a clear and predictable pathway to your project's approval.

What I Learned and Didn't Learn at Harvard

When I was at the Harvard Graduate School of Design (HGSD) I became known as the 'developer', as I took courses at both Massachusetts Institute of Technology (MIT) and the Harvard Business School in real estate development. Though schooled in design, I wanted to know more about the development process, planning law, and economics. Design school students were not generally encouraged to focus on business and real estate development, but I eventually became the teaching assistant to Miller Blew, the real estate development instructor at the HGSD. Lucky—or was I?

Lesson one: Wisdom informs best decisions

At the time, there was no formal master's degree in real estate development, so I had to cobble together a curriculum that gave me some development knowledge. The real estate instructor icon at MIT was Philip David, a protégé of William Zeckendorf Sr., a prominent American real estate developer who developed a significant portion of the New York City urban landscape through his development company, Webb and Knapp.

David flew up to Boston from New York City to teach our course each week. Did he have some stories of victories and failures! I wanted to know what not to do, and he certainly shared his war stories. I soaked up these stories and more as he furiously worked chalkboard after chalkboard of numbers relating to various cases, turning into a white cloud by the end of each lecture. His impeccable, shiny, Italian form-fitting suits and shiny bald head were transformed by a haze of chalk to look like workers' clothes, his shiny bald head muted by the dust. He was passionate about his subject, and we left the class dazed with numbers, and with his stories spinning in our heads. This was no superfluous salesman, though; he knew what he was doing and proved it with numbers.

I also did do some valuable applied research work as part of my courses at Harvard, in the Fort Point Channel area of Boston and the technology triangle at MIT, meeting industry icons from Rose and Associates in New York; Cabot, Cabot, and Forbes in Boston; and the Rouse Corporation in Baltimore. Some of my teammates in these class projects were brilliant (or so they thought) and brash. As the youngest in the crowd, I just listened and absorbed their insights and keen analytics, feeling that it was better to keep my head down and my ego in check amongst these heady students. Some of my colleagues had been bankers, developers, and businesspeople for years before they decided to go back to school to get their graduate degrees. Who was I to argue ideas with them?

Ultimately, the teamwork, case study method, and applied analytics I learned and experienced during my time at Harvard and MIT brought me to the conclusion that real estate, like most businesses, requires a team approach that will provide a comprehensive look at all dimensions. One perspective alone is doom; you need multiple perspectives to provide balanced and insightful strategy. Real estate development at a larger scale requires a number of thinkers to provide break-through strategies and ensure that wisdom prevails. In this way, developers find value where no one else sees it. He or she mines the ground until they hit gold—risky but certainly exciting for the adventurous.

Wisdom, the result of appropriate learning, should always prevail. Wisdom is your gut feeling, your wisdom prompter, and your core intelligence. If your gut feels good, it is an indicator of a conditional go but if it feels off, then something is wrong. Potential red flags for your projects deserve notice and further due diligence. Listen to inner and outer wisdom; these inform best decisions, which was my first lesson at Harvard.

Lesson two: Do your homework and come prepared

Miller Blew, my mentor at the HGSD during my teaching assistantship, was a tall, grey-haired, formidable man with a huge handle-bar mustache and what appeared to be size 13 black, Oxford shoes—or so it seemed when he put them up on his desk among his piles of papers. A white, preppy shirt, a large bow tie, and grey flannel pants finished the east-coast Ivy League wardrobe. He had a hard shell on the outside, but over time I found a soft core with good intentions underneath it.

Miller was an architect who had graduated with distinction from the Harvard Business School, meaning he graduated in the top five percent of his class—no small feat! Miller terrified his classes with his case study method and forthright piercing directness. His pace was fast and furious. You either had the right answer, or he moved on.

Early in my first course, I had worked almost all the way through the night with my international student team to do an Internal Rate of Return (IRR) on the Graybar Shopping Centre case. This exercise required us to use a hand-held calculator to determine a 20-year cashflow, with a sale of the property at the end of the term. There were no Excel spreadsheets at the time, so it was quite a chore. An archaic LOTUS 123 spreadsheet program was just on the horizon but was not quite yet available for us.

After figuring out our numbers, we were exhausted when we came to class the next day. We sat rigid with anticipation, expecting him to suddenly call people out, a classic business school tactic. As I sat in total fear, trembling in anticipation of Professor Blew's sudden call, he came to me for my team's IRR. "von Hausen, what did you get?" he asked sternly.

Fear enveloped me and I will never forget his tough, unforgiving character as he brushed me off when I said, "We got 16.65 percent."

Abruptly he replied, "Close, but no cigar." The exact answer was 16.9 percent. The other answers varied from 15 to 22 percent.

Miller was a tough cookie, but I knew he meant well. We students shook in our boots every class as Miller's ritual repeated itself, especially when the real estate developers would join us (which they did sometimes) and share with us that we were all essentially wrong, because one or more variables (like market absorption or sales price) had unexpectedly changed and therefore the project projections were radically altered.

Expect the unexpected, we learned, and be nimble enough to act on these changing variables. Finally, leave no stone unturned in your vigorous investigations. Miller once told me simply and directly, "He or she who is best prepared and has done their homework will do the best."

I have taken this credo through my career and regret the few times I did not come into a situation prepared. Miller was absolutely right. Come prepared—lesson two from Harvard.

Lesson three: Dig beyond the obvious to find real community and project values
Among all this study, there was never any real mention of the approvals processes we may need to face when we entered our new careers. Approvals were seen almost as a technical process; the idea was that you just follow the steps and obtain the permit—straightforward and simple. We learned the numbers and the variables from project type to project type; we even learned about tax incentives for historic preservation, and general tax considerations from project to project.

Then all that changed. Miller called me into his office and asked, "von Hausen, do you want to do something worthwhile and valuable?" I cautiously peered over his size 13 shoes that were, as usual, on his desk among his stacks of papers, to where he slouched back in his chair and asked, "And what is this opportunity?" Without hesitation, he promptly said that I had done a great job in presenting the Boston Stock Exchange case to the class and that he wanted me to write a business case study that would be published at the Harvard Business School, adding, "Do you realize that not many people ever get to write a case for the Business School?"

I considered the proposition for all of a few seconds, not realizing fully the intensity of what lay in front of me, and blurted out, "I'll do it." Fear and excitement enveloped me as I turned and left Miller's office. What had I just got myself into? That business study resulted in a case used for some time at Harvard.

So began an intensive process that involved me finding out as much as I could about the emerging Canadian real estate giant Olympia and York, based in Toronto. They had just purchased 13 buildings in New York City—all at one time! Private companies like Olympia and York do not divulge much information, so I had to get whatever I could through wits alone before I could develop the case content, questions, and basic market and project context numbers. As I did so, the complexity of the case began to reveal itself. What I found was that there were inherent conflicts between the developer and the heritage preservationists. The preservationists were led by Angus Crowe, a dedicated architect committed to saving Boston's valuable landmarks.

Angus and his group were well-organized, and a storm was brewing in city hall as the nay-sayers gained ground, as reflected in a stream of articles in local media, headed by the Boston Globe. The developer had originally one public option—the glass tower and no preservation—but to my surprise, I found out there was a second option, to conserve the façade of the Boston Stock Exchange building and build the glass tower *behind* it. But, in the early stages of planning, this second option was not public.

There was a lot at stake with a 22-floor area ratio (FAR) potential permitted density on site. In simple terms, the developer could, with permission, build up to 22 times the site area! With an average of 50 percent site coverage on these kinds of compact sites, that would mean up to 44 stories or approximately 137 metres (450 feet) of height. This was 1980 and was no small building even by Boston's standards.

What eventually was approved and built was option two, and today it stands in its sensitive and iconic glory at 50 State Street in Boston, reflective of the foundational community values that saved valuable heritage DNA by developing an iconic landmark within its historic wrappings. This insightful solution became an example that is used across North America in retaining our valued past (Figures 2.1a, and 2.1b below). The final building, completed in 1984, rises 40 floors from its foundations to a height of 155 metres (510 feet). It is the 14th highest building in the city of Boston.

In Vancouver, they have taken things one step farther by creating the *Heritage Revitalization Agreement*. This agreement is a policy tool that is used to transfer unused density (or 'air rights') to other receiving sites. In situations where a developer wants to retain heritage values, but is doing so at some cost, he can recoup by selling the air rights to a project that can have more density. So, the full heritage structure is not touched, and density is transferred elsewhere.

Lesson 3 at Harvard brings to life the value of listening and integrating community values in order to achieve success. Do so, and you will find more prosperity and support.

Figures 2.1a and 2-1 b: 50 State Street in Boston
The former Boston Stock Exchange building and redevelopment that integrated the historical façade

Lesson four: The three laws of reasonableness, facts, and martinis
Professor William Doebele was a memorable and well-established law professor at Harvard. He taught a full room of over 200 planning and design students, and captivated ears listened as he described the case law that shaped America's land use and development over the last century.

From the holdings of the foundational Euclid versus Ambler nuisance case of 1926 (in which the practice of zoning was argued in the U.S. Supreme Court), to some of today's contemporary, exclusionary zoning cases in New Jersey, all have relevance to the cumulative layers of common law and precedents used today. But beyond the 'case on case' of planning law, there are three laws that echo in my mind continually that have stood the test of time, and stand steadfast and universal today in the same way as when I first heard them.

First law: *If it is reasonable, go ahead.* This statement means that if a project is reasonable, or the assumptions behind it are reasonable, you should proceed further. If not, stop and reconsider.

Second law: *Facts win cases.* Win your case on facts, not speculation. In any real estate development project, the facts presented to municipal staff, council, and at public hearings are the credible foundation to build approvals on. To try to win your case without facts is a fool's errand.

Third law: *Three martinis with your circuit judge is worth three books of law.* This is not about bribery or illicit activities; this is about knowing what the backstory is, not simply the policy law. It is about understanding not only the face value of written words, but the meaning and *intention* of those words. This law is maybe the most important one for real estate development approvals, as it directs us to building relationships and trust. For planners and developers, those relationships include such diverse players as the director of planning, councillors, and community. You can't focus on property policy and legal rights in a vacuum. As I will elaborate on later, relationships and trust are crucial in obtaining consistent results in project approvals.

Lesson five: DAD and the approvals evolution

I didn't learn anything directly about approvals, especially as we know them today, at Harvard. When I was a student there, in the late 1970s, it was a different era and the real estate world was seen as a somewhat technocratic conglomeration of big money. Permit approvals without much public engagement were the norm, and there was no social media or internet to engage or inform people about what was going on in their neighbourhoods.

However, there was a rise of citizen activism of personalities like Jane Jacobs of New York/Toronto. Jacobs was an American-Canadian journalist, author, and activist who influenced urban studies, sociology, and economics and wrote the seminal book, *The Death and Life of Great American Cities*. There were isolated incidents of activism on big issues, but not on a daily basis at the time.[28] Decisions were determined largely by powerbrokers like Robert Moses. Robert Moses was an American public official in New York whose decision to favour highways over public transit helped create the suburbs of Long Island, influencing a generation of engineers, architects, and urban planners. Moses ruled from the top and maneuvered masterfully to obtain political support.[29]

I was certainly naïve to think I was tooled for the real world when I graduated. I had certainly learned some valuable things during my schooling in real estate development, but the live theatre of the real world would build on my educational foundation, particularly with regard to approvals processes. I was amazed that I hadn't been taught much about this. Why wasn't there more about community engagement, the politics of approvals, staff interaction, and how to build relationships to gain trust in my curriculum? Maybe because this was the era of top-down versus bottom-up planning, where the professionals and city hall determined the fate of city building with little input from the community.

---

28 Jane Jacobs, *The Death and Life of Great American Cities*, n.p.

29 Robert Caro, *The Power Broker*, n.p.

Certainly, the favoured technique at the time was the outmoded 'decide, announce, defend' (DAD) technique of public engagement, where projects were developed in isolation from the public (decide); then announced to the public as a finalized option (announce); and finally, presented to the public without flexibility and sensitivity (defend). This was the way I was taught to design and develop at the time. A defensive posture toward the public was the dominant stance of the day. On the development side, we would rationalize by asking ourselves, what do they know? What right do they have mucking in someone else's business? Community response to development and change was simply a sideshow, and a torturous phase of the process.

Following my completion of graduate school at Harvard, I spent ten years doing a variety of things including real estate development in Alberta; finance and venture capital in Vancouver; design and planning in Ottawa; and finally, teaching and consulting in Denver, Colorado. I was bouncing around to get my real-world education and find my niche. All this time, without being completely aware of it, I was learning about real estate approvals processes.

A further awakening awaited me when I joined the City of Vancouver in 1991. While it has never been easy to obtain approvals, especially for larger, complex projects, I was soon to become aware how different approvals processes are in different countries.

Take-aways from Vancouver City Hall Experience

I remember my stepmother, an astute businessperson in her own right and development partner with my father, constantly teasing me when I was at the City of Vancouver, saying, "What a waste of time working for government."

I would patiently and calmly respond, "Mom, I am learning how the inside works, so I can eventually work the system effectively from the outside."

American financier and banker J.P. Morgan once famously said, "I work for the bank, for that is where the money is." I did a similar thing to J.P. Morgan, but instead worked for a planning department because that is where the policy and approvals heart lies. I learned the inner workings, and how the process operates, from the inside out. I only realized the value years later when I started working from the outside in. My experience on both sides has given me the understanding that has made me a trusted third party in many municipal and private projects, which I will describe more fully later in the book.

Working for the city, I gained a healthy respect for what goes on inside, including staff duties, the increasing level of professional competency within, and the commitment to protect the public interest in what can be a very turbulent political environment that changes every few years.

Let's now look at some key take-aways from my experience on the inside of City Hall. First, bear in mind that these are not easy jobs. Let's put our feet in their shoes for a moment and see how we can soften our critical views by further understanding where power lies, who controls the agreements and why, and how we can possibly work more effectively with, not against, the system.

Take-away one: The municipality holds the pen

Approvals start and end with staff and ultimately council. Thinking that you as the developer or landowner hold the power with your property rights is a fool's dream. You may be partially right, but in terms of approvals, the balance of power rests with government. I've learned that receiving permission to build a proposal, even within existing zoning, can be an arduous task.

It is important to understand that this power to control what happens on private property is not intended to deprive the landowner of rights, but is instead intended to protect the public health, safety and interest of Canadians. Essentially, the *public's* interest is a higher aspiration in the minds of staff and council than individual property rights. Unfortunately, this public interest can sometimes be manipulated by self-interested political or community players, occasionally making it a wolf in sheep's clothing. Beware how sometimes things represented as community truths are actually self-interests. Peer behind the veil and see the enlightening real agenda that is frequently not obvious.

Another thing that can delay projects unnecessarily is innovative design, especially if council or staff have concerns. Norm Hotson, an eminent architect in Vancouver, in a class I facilitated at the Urban Development Institute, shared a story about the Capers Block courtyard on 4th Avenue, west of Vancouver's Burrard Street. Staff concerns regarding public safety of this courtyard delayed the project an additional six months, but the courtyard is now a landmark meeting place in Kitsilano and an innovative addition to the community. It is also an example of successful relationship-building with city staff to create a success, and it sets a precedent to follow.

Unfortunately, innovative ideas have not only delayed but sometimes eliminated well-intended project elements, which leads to my next point. Remember, take-away one is that the municipality holds the pen of approvals. Unfortunately, great ideas can be left on the cutting room floor if they are presented prematurely, victims of bias, unfounded judgements, and wrong timing.

Take-away two: The community holds the power

Without significant community support, your project is simply a failed application, unless council and staff have an exceptional reason to overrule community concerns. The exception is where your application complies with existing zoning and no public review is required. In the Vancouver region, and across Canada, there are sites that have been looked at continuously for project development, but the same conclusion is reached over and over—it's not the right time, or maybe it's the wrong design, or both.

Name a neighbourhood in the City of Vancouver—Kitsilano, Marpole, Mount Pleasant; in all of these places it's difficult at best, and a nightmare at worst, to obtain support for a project. No matter what goodies you provide, there are constant neighbourhood accusations of negative impacts; parking, transportation, safety, overshadowing, and community infrastructure intrusion, among others, are regularly listed, as well as associated potential crime in the community. Largely exaggerated misconceptions of these issues are actually the new normal whether you are in Halifax, Ottawa, Toronto, Calgary, or Vancouver.

Building support in the community starts at the beginning of a project, with an inclusive outreach and communications plan before any substantive site or building design begins. To do otherwise will undermine trust and eventual community support for the project. Recently, I was reminded yet again by the director of development services for a lower mainland municipality that it takes only one person to rise against a project at a public hearing to have council defer the third reading vote. In many cases, the project is approved eventually—but it is one more delay in approvals.

Remember, one apple drops and the whole apple cart can be upended if it is not balanced properly. It may be hard to imagine, but it happens if residents' concerns are not addressed to their, and council's satisfaction, prior to the public hearing. Do not miss turning over a stone in your community or dismiss a valid comment. Listen, listen, and listen some more. This is how you can achieve miraculous results. It is *their* community, not yours. They own it and are the experts, as many residents have lived there for decades. The community, in most instances, controls the vote of council, and so without their solid and substantive support, all is lost.

Adding community consultation to the technical approvals adds months and often years to a process, which may seem daunting. But I firmly believe in the rule that you must 'go slow to go fast'. If you have community support, the rest becomes a fairly predictable technical process, assuming explicit parameters for development. There is no short process now, even when it comes to outright applications that do not require rezoning. Consultation is king.

We will examine the various planning approval processes in more detail later as well as strategy drivers in chapter 8 to build support for your project. Take-away two: The community holds the power.

Take-away three: Staff holds the tools to approvals and a commitment to excellence
Too often we assume that staff are impediments to processes. Sometimes that is true, but often this assumption is false. At the city of Vancouver in the 1990s when I was on staff, for example, the city had a highly trained professional team of architects, landscape architects, and development planners. Complemented by a talented outside application development team, this made for relatively smooth approvals processes.

This commitment to urban design excellence and public participation was first embraced by Ray Spaxman, who headed Vancouver's planning department in the 1970s and 1980s. Spaxman set an innovative precedent with regard to planning in Vancouver that was carried on in the 1990s by Larry Beasley, who was responsible for forward thinking developments in both North False Creek, Vancouver's Downtown South and elsewhere.

Compromise was not an option under Beasley's leadership. For example, there were two options for building the specified 'public realm' alongside these projects. The developer could build it to specifications, or the City of Vancouver could build it at 150 percent of the cost, billed to the developer. Guess who built the public realm? The developer, to specifications of course (Figure 2.2).

Figure 2.2: The High Amenity Streetscape
Private and public realm improvements in Downtown South, Vancouver

Today, the City of Vancouver continues to strive for excellence. They have the largest engineering department in North America, with 2,800 personnel! They are currently building much of the public realm in the Cambie Street corridor to ensure it is executed with overall cohesion and consistency. What the City of Vancouver accomplished in the 1990s set the stage for the quality urban design that Vancouver is known for throughout the world, and what is now known as Vancouverism.[30] 'Vancouverism' is an urban planning and architectural phenomenon in Vancouver characterized by mixed-use developments, active street fronts, high quality public realm, reliance on mass public transit, view corridors and green spaces to support a large residential population.

Vancouverism appears to have rubbed off on other municipalities throughout the Lower Mainland over time. It is an ultimate credit to our committed development community who build these projects that they continue to be a testament for healthy living spaces and are setting the stage for the next generation. Vancouver continues to garner top world rankings for quality of life. Take-away three: Work with a committed staff to improve your project.

Take-away four: Community amenities are the tender for discretionary approvals
Community amenity contributions (CACs) were born in the 1990s as Vancouver was searching for ways to balance their budget while paying for community facilities needed

---

[30] Larry Beasley, *Vancouverism*, n.p.

due to rapid growth. Although always referred to as entirely 'voluntary', they are expected as part of development planning.

Originally CACs were negotiated on a site-by-site basis to extract funds for community facilities, either off-site or on-site, in exchange for additional density of normally discretionary residential uses. The extent of the financial contribution was determined based on the density granted and the value of the associated 'land lift' as a result of rezoning. 'Land lift' is the difference between the value of the existing property and the appraised value of the rezoned property. Vancouver and other municipalities have been known to require up to 80 percent of the land lift paid before construction begins.

We will learn later that most other municipalities have also pursued CACs as a source of community facility and other amenity funding. Take-away four: Community amenity contributions are here to stay and are important tender for approvals (Figures 2.3 and 2.4 below).

<u>Figure 2.3: Community Amenity Improvements</u>
North False Creek development and rich streetscape with mixed uses

Figure 2.4:
Waterfront pathway negotiated from 3 metre to 10 metre right-of-way.

Community Amenity Vision: City of Vancouver engineers initially insisted on the potential of a three-metre-wide (ten foot) pathway along the north side of False Creek, and it wouldn't necessarily be continuous. Through negotiations and inspirational drawings, planning staff convinced them that the minimum standard should be ten metres (33 feet) to include a separated bike and walking path continuous along the waterfront. Could you imagine a three-metre (10 foot) wide walkway? Vision is important and this continuous walkway and bikeway is now part of the lifeblood of the community, and Vancouver, today.

Take-away five: Community engagement is an art and a science of trust building
It is interesting to see the turnaround in a community. Building trust is at the core. Many neighbourhoods have had 'bad experiences' with development, because trust is sparse or not there.

In my experience with transportation projects, greenways planning, and development approvals, there is always suspicion between the players, and well-founded criticism is exchanged. When you build trust and deliver on even the smallest projects, however, there is genuine gratitude and, in some cases, disbelief that you've managed to deliver the project. If you, as a developer, deliver on your promises, you will be a hero for at least a week if not for all time. Memories are long in communities. Take-away five: Build community trust and it will pay endless dividends in approvals.

Take-away six: Don't assume anything until the ink is dry

The City of Vancouver instigated some innovative development process improvements during my tenure there. One aspect I believe to be transformative was the introduction of what I refer to as a 'front-end loaded process', in which they used a facilitator and a 'scoper' to help manage the efficiency and clarity of the process.

The scoper outlined potential roadblocks and requirements at the beginning of the process, while the facilitator guided the applicant through the process step-by-step. A pre-application meeting was organized so that the applicant could meet with the key departments and ensure all aspects of the application requirements were discussed—especially the red flags that could delay approvals.

In many projects, this refreshing approach worked well. Nevertheless, in other projects after many refreshing, enthusiastic first meetings, and false presumptions of approval, projects still managed to get bogged down in various requirements that were all but debilitating. No one was at fault, per se, but the system is such that any little thing can slow approvals to a crawl. Take-away six: Do not assume anything and keep your eye on the target and your hand on your smart phone.

Twenty Years of Learning Both Sides Outside Vancouver

Following my experience working at Vancouver City Hall, I started my own consulting practice, which opened my eyes to the world—literally. I worked in the United States, Mexico, Russia, and China and I also was fortunate enough to spread my wings from Vancouver to Halifax. What eye-opening experiences!

I worked as a public sector consultant for the City of Phoenix, Arizona, as well as the City of Edmonton, Alberta. I also worked for large private developers including Shape Properties in Vancouver, and development interests elsewhere such as Canada Mortgage and Housing Corporation (CMHC). CHMC sent me to work on international projects overseas in Russia and China where, as you will learn, top-down executive approvals are the modus operandi.

All these public and private experiences enriched my palette of approaches to the entire process of development approvals. They taught me valuable lessons I want to share with you so your own processes can be more robust, flexible, and responsive. I want to present what I have learned as rules, as they are essential in the 'approval skills' game. We always have to remind ourselves that there is much more than just the speed of approvals, although at the same time, unnecessary time delays is money wasted.

Rule one: Be nimble and adjust

I remember Krasnoyarsk, Russia—a city of over one million people located in mid-Siberia on the Yenisei River—clearly. My client, Alex Gobechev, looked me and said, "There is only one solution, and you will present it to the regional government."

I was somewhat shocked, as I was used to being flexible and leaving room to maneuver, especially in highly political international situations. But Alex's direction was a good reminder of where I was and how I should carry myself. This was Russia, and the power for decision-making rested solely at the top of the food chain. This was certain, and no other option was even considered.

I adjusted my presence to an assertive mode, and matched my presentation style accordingly. My consulting team and I rehearsed our presentation which we would be giving to the Krasnoyarsk regional government. The goal was approval of a new community for an estimated 25,000 residents. Alex was the former vice-mayor of the City of Krasnoyarsk, and he knew the politics of approvals very well.

When we actually did the presentation—in an environment similar to the House of Commons in Ottawa—it went off without a hitch. The regional governor and his staff were all set up for approval. The stage was set, and we presented the plan in less than 30 minutes, complete with translation. The result was unanimous endorsement and then the TV cameras were all on our client Alex Gobechev as he answered questions about this significant new development.

Rule one: Be nimble in your preparations and presentations and be prepared to modify them depending on the circumstances and the local style and etiquette. In that way, you get *your* way and they (the approval authority) get *their* way as well. Everybody wins!

Rule two: Use soft hands and carry carrots

The famous quote from Theodore Roosevelt, "Speak softly, but carry a big stick," comes to mind when discussing project negotiations, but I use it with a slightly gentler twist. I always approach my challenges, especially 'dead patients' (projects on the verge of failing) that need resuscitation with soft hands and carrots as a way to open up meaningful conversation and bring them back to life.

I am reminded of two recent projects that were almost turned into nightmares by hard and insensitive hands. My consulting group was brought in to develop a facility plan for a First Nations group. The project seemed straightforward, but somehow the First Nation's project manager's 'need' was to develop detailed facility programming plans with their user groups rather than through the process of more general community consultation. By not communicating well and not listening to needs of the client, a stalemate ensued.

Direct off-line private conversations with the project manager created the necessary understanding to correct the course of the proposal and get it back on track. We corrected the work program emphasis and the associated budget to match the *client's* 'needs' for ultimate success. The lesson was that we needed to listen intently to first understand the other party's point of view, before being understood. Sometimes it is difficult, but you have to ask the right questions to get the right answers.

Rule two: Carry a carrot called 'openness' and first seek understanding of the problem. Only then can you develop alternative solutions. Openness is your gateway to solutions that will cover all interests to the extent possible.

Rule three: Leave your ego at the door and walk together

We have all made the mistake of trying to take command of a room with emotion or enthusiasm rather than respectful communication. I am guilty more than I think I am, as I tend to overtalk in my enthusiasm. My wonderful wife sometimes nudges me, or gently kicks me under our large dining room table, to remind me that any guests in our house deserve to be listened to.

The same applies in a room full of staff or community members who want to be heard. Simple rules of desired behaviour are:

- When you hear yourself speak, it is time to be quiet; and
- Speak last rather than first, and only when necessary.

This latter rule reminds me of the purported wisdom of Zulu chiefs. According to legend, the chief speaks only if it is necessary, but otherwise remains silent. Sage advice.

I have trained myself to put on the quiet mantle of listener, just asking questions and probing for answers rather than directing meetings, and have found that inquiry is always more important than control. This approach has been affirmed many times for me. I hear constantly from the community, "Thank you for listening to us, it makes a big difference, and we feel that our issues were heard and dealt with genuinely as part of the development application process."

Rule three: Speak only when necessary. You were given two ears and one mouth so you can listen at least twice as much as you speak.

Rule four: Formal meetings are for approval, not agreement

I thought I had this rule ingrained in my practice, but it happened again recently that I wound up in a disaster of a meeting ruled by old, white men, who almost came to blows. Two developers with large egos met without prior contact and could not find common ground. I should have insisted on my protocol.

Previous to this meeting, which was between a large community group and our development group, I had suggested a preparation meeting with the leader of the community group, who was a distinguished land developer in his own right. I believed we needed to meet separately to create a personal connection and feel out the community interests and positions.

My goal had been to create a comfort and trust and perhaps an informal agreement in principle before the main meeting; however, the engineer, despite good intentions, did not get the preliminary meeting set up, and so we rolled into a 'gun fight'. The emotions of the community representatives were so high that nothing was accomplished, and a greater divide was created. Egos were not left at the door. A prior meeting could have helped all parties to work together to set a common agenda, allay concerns, and create a preliminary series of solutions to consider.

So, it is a good rule of thumb to have a meeting *before* the meeting, to get the teams moving in a common direction. By their nature, formal meetings are stressful, and so they should be simply for approval and refinement. The informal meeting is for 'peace-making' and outlining agreement options. This same principle applies to development agreements and public hearings. You want to get the job done *before* the public hearing, not *at* the public hearing. If you try to hash complicated issues out at a public hearing, good intentions will normally end in disaster. Remember, in a public forum, bad news is good news for the naysayers.

Rule four: Agree on decisions before the formal meeting to attain a mutually supported solution.

Rule five: Break through with a third-party facilitator

Many projects need a third party who has 'no skin in the game', therefore no conflict of interest or bias toward a specific outcome, to broker a deal. I often take on this role. In Alberta, for example, I have worked in facilitating annexations for up to 4,000 hectares (10,000 acres), and I have helped unblock approvals in various municipalities.

I have learned that the role of facilitator is invaluable. To attempt this type of complex negotiation, it is essential to test the chemistry of the situation, assess the project, and create a workplan. I first try to understand what the parties want to accomplish, and then I build a series of principles, goals, and common interests. I then take them through a process of joint problem-solving to find solutions they both can support. I am simply a coach in the process, but I am also a crucial player. The importance of a facilitator in complex situations cannot be understated. (See Appendix B: *Building Agreement Through a Consensual Process* as a further resource.)

Rule five: When you use the tool of the third-party facilitation correctly, it can be a great asset. A facilitator can solve what might otherwise be an impossible impasse between two parties. I will discuss the third-party tool further in Chapter 6 of this book (Figure 2.5 below).

Figure 2.5: The third-party facilitator can help bridge common interests

Realities You Don't Want to Hear About

They don't have to approve anything

I was in denial when I first heard this statement: "They don't have to approve anything". I thought to myself, *how can this statement be true? Don't we have inherent rights that come with a piece of land?* However, the statement above was said to me by a close colleague and friend, a former chief administrative officer (CAO) for a municipality in Metro Vancouver, and he knew what he was talking about.

What really shocked me is not what he said but what he meant. Imagine for a moment that there is no basic right to at least build what is permitted under current zoning, or under the current official community plan. This idea goes against my core understanding of real estate development approvals and planning. What it means is that essentially, if a council or board of directors (as manage regional districts in B.C.) do not want to approve a project for some reason, even if it's for purely political reasons, they will find a way to defer approvals indefinitely.

This is generally done by asking (again and again) for more information, or clarification on technical details, which essentially stone-walls progress through the approvals process. This technique can go on indefinitely, to their advantage. A politician's best position when there is perceived or real risk, or doubt, is to defer decision.

I learned this years ago, when the former chief administration officer for a city in Alberta shared the stark reality of the extent of power held by councils. In a private strategy session, he said, "You don't know the extent of the tools they (municipal councils) have to control outcomes. You are powerless unless they support you."

In other words, in many approvals situations, the powers vested in council and the approving officer can result in refusal based on obscure terms or policies, as long as those terms and policies appear legitimate in the minds of the approvers and are legally supportable. This can be enough to defer projects, sometimes indefinitely.

Community sentiment determines outcome

Unfortunately, community feelings toward a project are largely overlooked by real estate developers. They are frequently discounted or denied as secondary and many developers don't think such public sentiment really affects the approvability of a project. Yet such presumption is often a fatal flaw in the approvals process, as the developer gets blind-sided at the public hearing, having been in denial throughout the process. When the project is flatly turned down, sometimes by what appears to be a close vote at council, the developer scratches his or her head and wonders why.

The ability to really hear others' concerns and be proactive in outreach is critical to the success of any development approvals process. The City of Vancouver instigated a 'good neighbour' program years ago that required developers to reach out to adjacent landowners before a formal application was actually made to ensure the neighbours were aware of the project and could voice their concerns early. There is merit in starting early and knowing the valid concerns of neighbours. Ultimately, this approach—being aware of others' concerns—will save you time and money. It may even help you help birth a support group. I will discuss this concept further in the *Approvals+* process and framework sections in Chapters 6 and 7.

Staff can frequently be on the other side

Early conversations with staff are worth three books of law, as I pointed out earlier in this chapter. Sometimes, staff are not really approachable, or do not return calls immediately. If this occurs with your project, it is a sign that something is going on. It may be related to bigger issues, such as past development applications, or it could be that they simply don't support the development or a rezoning of the property for various reasons. With planners, it may be that there are no supportive policies; with engineers, it may be because transportation or servicing issues are larger than the land development proposal in question.

This situation is difficult at best, and may provide a basis to consider another property. Ensure that you visit with an approving officer, and other key players in the municipality, before you close the sale on the property. You don't want to walk into a pre-application meeting to a cool reception where everyone is smiling and cordial, but no move is made to advance the project— except requirements for all sorts of costly studies. Worse still, you will find yourself dead in the water if the development or planning director indicates that they can't support your application on policy or technical grounds. A final killer is associated political risk. If there is such risk, chances are council will not favour you; after all, saying no is easier than saying yes in many situations. So, the biggest question to ask yourself before taking your proposal to them is, "Why should they say 'yes'?" Then give them reasons to tip the scales in your favour.

Council is a wild card

Understanding the motivation and political interests of municipal or regional councils is important for their winning vote. I use the phrase, "One vote can determine outcomes," and it is so true when it comes to approvals, at council or otherwise.

In many cases, voting can be close but still doesn't indicate the 'behind-the-scenes' position of any given council. Votes often favour the political whims of the day and can turn on a dime if your relationships with these people are not managed properly and sensitively. Lobbying at council should be on the 'continuing work' program of the developer to ensure a favoured position all the way to the public hearing, and potential final adoption of the project.

I distinctly remember veteran Vancouver councillor and lawyer Harry Rankin saying that, "It is the last man standing who ultimately wins." He was referring to the approvals process, and its associated political and community review rigours. Never assume you have the council's vote, and work towards unanimous approval if possible … otherwise it is a flip of the coin, which is far too risky. You have to wait to count the votes until the very end, and councillors can flip-flop at the last minute. It is fascinating to watch the ebb and flow of the changing tides in these meetings, as the mood can shift with one compelling speaker. That is why you must work to bring many supportive speakers to the public hearing, so you can ensure a 'love-in' for the project, if possible. I will describe these strategies in further detail in Chapter 8, as 'successful strategy drivers'.

Don't fall in love with your project

If the deal or approvals appear impossible, find another property. If you hear, as I have heard a few times from senior municipal or district planners, "You have a great design, but it is on the wrong site," this means there is little hope for obtaining staff and council endorsement for the project. This is just good business. For example, after years of haggling and trying to get through community and council obstructions, the president of an eminent development company phoned me and said, "Find me another site for this great idea." Drop the option or sell the property if it's not working out, otherwise, as captain of the ship, you could go down with your property's disapprovals.

One technique to ensure that your love affair with the property does not continue is to develop a set of objective criteria and targets for each of your projects. These are measured performance triggers designed to make you reconsider the project and turn you away from moving forward in one direction without considering another.

We will speak further on risk and assessment in Chapter 5, as due diligence is critical for being able to distinguish realistic vision from fantasy that is doomed to fail.

There is always something in approvals

One of the greatest threats to a development is uncertainty. Approvals are a subjective process in the end, as votes are cast based on both technical and non-technical information. The aspect of subjectivity, or non-objective measurement, can make the blood of lawyers, bankers, consultants, and developers run cold. One thing *is* certain; there are large gaps of uncertainty in the development approvals process, and requirements are not always evident or outlined clearly.

A development colleague likes to remind me that there is always *something* that is an issue in approvals. It can be regular issues, like transportation, noise, parking, density, or simply lighting and safety that create perceived or real threats about a new development application. In some communities, there is an unspoken belief that if they can prevent one development, then there won't be further threats to their established communities. This 'no change is good' mindset means that they will resist any change because change is a threat to their status quo. Even when housing affordability is a community's number one issue, it is hard for people to accept increased density, or the 'intrusion' of townhomes or duplexes into, for example, a community of primarily single-family, detached homes. Such citizens are also blind to their own future need to down-size, or 'right-size' so they can age in their community.

The lessons, take-aways, rules, and associated enlightenments examined in this chapter have given a context for the 'game' of development and approvals. Moving forward, we will now examine how the world of development approvals is changing by looking at current practices and the rules of the game. We will carefully consider where there is flexibility, and where the law rules—in some cases to the developer's advantage and in others, not so much.

Going forward, it appears the burdens and requirements of approvals are not becoming easier, but let's keep our chins up and our smiles intact as we discover more opportunities, as a positive attitude is the developer's key advantage. Successful developers find value where others have overlooked it.

PART 2: CHANGE AGENTS

3. THE RULES OF THE GAME

You can't bully a building into being built anymore. While force and energy are still required, patience, persuasion, persistence, partnerships, and participation are increasingly what it takes.

—Joe Berridge, Perfect City (2019)

The old rules that the 'squeaky wheel gets the grease' don't often apply anymore. In other words, bullying and intimidation tactics don't work in the project approvals game. In fact, these tactics can hamper approvals and slow the process down. A better way to get your project through approvals is to know the rules and create a streamlined method to make those rules work for you in the best ways possible.

This chapter outlines the current approval process in British Columbia and as such, creates the foundation for subsequent discussion in the following chapters. Understanding the approval process as well as regulatory requirements governing policies is crucial for a real estate development project's success.

The first discussion of development process, then, is set within the context of the overall real estate development business and provides primers on due diligence, financial viability, and market context. Each in its own way affects approvals and the viability of a project as it proceeds.

These overall project components are intrinsically connected to each other, especially since municipalities take an active role in real estate transactions, either directly or indirectly, through community amenity contributions or bonus density considerations, which we will discuss in this chapter.

General Governance in British Columbia

It is one thing to complain about a process you don't understand, and another to fully understand and work a process that you *do* know and understand. But both can end up without approval if processes aren't skillfully coordinated and monitored.

When you enter a municipality informed with knowledge and experience rather than mere opinions or, worse still, preconceived judgements, there is a greater possibility for building respect and understanding with various staff members. When you or your consulting team are fully informed and have already had dealings with various staff members, the process can be smoother. Familiarity and positive, local relationships will help grease the wheels of approvals.

At the same time, admittedly, approval processes have become more complex and, in some cases, largely incomprehensible unless you have the benefit of the eagle eye of an experienced professional planner. But even then, I would suggest further internal interpretation of what is required, otherwise conflicting views are inevitable. Staff approvals and council approvals are two different things, and one does not necessarily follow the other.

In British Columbia, provincial planning powers are delegated to the municipalities through the *Local Government Act* (LGA). The LGA empowers municipalities to govern their local approvals, with the exception of those permissions that require a higher level of provincial and federal approvals (such as highways, water courses, and Crown lands).

There are also approvals required that pertain to railways and utilities. If you have an active railway or utility right-of-way running through, or adjacent to your property, you must ensure that you have the appropriate permits to work around, under, over or through it. In addition, consultation is required if your project is located on First Nations territory, as per B.C.'s Bill 41.

As I've mentioned earlier in the book, Vancouver is special in that it has its own charter which is separate from the LGA. Its governance is different from other municipalities. I will discuss this further in the next chapter. If you are doing business in the Vancouver area, make sure you study this charter diligently, as what applies *outside* Vancouver does not necessarily apply within its boundaries. Further, even while other municipalities are under the umbrella of the LGA, at the same time each municipality has its own system of policies and approval methods—call them refinements—that apply to their system, and you must be familiar with them as well.

That is why it is important to have someone who knows local process and details on your team. That familiarity can save time, money, and resources. Remember also that policies can and will change, so always check on the most recent amendments to policy to ensure these amendments have not affected your property's development potential in terms of use and density. That is where the 'three martinis' law I mentioned earlier comes in: meeting with your local director of planning is worth three books of law and policy (Figure 3.1 below).

Figure 3.1: Critical to success is local knowledge and relationships

Hierarchy of Plans

There is a distinct hierarchy of plans that govern approvals, starting at the regional level of influence and moving down to the site level. Each has their own specifics, but from an approval standpoint, the higher-level documents require more complex and longer approvals processes, including broader consultation, and are therefore riskier in terms of support. The following chart (Figure 3.2 below) generalizes the hierarchy of plans, bylaws, and permits an applicant must follow for reference, potential amendments, and approvals depending on the site.

Plans/Bylaws/Permits	Purpose	Approvals/Amendments
Regional Growth Strategy	Regional goals, growth areas, and general land uses.	*Major regional government approvals.
Official Community Plan (OCP)	Municipality or regional district policies, objectives, and land use designations.	*Local government overall plan amendments (can run concurrently with Area Plan and rezoning).
Area/Local/Neighbourhood Plan	Specific local area plans that include further detailed land use designations and policies.	*Local area amendment (can run concurrently with OCP and rezoning).
Zoning Bylaw	Permitted uses, building envelopes, density, coverage, and setbacks.	*Rezoning sometimes completed concurrently with area plan and OCP.
Subdivision Bylaw	Parcels divisions layout (PLA) and servicing concept framework.	Subdivision is a technical process requiring approval from the Ministry of Transportation and Infrastructure (MOTI) for rural sites; bond and works and services agreement for off-site costs; complete sales. Option: Subdivision Appeal Board
Development Permit	Design development for parcels including architecture, landscape architecture, conceptual drawings; class C costing (zoned, serviced, legal parcel).	Local municipal approvals without public review. Option: Development Appeal Board
Development Variance Permit	Specific variance to development application.	Variance considered but not for use or density (e.g., building setback) Option: Board of Variance
Building Permit	Detailed construction drawings and class B costing (Building Code focus).	Local municipal technical approvals without public review.
Occupancy Permit	All approvals and building and site inspections complete.	Building and site inspectors have completed their final inspections and approvals complete; presales complete.

* Requires public review process.

Figure 3.2: Hierarchy of Plans and Permits in British Columbia

Let me illustrate this hierarchy of plans concept further by examining Rocky View County in Alberta. Rocky View County surrounds the west, north and east areas of Calgary, constituting 400,000 hectares (1 million acres). In Alberta, municipalities and counties are governed by the Municipal Government Act (MGA), and a similar hierarchy of plans to those of other Canadian provinces (but with different names and contents) is in place (Figure 3.3 below).

In Alberta, for example, the Official Community Plan is called the Municipal Development Plan (MDP), and the Area/Local/Neighbourhood Plan is known as the Area Structure Plan (ASP). Both the cities of Calgary and Edmonton currently have regional approval boards that govern approvals to varying degrees, depending on a project's size and potential impact on land use and density. In contrast, Metro Vancouver indirectly governs approvals through growth targets (Regional Context Statements), and the provision of regional infrastructure.

There are some unique governance variations in Alberta that could inform planning in British Columbia. For example, in Alberta they have an Inter-Municipal Development Plan (IDP) to manage growth in border areas between counties and municipalities, or between counties. In addition, they use 'conceptual schemes' or the 'master site development plans' to provide further area or parcel plans prior to subdivision.

RELATED PLANS & POLICIES

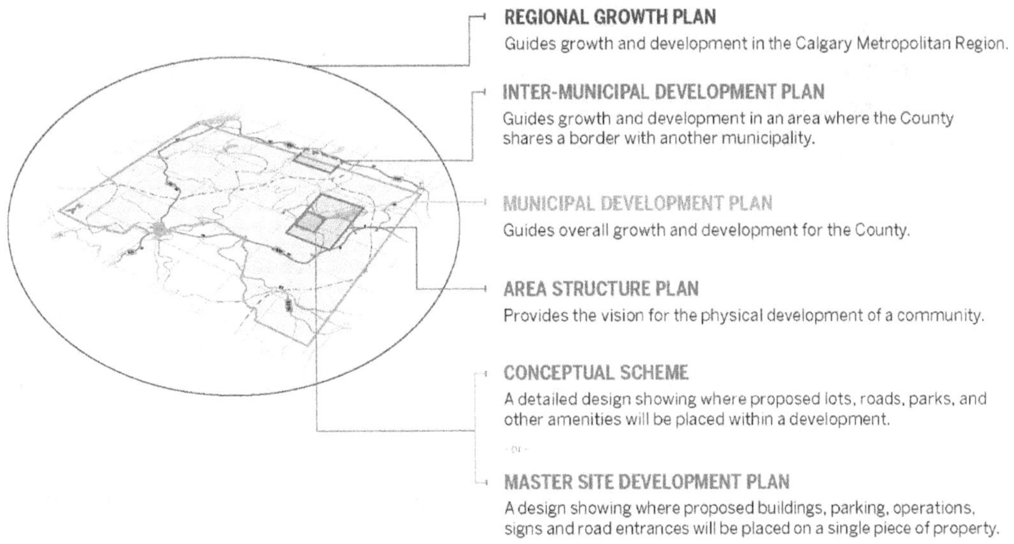

REGIONAL GROWTH PLAN
Guides growth and development in the Calgary Metropolitan Region.
INTER-MUNICIPAL DEVELOPMENT PLAN
Guides growth and development in an area where the County shares a border with another municipality.
MUNICIPAL DEVELOPMENT PLAN
Guides overall growth and development for the County.
AREA STRUCTURE PLAN
Provides the vision for the physical development of a community.
CONCEPTUAL SCHEME
A detailed design showing where proposed lots, roads, parks, and other amenities will be placed within a development.
- or -
MASTER SITE DEVELOPMENT PLAN
A design showing where proposed buildings, parking, operations, signs and road entrances will be placed on a single piece of property.

Figure 3.3: Rocky View County, Alberta Hierarchy of Plans and Policies

Below, I will discuss each of the British Columbia plans, with emphasis on Metro Vancouver. I will start at the regional level and move down to the final building occupancy permit and provide a thorough explanation of the uniqueness of each plan, bylaw, and permit, as well as the relationships between each and their implications on site applications approval requirements.

Regional and Local Plans

In the Vancouver region (also referred to as the Lower Mainland), the regional plan currently in use is called, *Shaping Our Future—Metro Vancouver 2040,* and it is under the jurisdiction of Metro Vancouver. This regional plan is the collective vision for how growth (population, housing, and jobs) will be managed to support the creation of complete, connected, and resilient communities.[31] Metro Vancouver is a federation of 21 municipalities, one Electoral Area, and one Treaty First Nation.

The Vancouver region stretches from the City of Vancouver on the west, to Abbotsford on the east, to White Rock on the south, to the municipalities of the District and City of North Vancouver and West Vancouver on the north shore. The City of Vancouver is currently updating the 2040 Plan to *Metro 2050* and this new plan is due for completion in 2022. Although Metro Vancouver's Regional Plan is not a detailed land use plan per se, it does lay out expectations for land use and density indirectly through plans for the provision of water and sewer services to the region.

Each municipality within the Vancouver region is required to complete a 'regional context statement' that illustrates how they are going to conform to the growth projections and land use targets as a component of the region. The Vancouver Regional Board of Directors consists of the mayors from the membership municipalities, as well as representation from the electoral area and the Tsawwassen First Nation.

Other municipalities and rural areas in British Columbia are required to complete a Regional Growth Strategy (RGS) that directs growth at a regional level. These regional plans, when knit together, cover the whole province. The point here is the rural regional plans cover large areas, most of it rural and resource-based lands, such as Crown lands, provincial parks, or First Nations' lands.

Regional Plan amendments are required when the land use designation, or nature of the use, is modified. In general terms, if the use or density of an area is changed as a result of a proposed development project, then a regional plan amendment will be required. What constitutes a change is a tricky business; you could be following local land use designations, but perhaps you are adjusting the density and use allocations on various

31 Metro Vancouver, *Metro 2040*, n.p.

parts of the property. This would normally be deemed as changing use or density. In many instances, much of this is up to interpretation; however, when there is any doubt about an applicant's intentions, a full regional plan amendment is required. The sticking point here is that a plan amendment requires the approval of all the board members representing various areas within the region. The areas with greater populations in a particular region, for example Nanaimo in the Regional District of Nanaimo (RDN), or Whistler and Squamish in the Squamish Lillooet Regional District (SLRD), have a greater vote count and therefore have greater influence in the decisions.

Generally speaking, amendments to regional plans are significant and are not the policy amendment of choice, as they are risky and can take significant time and resources with no guarantee of a successful outcome. Unless there is support from staff and local council, there is little hope of success in getting a regional plan changed. Even with local support, there could be significant political resistance to change, especially if an updated regional plan recently came into effect. There is reason for the general land use designations within the regional plans. Unless your land is an anomaly and has justification for change, regional plans tend to stand.

Agricultural Land Reserve: More than 50,000 hectares (124,000 acres) of land within Metro Vancouver is dedicated to agricultural use.[32] This agricultural land is preserved within the Agricultural Land Reserve (ALR) boundaries and is overseen by the province under the governance of the Agricultural Land Commission (ALC). This appointed board makes decisions, and gives direction, on behalf of the province. The land in the ALR not only provides arable land for farming and other agricultural use, but it also provides a greenbelt that limits sprawl and is a growth containment boundary between municipalities. Quebec, Ontario, and Oregon have also created similar Land Commissions.

Nearly 75 percent of the Township of Langley is in the ALR (Figure 3.4 below). The balance has been left for development, or other uses. That is why more compact forms of housing, instead of detached single-family homes, have become the norm in the Langley area as when development, or redevelopment, is being considered. As land prices continue to increase, the move to higher density housing increases as well, as exemplified by the Willoughby Town Centre area of the Township of Langley, and other growth centres in the region.

---

[32] Metro Vancouver, *Metro 2040*, 8.

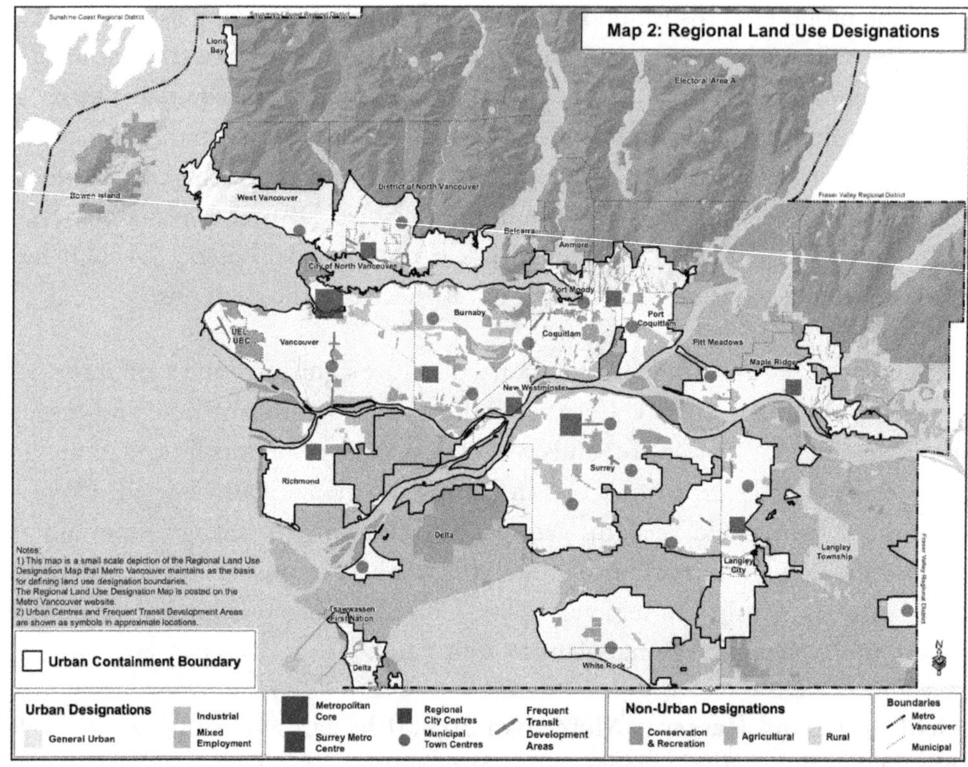

<u>Figure 3.4: Metro 2040</u>
Metro 2040, Regional Growth Strategy Maps, Section 6.12, Map 2, Land Use Designations
(Source: Metro Vancouver)

The Agricultural Land Reserve is a form of zoning that protects the land from non-agricultural development and limits land use to agricultural use, or other uses that do not diminish the land from producing crops.[33] Only five percent of British Columbia is actually arable, and of that only one percent is Class One agricultural land. Considering that British Columbia has a land mass that is three times as big as France (one million square kilometers), this small portion of arable land is precious and requires such protection. Until the establishment of the ALR, the province was losing 6,000 hectares a year of arable land; now the reserve holds steady at five percent (or 4.7 million hectares) of B.C.'s landmass, supporting 50 percent of the food, 20,000 jobs, and $2.2 billion in farm income.[34]

Adjusting ALR boundaries, or taking lands out of the ALR, is a significant undertaking and permission is only given under exceptional circumstances that are acceptable to the commission. Unless the lands in question can be replaced with similar lands elsewhere

33 Mike Harcourt and Ken Cameron, *City Making in Paradise*, 69.
34 Mike Harcourt and Ken Cameron, *City Making in Paradise*, 60, 75.

(an exchange for equal or better for agricultural land), then the permission will not be granted. ALR land is deemed 'sacred' in the lexicon of land designations, and it's not frequently changed.

Similarly, industrial lands are important to regional job growth and their designations are not easily changed either. The retention of industrial lands is important as a way to balance jobs and housing across the region. It puts the industrial jobs in proximity to residents and other businesses, reducing commuting.

Finally, regional growth centres are central hubs for residential and business intensification. They are normally along transit routes in the Lower Mainland. In these areas, higher density and mixed use are invited as part of the desired growth patterns in the future.

As Metro Vancouver grows, it's obvious we have to find ways to create more compact communities on our existing footprint. Vancouver has found lane homes and secondary suites can triple density without changing the character of the neighbourhood. Lane homes are considered by the City of Vancouver as an outright use that does not require rezoning of the property. The overall growth management structure for the region provides significant lessons and creates the framework for each municipality to work together in designing and planning their edges. The structure also informs a number of enlightened policy directions for other metropolitan regions to follow, including the following (Figure 3.5 below):

- Concentrating commercial and job growth in a few priority growth centers in the municipalities that also contain key public facilities (libraries, schools).
- Linking these centers with fast, efficient transit and creating multimodal link opportunities to buses and other modes of transportation.
- Intensifying town centers with high-density residential uses to support commercial uses throughout the day and evening.
- Planning for regional growth management and transportation in an integrated, iterative way so that transportation reinforces growth management, and vice versa.
- Planning infrastructure and servicing based on a more concentrated model for efficiency, and conserving the valuable green zones for recreation, as well as environmental and agricultural protection.
- Creating a spirit of collaboration and cooperation among member municipalities and other public authorities that translates into the collective power of shaping an outstanding region.
- Bringing planning, financing, and operations for transit, roads, transportation demand management, and cycling together under one agency financed primarily with revenues from transportation users (i.e., fares, fuel taxes, parking levies, etc.).

In the past 40 years, the region has continued its transformation from primarily single-family housing sprawl to a variety of more compact housing forms and regional centers. The proportion of new single-family, detached homes was 56 percent in 1980; by 2010 it had dropped to 30 percent and continues to decline.

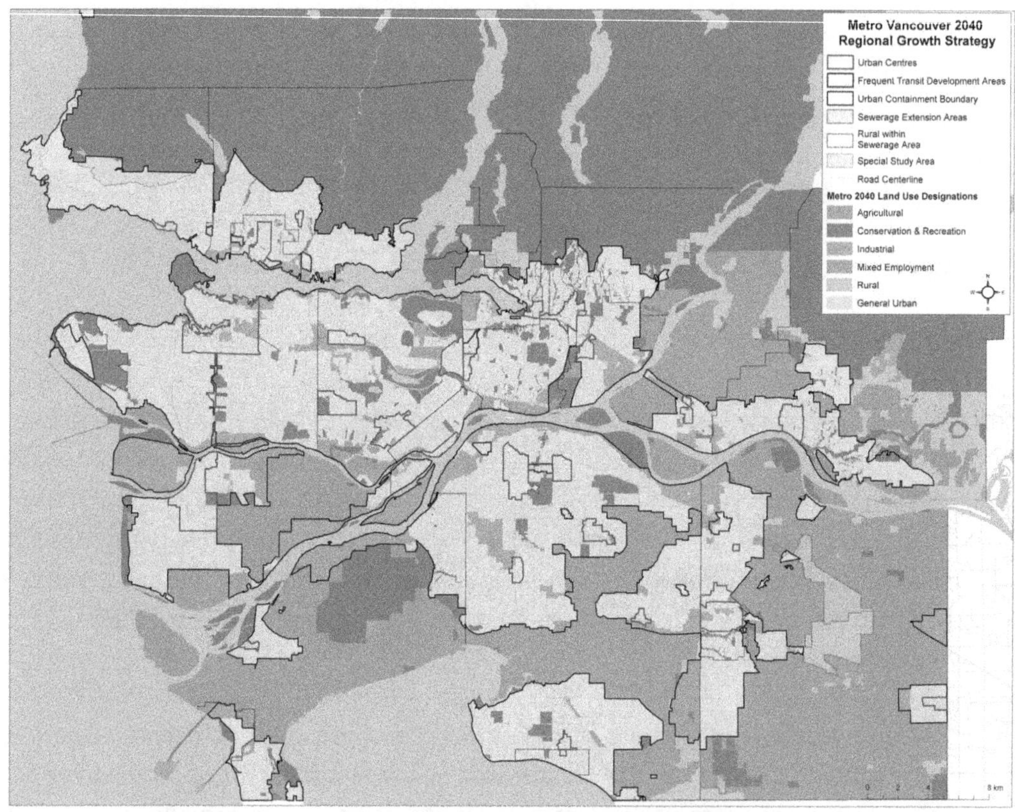

<u>Figure 3.5: Metro Vancouver 2040</u>
Regional Growth Strategy parcel-based land use designation map
(Source: Metro Vancouver)

Official Community Plans: Municipalities in British Columbia are given the authority to adopt an official community plan (OCP) by the province through the *Local Government Act* (LGA). Sections 473, 474, and 488 of the LGA specify the content and process requirements, policy statements that may be included, and designation of development permit areas (DPAs) which form the core of the plan.

The OCP is the overall plan for each municipality. It sets out how and where a municipality can grow, and how land can be used. The planning horizon for OCPs is normally 20 to 30 years, with five-year interim reviews to ensure that the objectives and policies are current and land use designations are updated. The OCP sets out development areas as well as associated objectives and policies for each of the land use designations.

Many OCPs also have DPAs designated within their boundaries to enable the introduction of development permit area guidelines that further direct form and character of development in each area. In many cases, these development permit guidelines can be very specific and can somewhat overstep their boundaries of general direction and intent. Guidelines may vary from 'may' and 'can', which are voluntary directions, to 'shall' and 'must', which are required to be followed. The difference between the two wordings is significant.

Normally guidelines are meant to provide general direction for development, and not limit it; but more recently the wording has changed to require development to *conform* to the guidelines, changing these guidelines to standards that can be rigid and inflexible. In some municipalities, the flexibility is maintained through 'equivalencies', or alternative treatments, that are deemed to be similar and acceptable.

OCP amendments can be significant undertakings, as they require the consideration of the entire municipality's interests in considering a 're-designation' of a parcel, or parcels, of land. The greater community interest comes into consideration. From an approvals' perspective, this can extend the process up to two years depending on complexity and scale of the proposal.

However, frequently the review and approval process can proceed concurrently with a rezoning application of the parcel, which is normally required, as both the overall OCP and the specific site zoning need amendments for the project to proceed.

Area/Local/Neighbourhood Plans: These plans are prepared as a subset of the OCP, and they provide further detail specific to the site. For example, the Marpole Plan in the City of Vancouver, the Olympic View Area Plan in the City of Colwood, and the Yorkson Plan in the Township of Langley are each subset to the OCP. These plans bring into focus the needs and growth of particular areas. Each of these plans may include growth forecasts, vision, site analysis and development capability, as well as examination of land use, historic conservation, building siting, architectural and landscape guidelines, amenity requirements, and infrastructure strategies.

If you are in a position where you may have to get an amendment to a lower-level area/local/neighbourhood plan, you may need to amend the OCP as well, and these efforts should be coordinated. Each amendment will require public review and scrutiny. Further, once a plan adjustment goes public, an additional variable is added to the approval's equation. It may be risky and uncertain, but it can lead to a better plan for the community and a smoother process for the developer.

Human nature is unpredictable, and if threatened with change, the public can easily resist by simply saying 'no'. Council will follow the flow, especially in an election year. Keep in mind that in a council election year (referred to as 'silly season') no significant approvals decisions are normally made within six months of the election date. Therefore, with a November election date, no decisions of any consequence are made after May or June of the election year. This delay alone can add six months to an application approvals process.

There is also the potential threat that Council may challenge your development application, even after second reading, or that there may be push-back from the community if they mount a campaign against the project. This happened recently in one municipality. The proposal conformed to local plans and had gone through a rigorous design and planning process with municipal staff for nearly two years. Then, after all that work, the municipal council started to question the fundamentals of the design, and land use, at the second reading of the application. Fortunately, while the council had some valid points, their proposals actually contravened the existing OCP, the local plans and the zoning bylaw. Each one of these plans would have to be amended to enable the new views of council. In the end, council reconsidered and approved the project essentially in its original form.

External Circulation: When your application is circulated externally by municipal or regional staff, a number of provincial and federal laws have to be reviewed to ensure conformance, or the necessity for special consideration. There are numerous federal and provincial laws that may apply to a property, especially when it comes to streams and wildlife.

Federal

Fisheries Act (FA): This Act prohibits polluting watercourses with substances damaging to fish or fish habitat, and any works that may result in serious harm to fish. Serious harm to fish is defined as mortality or habitat loss.

Migratory Birds Convention Act (MBCA): This Act prohibits any actions that may cause harm to migratory birds including populations, individuals, or their active nests. Works should be completed outside nesting season. If a nest is found on site by a qualified environmental professional (QEP), then the QEP will determine the appropriate setback buffer to protect the nest from disturbance until it is no longer active.

Provincial

Riparian Areas Protection Act (RAPA): RAPA provides directive from the federal ministry of Fisheries and Oceans (DFO) and the Ministry of Environment and Climate Change Strategy (MOECH) to municipalities and regional districts to protect streams and adjacent riparian areas for fish and fish habitat using Riparian Area Protection

Regulation (RAPR) to determine appropriate development setbacks from the top of bank (high water mark).

BC Wildlife Act (BCWA): The *BC Wildlife Act* prohibits any activity that may be harmful to a species and/or their habitat unless authorized by permitting. Section 34 of the Act primarily protects eagles, herons, peregrine falcons, osprey, gyrfalcon, and burrowing owls. The Act also prohibits any actions that may cause harm to migratory birds including populations, individuals, or their active nests.

Other Legislation, Policies, Bylaws, Plans, and Permits

The following legislation, policies, bylaws, plans, and permits may also apply to the property you are hoping to develop. It is worth considering each one of these early so you can anticipate their requirements and the effects they may have, singly or collectively, on your development. Keep in mind that this is not an exhaustive list and it may vary from municipality to municipality, and regional district to regional district.

1. Strategic Plan
2. Climate Action Plan
3. Transportation Plan
4. Sustainability Plan
5. Greenways Plan
6. Affordable Housing Plan
7. Parks, Recreation, and Trails Plan
8. Cultural Services Plan
9. Economic Development Plan
10. Financial Plan
11. Tourism Plan
12. Public Art Policy and Program Plan
13. Heritage Landscapes and Structures Plan
14. Stream and Drainage System Protection Bylaw
15. Conservation Bylaw
16. Tree Management Bylaw
17. Development Procedures Bylaw
18. Sign Bylaw
19. Archeological Protection
20. Site Profile and Soil Contamination
21. Clean Water Act and Pollution
22. Environmental Setbacks (also including steep slopes, hazard conditions, and flood levels)
23. Tree Permit
24. Demolition Permit
25. Conservation Permit
26. Foundation Permit
27. Building Permit
28. Occupancy Permit

Zoning Bylaws

A zoning bylaw describes what a property owner can build on a property in a specific area or 'zone'. It may describe existing conditions or reflect desirable form and location of development. Specific zones specify what the owner is entitled to build with his 'bundle of rights' associated with the property.

Each zoning bylaw normally describes permitted uses and, in certain circumstances, discretionary uses subject to review and provision of specific requirements. These bylaws also specify building setbacks, height, coverage, and permitted density in units per hectare/acre, or floor space ratio (FSR), or floor area ratio (FAR) (which are defined the same). FSR is the total allowable building area as a proportion of the site area. For example, a 2.0 FSR equals a gross building area that is two times the site area, or two storeys. If building coverage is limited to 50 percent of the site in the specific zone, then the building will be four storeys, as only half the site is covered with building. In simple terms, units per hectare/acre defines density in two-dimensional space, whereas FSR/FAR defines density in three-dimensional volume.

Front yard, rear yard, and side yard setbacks vary from property to property, but there are normally standard setbacks for each type of use. For example, standard setbacks for single-family homes are normally six metres for the front yard and seven metres for the rear yard, with front garages. Standard side yards are normally 1.5 metres to allow at least 3 metres between homes. There has been a trend to reducing front yard setbacks, at least for the front porch, to 3.5 metres to bring the house closer to the street, especially where there is a rear lane and the garage is in the rear.

Building height is another measurement that deserves further clarification, as it impacts views and potential obstruction of views. Building height is often measured to halfway between the eave and the peak of roof, or the top of the roof where the building has a flat roof. The other measurement to keep in mind is the determination of finished floor elevation. The difference between the roof and the finished floor elevation is the allowable height, normally 8.0 to 10.0 metres for 2 to 2.5 storey homes.

In locations where a number of different uses are permitted, and the property is sizable and has a customized site plan or master plan that requires special considerations, a comprehensive development (CD) zone, or district, may be considered. In these cases, a specific CD zone is created in the zoning bylaw. The CD zone has tailored specifications including permitted uses, discretionary uses, setback requirements, building heights, and densities on various parts of the site area. Environmentally sensitive sites and larger complex sites are often appropriate for this CD zone consideration.

In Vancouver, much of zoning is discretionary in that, in addition to the base zoning, other additional bonuses in density and uses can be provided in return for specific desirable uses and amenities. This is the road of the future—flexibility, compact form, with amenities.

In the case of re-zoning, it is important to understand that when you proceed from an outright zoning application to a re-zoning application, the whole approvals process changes. Instead of a process that is relatively straight-forward with no public review process, re-zoning is a process that requires a public review, including a public hearing. These re-zoning processes can take, in conservative terms, up to two to three years due to the additional complexities and public reviews.

In simple terms, you are requesting an increase in density and/or land use. This request increases your rights on the property but in return the jurisdiction will increase their required process and probably your financial contributions. With respect to re-zonings, many municipalities have adopted community amenity contribution (CAC) policies. These are in addition to development cost charges (DCCs) which are required to upgrades to sewer, water, streets, and the provision of park space. The CAC contributions are meant for additional amenities necessary as a result of the development including daycare, community centres, and other elements.

In some cases, the developer is required to pay for infrastructure servicing up front to allow the development to proceed on his or her property, as part of a larger development area. For example, an oversized sanitary sewer pipe might be required to service the property and allow for additional growth in the area. The developer, if he or she wants to proceed, is required to pay the full amount for this and must recover the excess (oversize of pipe) by way of a 'late-comers' agreement specifying a cost-recovery contribution from adjoining parcels, should they develop some time in the future. If the municipal community centre or a future district school has an interest in the area, they will also be obligated to pay their fair share of the infrastructure improvements.

When financial contribution is part of your development deal, ensure that your contributions are specific, if possible, and that they represent your equitable contribution to the upgrades. For example, if there are four communities that will impact a specific intersection, then your contribution should represent the percentage of units and/or floor area contributing to that growth, not more. The calculations can be complex, but care should be taken to determine what the fair contribution is. Do this, and then contribute accordingly.

Submission requirements for re-zonings can be significant. These may include site context, analysis of land use; community benefits and amenities; transit and mobility analysis; market impact analysis; replacement housing analysis; environmental impacts; biophysical analysis and retention strategies; view impact analysis (both on- and off-site); geotechnical and soils analysis; wildlife impact analysis; archeological survey; traffic impact analysis; economic supply and demand analysis; site infrastructure and servicing studies; green building and site analysis; architectural drawings with sections, elevations; building materials boards; landscape plan and tree retention/replacement plan.

The approvals process for OCP amendments and re-zonings, as mentioned earlier, can run concurrently—that is, in a parallel process where the two applications are completed and reviewed at the same time to save time and unnecessary complications.

The following is an ingenious method of personally informing mayor and council of your rezoning proposal, and it follows a checklist from the City of Victoria (Figure 3.6).

Sustainable Planning and Community Development
1 Centennial Square
Victoria, BC V8W 1P6
T 250.361.0283 E DevelopmentServices@victoria.ca

Rezoning Information

Letter to Mayor and Council

A letter addressed to Mayor and Council detailing the following information must be submitted.

The amount of detail may vary on the nature of the application. Please discuss with your Neighbourhood Planner if you require further direction.

Description of proposal	Provide a summary of the proposal: • land use/zoning change • density changes • type of tenure (rental, strata ownership) • number, description and type of dwelling units • inclusion of adaptable housing features
Government policies	Does the proposal conform to the *Official Community Plan*? The Neighbourhood/Precinct Plan? If a change to the *Official Community Plan* is requested, provide a rationale.
Project benefits and amenities	What are the economic, environmental and social benefits to the City and neighbourhood? Will there be any public amenities associated with this development, such as play areas for children, public art, streetscape improvements?
Need and demand	What is the demonstrated public need for the proposal? Does the location meet a need or demand which is not or could not be met in land already zoned? For example, is this a change of permitted use or an increase in density?
Neighbourhood	What is different or unique about the site to warrant rezoning, e.g., lot size, topography, context, existing site and neighbouring development? How well does the proposed development relate to the neighbourhood?
Impacts	Would the development complement or improve conditions existing in the surrounding area? What other effects would this proposal have on the immediate neighbours? Consider noise and activity levels.
Design and development permit guidelines	Please reference the applicable design guidelines. Indicate how the proposal complies with the guidelines. Note that a development permit application may be required for some applications.
Safety and security	Address CPTED (Crime Prevention Through Environmental Design)
Transportation	Does the project meet the vehicle parking standards of Schedule C - Off-Street Parking? How will a shortfall in parking be satisfied? Does the project meet the bicycle parking standards of Schedule C - Off-Street Parking? Will the project include bicycle facilities above the requirements? Is the parcel on a Greenway? Are there any anticipated improvements to the Greenway resulting from this project?
Heritage	What is the heritage status of the buildings on the property? How are the heritage buildings impacted by the development? Note that a Conservation Plan is required for rezoning applications involving a heritage designated or registered building.
Green building features	Using the Green Building Indicators (as follows) as a guide, indicate what green building features will be incorporated into the development. Provide appropriate documentation as required.
Infrastructure	Are there adequate public infrastructure and community/recreation services available to meet the proposal (e.g., sewer, water, sidewalks, roads, parks)? If not, how would the proposal address infrastructure and service requirements?

Figure 3.6: City of Victoria letter to mayor and council

The following is a helpful diagram of a rezoning approval process from the City of Colwood on Vancouver Island. Note the approval timeline does not consider the time for all the study requirements (Figure 3.7).

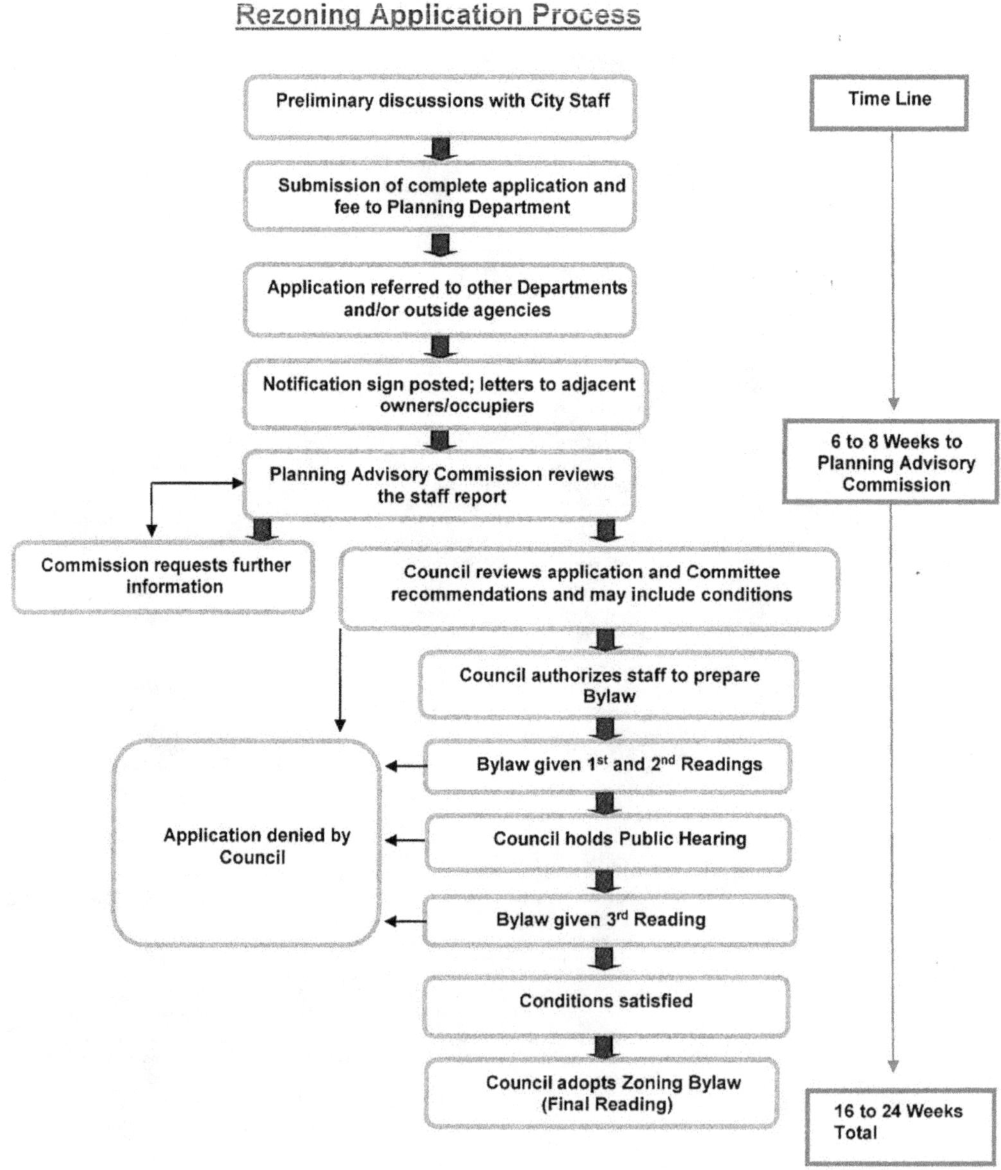

Figure 3.7: Rezoning Application Process, Colwood, British Columbia

The City of Colwood's approval process is based on a complete application with no requirements for further studies, further refinements of studies or other approvals such as development agreements, development permits, or development variance permits.

In this example, once the application is reviewed and accepted by staff as complete, the application, accompanied by a staff report, can go before council for consideration.

- Public workshops or open houses are normally required before first reading to determine the extent of public support and concerns about the proposal.
- If council or the regional district deem the application complete, they can recommend and approve FIRST READING of the re-zoning bylaw.
- Further public workshops and open houses may be required to respond to concerns about amended drawings that reflect an alternative development concept.
- SECOND READING occurs, following a PUBLIC HEARING[35] where the public is provided the opportunity to speak before council in support of, or against, the application.
- Then THIRD READING by council occurs.
- Then, the FOURTH and final reading by council, and final adoption of the bylaw, occur once the development agreement between the municipality and developer is executed.

Phased Development Agreement: A phased development agreement (PDA) or 'master' development agreement is required prior to fourth and final reading. This is a legal agreement (affirmed by municipal bylaw) between the developer and the municipality (or regional district) that is normally in place for a period of 10 years, with possible extension of two five-year periods.

This agreement secures amenities for the community and development rights for the developer, as well as outlining realistic phasing of development rights and associated amenities.

---

[35] In British Columbia, the Public Hearing is required after first reading and before third reading of the bylaw in accordance with the Local Government Act (LGA). In Alberta, the Public Hearing is required before second reading of the bylaw in accordance with the Municipal Government Act (MGA).

Development Permits

Once zoning, or re-zoning, is in place, and the OCP amendment is complete, the development permit application (DP) can proceed. All buildings require a DP except single-family houses. The DP requires detailed drawings of architecture, landscape architecture, and engineering, as well as other professional studies. It may also require further detailed studies beyond the rezoning submission. Some professionals term this 'design development' with a Class 'C' cost estimate associated with the degree of completion.

From this submission comes a response from the municipality, normally referred to as 'pre-conditions' for approval. This sets conditions that impact the following aspects of the project: architecture, landscape architecture, parks, environmental concerns, geotechnical impacts, potential contamination, installation of utilities, emergency (fire and police) accessibility, traffic engineering, and other services and conditions from different departments, depending on their extent of interest and responsibilities.

Outside agencies may have conditions for approvals, depending on location and adjoining ownership, including the Ministry of Transportation and Infrastructure (roads, access and so on); Federal Department of Fisheries (streams and waterbodies, railways); BC Hydro; Ministry of Environment and Climate Change Strategy (contamination); First Nations; and others.

First Nations are becoming active players when it comes to developing their lands and traditional territories. The need to proactively consult with indigenous people, separate from the formal municipal or regional district reviews, is important to ensure they feel respected and actively integrated in the approvals process. Sometimes, active consultation with First Nations can result in cultural recognition in site planning and design, which is one aspect of planning that can positively impact your project and provide you with firm support for the application. In some cases, joint venture or partnerships with First Nations may be contemplated.

The example below of a development permit application process from the City of Colwood provides an interesting example of a B.C. approvals process (Figure 3.8). It includes staff discussions; signposting on the proposed development site (intentions and submission); formal review by staff, and letter response; and director of planning (approval officer) approval of the application.

In this case, if the application is denied, reconsideration can be requested, and the application is then referred to the Planning Advisory Commission (PAC) for deliberation. Assuming approval by the PAC, the application then is forwarded to Colwood City

Council. Council approves the application or amends the approval officer's decision. The approval officer then executes the associated development permit document, and it is filed with the Land Title Office.

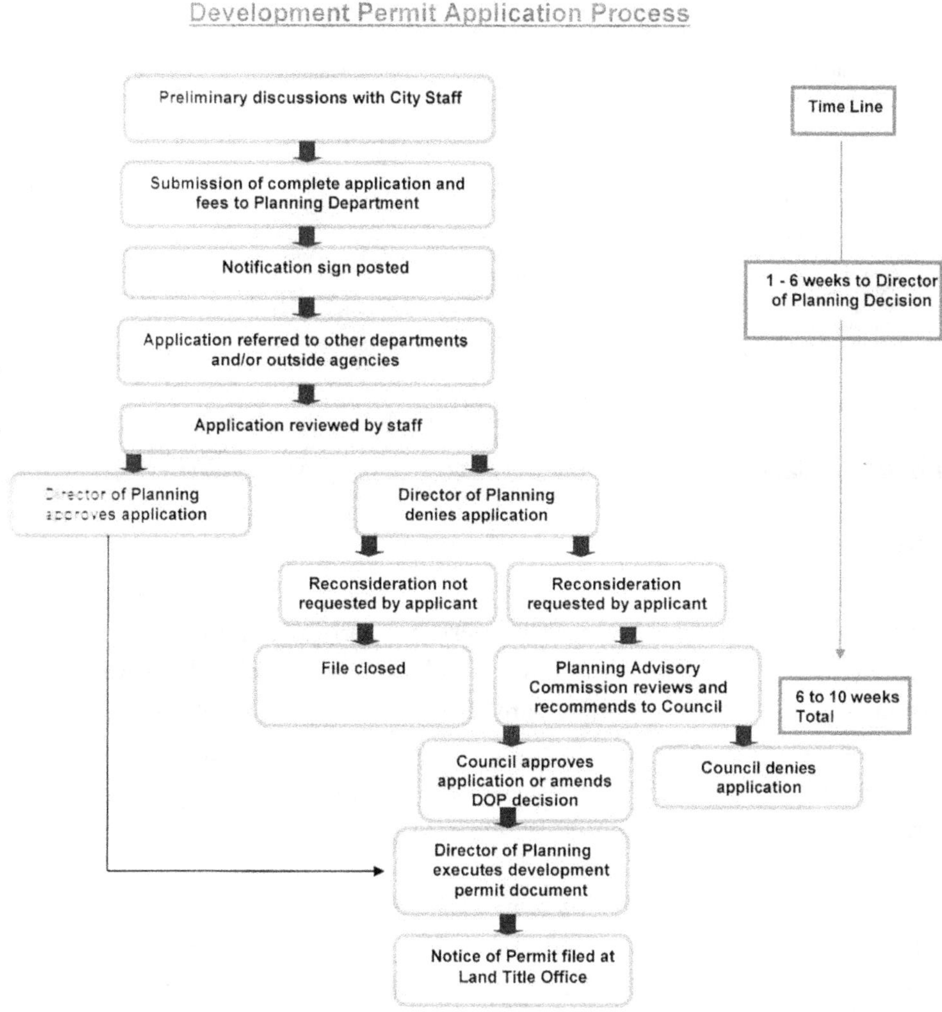

Figure 3.8: Development Permit Application Process, Colwood, British Columbia

These approval processes vary from municipality to municipality and regional district to regional district, but they have to conform to LGA requirements and procedures.

The following is an example of a City of Surrey development permit, and its subdivision approval processes.

City of Surrey Development Permit: The development permit assumes that the property is zoned for the use and density proposed by the developer. It does not require public review, though it may be reported to council if there are exceptional circumstances, or if it is a major project of interest. Once the conditions are met, staff approves or sends it to council for formal approval (Figure 3.9 below).

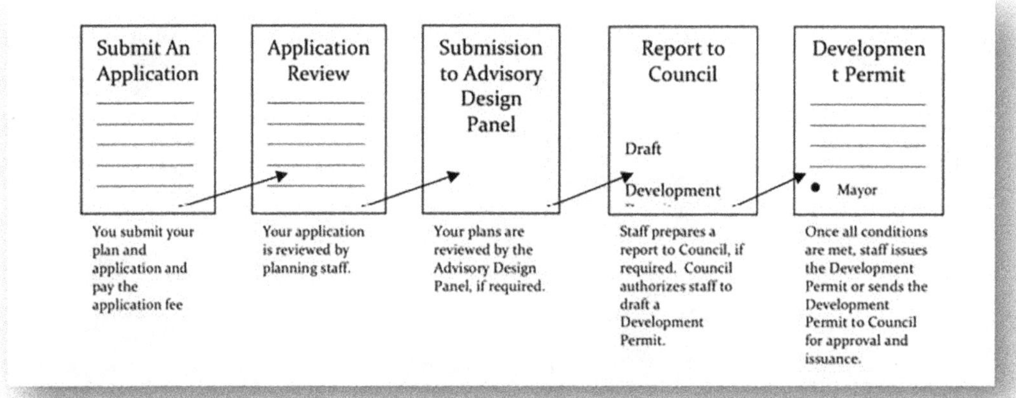

Figure 3.9: Development Application Process, City of Surrey, British Columbia

Subdivision

Following re-zoning and development permit approvals, land normally requires subdivision so that the development's first phase can proceed. Subdivision means a division of the lands into smaller parcels, or a consolidation of parcels, to permit development to proceed in a planned, phased manner, one step at a time. The subdivision triggers fees that must be paid in advance of the building permit approvals that follow (Figure 3.10 below).

Fee payment varies from municipality to municipality. For example, community amenity contributions (CACs) can be required as part of development permit approvals. Check as to what various fees and contributions are required, and when, as some are significant (like CACs) and require external funding. It is interesting to note that CACs are now included as a separate line item in proformas (financial analysis), as they are normally a significant item.

Also keep in mind that in regional districts (rural areas) outside municipalities in British Columbia, the Ministry of Transportation and Infrastructure (MOTI) holds the power of subdivision approvals; therefore, transportation and access are key to getting your project approved in these areas. However, one issue is that innovative road design standards require privatization (strata or other ownership), as MOTI's road standards are conventional and generally large-sized.

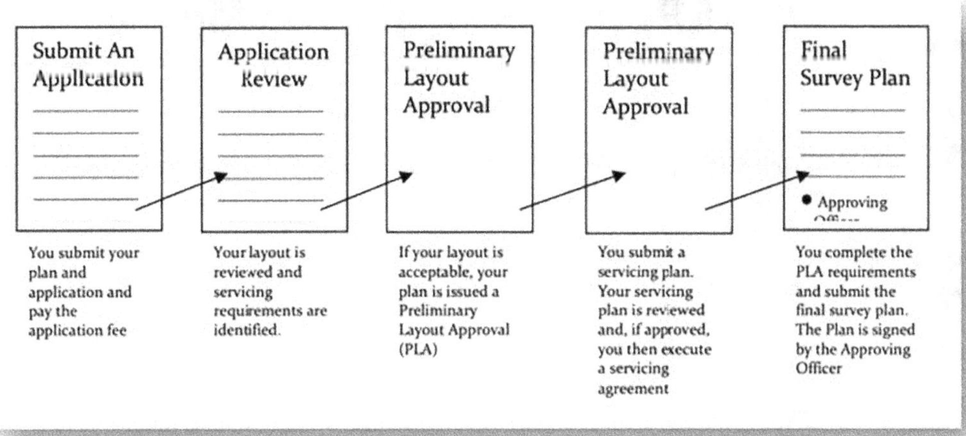

Figure 3.10: City of Surrey Subdivision Application Process

Building and Occupancy Permits

Building Permit: Building permit submissions require detailed construction drawings, normally with class 'B' costs estimates that reflect the detailed level of design. Building inspectors employed by the governing municipality or regional district ensure that the buildings comply with the B.C. Building Code. This is an area that deserves another book, or at least another chapter, but it is not part of this discussion.

Occupancy Permit: Once the construction is complete and the required building inspections are done with, and appropriate improvements or rectifications of detail have been made, then the occupancy permit can be awarded by the jurisdiction.

From the regional plan and official community plan amendments, to rezoning and building permit approvals, it is a long stretch to get a project underway. However, now that you understand the many different factors you must consider, it is important to remember that these are all separate and complex processes in *themselves*. Taken together, they can be overwhelming, but they should not be taken lightly. It takes constant diligence and focus to maintain agreements, and constancy can be a challenge, as individuals change jobs within these municipalities or regional districts which can further complicate matters.

4. VARIABLES IN THE GAME

When dealing with people, let us remember we are not dealing with creatures of logic. We are dealing with creatures of emotion, creatures bristling with prejudices and motivated by pride and vanity.
—Dale Carnegie, How to Win Friends and Influence People (1981)

Vancouver's Unique Model

The City of Vancouver is unique in British Columbia as it is guided by the *Vancouver Charter*. The charter sets out a specific legislative framework to guide planning and development. Other parts of British Columbia, as we learned earlier, are guided by the *Local Government Act* (LGA) which enables municipalities and regional districts to oversee planning and development as per the unique features of that municipality or regional district, while under the governance of the LGA. Uniquely so, the City of Vancouver guides its own direction, within the context of the *Metro Vancouver Plan 2040* that sets growth parameters for the region.

Policy framework: The family of plans

The city of Vancouver, under the liberation of its city charter, is in the process of creating a more prescriptive, city-wide plan, similar to the official community plans other municipalities in British Columbia are mandated to have and update every five years. The city developed a general direction city plan in 1995 which outlined individual visions for neighbourhoods. Since then, other functional plans—for example, the Transportation Plan, and the Greenways Plan—have provided more specific directions on special topics throughout the city. Vancouver's downtown and major development sites are also governed by specific official development plans (ODPs) that delineate comprehensive development policy for each area. The megaprojects of North False Creek, Coal Harbour, Southeast False Creek, Downtown South, Arbutus Neighbourhood, Collingwood Village, and East Fraser Lands [36] are examples of sites that are governed by these plans.

Discretionary zoning

Zoning in Vancouver provides a basis for innovation and incentives. It is essentially a negotiated process that requires community amenities and other considerations in return for additional floor space (normally residential). Within downtown neighbourhoods, the floor space ratio (FSR) has a significant range based on location and land use. This translates most often into mid-rise to high-rise towers with sufficient density

36 Michael von Hausen. *Dynamic Urban Design*, 424-430.

to compensate for increased amenities. This discretion allows the city to attain an expansive, customized public realm, and amenity packages for each neighbourhood as they expand and need additional services.

In terms of negotiating design alternatives and public amenities in re-zonings, ODPs are important to highlight. In some situations (e.g., Downtown South), the projects already have a street structure in place and involve multiple developers on relatively small parcels. This contrasts with some more recent megaprojects, such as North False Creek. North False Creek had one developer working with a large piece of land, and it required a new street and block structure. Megaprojects such as this, where one developer has large land holdings, allow the developer more flexibility in negotiating and exploring innovations in urban form, as well as amenities, especially when the acquisition price is reasonable, as was the case for North False Creek.

Design guidelines, special policies, and principles

The city of Vancouver continues to play a leadership role in setting policy framework for development. Vancouver has developed a series of design guidelines customized to different locations that are framed by overarching principles and policies. These principles, policies, and guidelines collectively translate to different design treatments which create variety, but fit each location within the city.

The following 'living first' principles set the guiding rules that shaped residential emphasis in downtown Vancouver.

- Limit commuter access into the downtown.
- Prioritize walking, cycling, and transit.
- Integrate new development by extending and connecting with existing patterns.
- Develop complete neighbourhood units with supportive commercial services, including community amenities and schools.
- Provide a diversity of housing types, including both market and nonmarket housing (20 percent target for nonmarket and 25 percent suitable for families), mixed incomes, family and nonfamily households, special needs housing, and unique housing choices (floating homes and lofts).
- Encourage fine-grained mixed use and proximity of live, work, and play both vertically and horizontally.
- Expand sidewalks as outdoor rooms and 'third places' for social activity and interaction, supported by special design guidelines and unique treatments in different areas.
- Create park and greenway connections to extend and include developments in the Metro Vancouver mobility and recreation network.[37]

[37] Larry Beasley, *Vancouverism*, 51.

Review and approval processes for major projects

Overall, major projects in Vancouver require a special approvals process that involves the developers, public, and politicians in liaison with assigned staff. The project is scrutinized through many filters, and this process allows for consensus-building on large-scale conceptual issues at the beginning, and for detailed design at the end.

The design development and approval process consists of the following distinct steps:

- Development of policy broadsheet (ODP) by staff and developers while engaging in a series of public workshops and council reviews.
- Building of the development framework plan by staff and developer, refined through public workshops and council hearings.
- Development of detailed design guidelines within each block of the neighbourhood, with architects and landscape architects consulting with local stakeholders, and with feedback from city council.
- Submission of rezoning application based on development plan and design guidelines, with formal staff review; Urban Design Panel (an independent, council-appointed advisory group of design experts) review; and review by the Development Permit Board.
- Final public hearing by city council.

Vancouver pays attention to implementation details, as does the majority of municipalities and regional districts in B.C. Whether it be building or landscape inspections supported by consulting architects, landscape architects, and engineers, design drawings are carefully implemented on-site through monitoring and inspections. This scrupulous attention to detail is the difference between excellence and sub-standard performance. Building material application, attention to details, and material quality are all variables that need constant monitoring and managing, otherwise, good intentions can be lost at the hands of a contractor. Ensuring a high standard in construction is critical to success, especially in complex projects where multiple steps are occurring at the same time, or in close succession.

Financing Vancouver's growth

The city of Vancouver requires that the developers pay for growth associated with development so that the taxpayer does not shoulder this burden. The overriding principle is that all developers should pay their fair share for public utilities and facilities.

Developers are responsible for site and streetscape improvements that affect sites adjoining their projects. If they don't build the street improvements, the city will do so on their behalf. Off-site improvements related to development are normally funded by cost levies paid by the developer to cover parks, daycare, replacement housing, and basic infrastructure. Community amenity contributions pay for additional public amenities, such as community centers and social housing. In contrast, public amenity contributions cover libraries, schools, public art, and specialty items required by the project. These contributions help ensure, along with quality implementation monitoring, that the project is not only implemented properly, but that the community as a whole benefits as it grows.

It is worth noting that Vancouver is a leader in developing progressive policy and approvals frameworks, but at the same time it is an island distinguishing itself from other lower mainland municipalities. Each municipality and regional district has its own idiosyncrasies that have evolved over the years, but all must still conform to the overarching LGA. It is wise to remember that a detailed knowledge of local applications processes and requirements is important. Otherwise, presumption will lead to disappointment.

City of Vancouver Development Regulation and Approval Improvements

Like most municipalities, Vancouver strives to continually improve their approval processes, especially priority areas. For example, in 2018 the City completed the following to expedite and improve city approval processes for specific housing priority sectors:

- Approval of over 900 affordable housing units permitted in half the average development time under the *Social Housing or Rental Tenure* (SHORT) pilot program with over 2,000 units in the pipeline.
- Efforts to remove barriers for ground-oriented housing resulted in 75 percent of permits turned around in under 12 weeks in 2018 versus 41 percent in 2017, and reduction of 50 percent permit backlog.
- Launching of the *Applicant Supported and Assisted Program* (ASAP) pilot program to prioritize one- and two-family and laneway homes through an accelerated permit approval process resulted in permits issued in six weeks versus the previous average of 35 weeks.
- Introduction of new fixed rate community amenity contribution (CAC) targets in the Cambie Corridor Plan resulted in 93 percent of the lots having certainty for future rezoning applications.
- Pre-zoning of select sites identified for townhouses in the Cambie Corridor Plan, to expedite the delivery of ground-oriented, missing-middle housing.
- Implementation of the *Regulation Redesign* project, which approved several regulation changes—including updates to RS Zones (single-family zones)—to clarify decision-making authority, provided more flexibility for artist live-work spaces, simplified review processes, and repealed outdated policies.[38]

---

[38] City of Vancouver, *Housing Vancouver Strategy*, 170.

We will now learn about further variables in the approvals process, including other tools to finance growth, multiple viewpoints of approvals, and who controls approvals.

Funding Growth

Communities are more than houses, apartments, commercial buildings, industrial warehouses, and institutional uses. Parks, streets, sewers, water pipes, and other amenities are required as part of growth. These public components make up 30 to 40 percent of the financial outlay of our municipalities. More people require more support services, which often goes beyond the boundaries of the site under development. Municipalities and regional districts select their methods for funding this growth in accordance with the LGA.

Development cost charges

Municipalities and regional districts can charge for off-site improvements relating to infrastructure under their development cost charge (DCC) bylaw. This is the primary method for new development to contribute to off-site infrastructure improvements, including transportation, parkland acquisition, park improvement, drainage, sanitary sewer, and water systems. These DCCs are enabled by sections 932 to 937 of British Columbia's LGA.

DCCs apply when subdividing land, constructing a new building, or altering an existing building. Each year councils or regional directors determine which capital projects DCC funds will be allocated to. However, provincial legislation limits what services and amenities DCC funds can be spent on. Specifically excluded are community facilities and recreation centres, fire stations, sports courts and spray parks, public art, public buildings, libraries, transit infrastructure, streetscape enhancements, and affordable housing.

The following chart illustrates the significance of DCCs on the cost and affordability of housing in the Township of Langley (Figure 4.1 below). There is a one-year grace period and no stepped transition to new fees, and the fees have not changed since 2012. The interesting point is that this does not appear to help the affordability crisis, as the cost per acre has significantly increased by almost 80 percent.[39]

[39] Frontline Real Estate Services Ltd., *Newsletter*, April 2020, 1.

Residential Land Use	2012 Rate Per Unit	2020 Rate Per Unit	% Increase	Additional Cost Per Acre (Assumed Density)
Single Family (< 6 units per acre)	$26,629.14	$47,366.00	78%	$124,421 (6 units per acre)
Single Family & Low Density Townhouse (6 to 18 units per acre)	$21,954.93	$39,140.00	78%	$257,776 (15 units per acre)
Townhouse (18 to 30 units per acre)	$17,824.02	$31,864.00	79%	$308,880 (22 units per acre)
Apartment (> 30 units per acre)	$14,437.47	$25,905.00	79%	$688,052 (60 units per acre)

Figure 4.1: 2020 Township of Langley Development Cost Charges Increase
(Source: Frontline Real Estate Services Ltd., Newsletter, April 2020)

Density Bonusing
In some municipalities a financial contribution is made by the developer when the jurisdiction approves additional density at the time of rezoning. The amount of additional density and financial contribution is normally set out in the zoning bylaw. The financial contribution is a specified portion of the increased land value that occurs at the time of rezoning. For example, the City of Coquitlam density bonus program applies to floorspace above 2.5 floor area ratio (FAR). Density bonus contributions can be spent on a wide range of amenities and infrastructure, as determined by city council.

Community amenity contributions
Community amenity contributions (CACs) are an additional tool used to fund other community amenities (including those listed before, as well as affordable housing, daycare facilities, performing art centres, and others). CACs only apply to rezoning where the applicant is applying for a change of use and/or density increase for the property.

CACs are deemed voluntary contributions, and they are negotiated or have a per square metre requirement, depending on the jurisdiction. In the past, there has been constant tension between municipalities and developers about CACs, as CAC negotiations elongated the approvals process and resulted in charges up to 75 to 80 percent of the land lift.

The land lift is the difference between the value of the land prior to rezoning and the value of the land after the rezoning. In simple terms, if the land yields 100 units before the rezoning (existing zone) and the rezoning results in 500 condominium units, the net difference is 400 units which increases (lifts) the land value significantly. In extreme cases, up to 80 percent of the increase in value might be required as a CAC. Recently, there has be a trend to specify CACs, as happened with the Cambie Corridor development in Vancouver. This creates more certainty and less risk for the developer.

Subdivision Servicing

In a new subdivision where there is no servicing in place, the developer is required to build all the streets, sidewalks, streetlights, water pipes, and sewer pipes. This infrastructure will be turned over to the jurisdiction upon completion. If the streets are public streets they are turned over to the jurisdiction as well; otherwise, they remain private (strata-titled) and are maintained by the owners. Other infrastructure such as electric power, natural gas, telephone, and cable are also installed by the developer in coordination with the utility companies.

Existing Neighbourhood Servicing

In an existing neighbourhood, developers of new developments are expected to upgrade water and sewer pipes needed to service the development, and to upgrade the streets and lanes to current standard (curbs, sidewalks, streetlights and street trees) unless they are building single-family houses. In some cases, existing overhead power and phone lines may need to be placed underground, depending on BC Hydro requirements.

The Municipal, Community and First Nations Perspectives

Municipal and community perspectives are different from development interests. They have public interest at their core, but they also have other interests that need to be understood and respected before any kind of informed conversation with them can take place.

Benjamin Franklin once said, "Any fool can criticize, condemn or complain—and many fools do. It takes character and self-control to be understanding and forgiving." Ultimately, any negative actions you take will undermine your intention to get what you want. Instead, give support and praise to those you want something from and make them want to do what you want them to do in balance with their own interests.[40]

Municipal and Regional Perspectives

Unfortunately, rather than first understanding the responsibilities and motivations of the other party, then responding with empathy and support, people tend to fall into old, bad habits. For a moment, put yourself in the place of the director of planning, or approval officer, for a city in the Lower Mainland. They are responsible for development approvals, and are charged with protecting the public interest. This means they are responsible for all the details associated with development review and design—a

[40] Dale Carnegie, *How to Win Friends and Influence People*, 13.

huge responsibility. Think now of the city engineer. He or she is responsible for the infrastructure that services your site, and even the sidewalks and other elements of the public realm that border your site. The municipalities and regional districts are essentially responsible for building 40 to 50 percent, or more, of the area around your building site. They have a lot at risk.

In many municipalities, there are 40 to 100 development applications at various stages of approvals going across these people's desk at the same time. Stress is high and time is short. You may believe they are dragging their feet, but their job is to ensure that all the required conditions are fulfilled, and the development agreements and designs are inclusive, comprehensive and safe. If something goes wrong, they could be part of the court proceedings. For those of you who have experienced court, you probably know that this is generally not a positive experience. In this context, then, it becomes clear that any innovation or change to the 'normal' by the developer could easily be seen as potential risk to the municipality, as it is not the standard way of doing things. So remember, the next time you are ready to criticize a municipal or regional district staff member, think for a moment before you speak. They have a job to do and their career is on the line. Walk in their shoes and you will know their dilemma and challenges.

I worked for the City of Vancouver for almost 10 years. In chapter 2, I reflected on the many lessons I learned working on the inside. Now that experience has given me empathy for municipal and regional staff. I understand their job requirements and their role in the applications and approvals process. This sentiment is difficult to understand for many developers who only see delay, excuses, and barriers to approvals when working with municipalities or regional districts. Further, in defense of these people, as I discussed earlier, the provincial and federal governments each have their own legislation and laws to adhere to in approving applications. Staff have to look at projects through both a provincial and federal lens, and the requirements are not flexible. It is the law.

Community Perspectives

The community, as I will discuss in further detail in Chapter 6, brings divergent personal or special interests that may be veiled as community interests, though they might not see it as so. Part of the challenge of every developer is to eventually differentiate between the two, and address those that are valid and substantiated.

Most of us have heard many of the community issues before. The community doesn't want the noise, parking issues, traffic, safety, height, density, real estate value decrease, loss of green space ... and the list goes on. All these issues should be regarded as passionate and personal concerns, but they are worth considering seriously, as even one of these concerns can undermine approvals. The process of addressing these concerns is outlined in Chapter 7.

A number of acronyms have evolved to signify the intensity and bias surrounding community opposition.[41]

ACRONYMS FOR DEVELOPMENT OPPOSITION
NIMBY: Not in My Backyard
BANANA: Build Absolutely Nothing Near Anything
CAVE: Citizens Against Virtually Everything
NIMTO: Not In My Term Of Office
NOPE: Not On Planet Earth

Emerging positive acronym:
YIMBY: Yes In My Backyard

First Nations Perspectives

In tandem with community and municipal/regional district perspectives, First Nations come to the table with their own unique views in mind, which should be addressed separately from those of other communities. With First Nations, their territory and lands are precious to them. Care should be taken to actively consult with them and listen to their needs and concerns. Respect and acknowledgement, along with heartfelt sincerity and sharing, are at the core of building constructive understanding and relationships with First Nations, and with all concerned citizens. We will discuss the importance of appropriate consultation with First Nations further in Chapter 6, when we examine working with multiple interests.[42]

When you train yourself to understand various points of view, you will understand how complicated the emotional side of development approvals can be. Technical aspects are important, but they tend to take a back seat to ultimate decisions if the emotional needs of the various parties are not met. You must ask yourself, what are the municipal, district, provincial, federal, First Nations, and community goals, strategies, and potential risks/rewards in a project? Without this multiple stakeholder analysis, various interests are either not adequately addressed or are left out altogether.

The following *Stakeholder Benefits Chart* (Figure 4.2 below) is a tool for analyzing the goals and interests, as well as measures for success, of each of the approvals' players. The benefits and risk/reward columns could be filled in based on specific projects, to address each participants' goals and interests. The intention is to build support for your project by addressing specific needs and aspirations, and not to provide generic responses that do not match individual concerns.

---

41 Frederick D. Jarvis, *Site Planning and Community Design*, 6.

42 Bob Joseph, Cynthia F. Joseph, *Indigenous Relations*, 106, 107.

Stakeholders	Goals/interests	Benefits	Measures	Risk/Reward
Private	short-term, medium-term, and long-term profit as well as corporate image	- return on investment - value increase - general support	timing of approvals, costs, revenues, return on investment, and support	- delays - demands - no approvals - investment - devaluation
Municipal	services, cost/revenue, land values, taxes, affordability, and equity	-improved amenities -additional services -community needs	value/spin-offs, taxes, quantity of development, and community support	- low quality - few amenities - little value-added
Community	Services, amenities/facilities, taxes, safety and security, traffic, environment, noise, and real estate values, cultural values and language	- additional amenities - diversity of housing - conservation of environmental areas - sensitivity to existing development - necessary facilities	community improvements: services, taxes, safety and security, traffic, environment, noise, and real estate values	- low quality - few amenities - high impacts - devaluation - community loss
Provincial	policies, regulations, and greater public interest	- housing - environmental - public interests	conformance to policies and regulations	- low quality - marginal housing - degradation
Federal	policies, regulations, and greater public interest	- housing - environmental - public interests	conformance to policies and regulations	- low quality - marginal housing - degradation
First Nations	territory, claims, and the right to be consulted, environment, culture and language, identity, respect and recognition	- partnerships - joint ventures - economic development - social/cultural recognition and identity	community improvements, employment, member benefits, and financial contributions or partnerships	- respect and acknowledgement - genuine partnership - no real socio/cultural gain - no economic development
Other Special Interests Affordability Environment Wildlife etc.	preservation and conservation of natural assets and increasing affordability	- affordable housing - environmental stewardship - wildlife conservation	conservation measures, increased affordability, and climate change	-little or no affordable housing, environmental gains, and community gains

Figure 4.2: Stakeholder Benefits Chart

Approval Controls and Influencers

Who really holds the power?

The ancient biblical story of David and Goliath, illustrated below (Figure 4.3), has many lessons and questions to ponder, especially when real estate developments approvals come to mind.

Questions:

1. Who holds the real power in the approvals process in the end?
2. Is finding out the power sources critical to approvals?
3. Is there support at the top?
4. Can you win without fighting, and can it be a supportive partnership?

Lessons:

1. Think tactically and smartly to overcome what could be obvious, and somewhat overwhelming, barriers.
2. Don't be presumptuous and assume victory at any point in the process.
3. Strength can be measured in different ways.
4. Remember the message of Sun Zu—great generals only fight when they know they can win.[43]

Figure 4.3: David and Goliath
(source: Wikipedia)

[43] Sun Zu, *Art of War*, 10.

Something that continues to fascinate me is the strange and uncertain alchemy that occurs when combining bylaws, interpretation, politics, and the various players involved in approvals. You may have the zoning on your side, and the request for rezoning may make perfect sense, but there are vested interests … and votes for politicians really matter more. The following discussion covers these unwritten variables. They require understanding (to the extent possible) and vigilance for beneficial results.

I come back to the 'three martini law' that I discussed in Chapter 2. That law is that three martinis with your local director of development services, or planning director, is worth three books of law. It may even be advisable to touch base with your local council and mayor to ensure there is support for development in the area. In other words, there is the politics of the case and then there are the apparent facts, or precedent cases. Really, each informs the other, but the politics of the land is as important, or more important, than the facts.

The Politics of Shifting Sands

In real estate development this legal parallel means that, although all the material facts and policies are in support of your proposed development, the political alignment, among other factors, may not be. No matter what the policy and bylaws state, a difference in opinion or an emerging new policy, even if it's not yet written, could affect the 'approvability' of the application. That is why, before even closing the sale on the land, there is a necessity to meet with the key players on the technical side (the director of planning or development services) and the political side (the mayor, or chair of the regional district, as well as influential councillors or regional directors in rural areas).

It is important that developers themselves meet with the municipalities or regional districts to ensure direct relationships are established. This will be beneficial to development interests. Having the developer's representative present (along with the planner and/or architect) may also provide continuity, as the process proceeds with staff. On the other hand, a confidential meeting between the developer and those presenting high-level public interests may be better, depending on the situation.

Political factors affecting approvability:

- Does the application have staff support?
- Is the mayor solidly behind the ideas?
- Is the application submitted during 'silly season' (approximately six months prior to elections) when no decisions are made?
- Who is the key local councillor or regional director who needs to be the foundation for the vote to move forward?
- Does the application threaten the councillors or regional directors?

- Is there uncertainty associated with the application, or unanswered questions about, for example, transportation, environmental, and housing types?
- What community, municipal or regional benefits will the application bring to the area?

Don't confuse the pre-application meeting with informal meetings required to obtain important intelligence on the project's risks and associated political barriers. Multiple meetings need to be undertaken with the various players to ensure consistent alignment up and down the approving organization. Also, remember that for many of these people, saying 'no' is easier than saying 'yes', as 'no' has no apparent risks associated with it. The risks approvers are staring at if they should approve your project and it causes harm in the community include career, liability, and isolation through the staff ranks.

That said, staff generally stick together and protect their own. Be aware that staff and politicians can be chameleons who change their skin colour in self-defense depending on the situation. This chameleon metaphor[44] does not mean they are dishonest, but that they sometimes change their minds based on new information and associated further risk, especially when a significant number of community members stand up against an application at the public hearing.

Also be aware that there will be a need for course corrections through the process. Stack the 'yes' votes in your favour at the public hearing by building support for the project from the beginning. This process takes time and commitment. At the public hearing, you want support stacked in your favour. The case that follows is an example of council changes that spelled major changes for development intentions. This can happen even if you have a development permit!

In the case (further detailed on page 106), town council in White Rock changed their development policy while developer G.S.R. was in the process of trying to get a 12-storey building project off the ground. The developer was vulnerable to changes in the proposed municipal policies, which essentially reduced the height of the development-permit-approved, 12-storey building—essentially 'down-zoning' the property—to half the height, at 6 stories. Once the council went ahead with their intended policy changes, the development permit became null and void unless the developer submitted their building permit application within seven days of approval. G.S.R. did not comply with the seven-day submission requirement and therefore could not proceed with their development as approved in compliance with their prior development permit.

---

44 Chameleon can mean a changeable or inconstant person (Source: Wordnik.com) or a person who often changes his or her beliefs or behaviour in order to please others or succeed (Source: Merriam-Webster.com).

The developer took the city of White Rock to court, as they already had an approved development permit, but B.C. Supreme Court Justice Carla Forth sided with the city on the grounds that the city's adoption of the OCP and Zoning bylaw amendments were reasonable and lawful.[45] In accordance with Section 463 of the LGA, the city was able to block the development because, while it complied with *existing* zoning, it conflicted with *proposed* zoning, which the city was in the process of preparing. Section 463 gives some relief to developers; in that it provides seven days for the applicant to submit a building permit application based on the prior zoning. White Rock mayor Darryl Walker stated that, "City council did what they thought was in the public interest for the city of White Rock with regard to the height in the Lower Town Centre in White Rock. The city must ensure development meets the needs of the community, while helping to create the White Rock we want to see in the future." [46]

45 BC Supreme Court decision March 31, 2020.

46 Vancouver Sun, Keith Fraser, April 1, 2020, n.p.

SHIFTING SANDS WITH COUNCIL
The 2020 Case of Lady Alexandra

White Rock mayor Darryl Walker and council took office in the city of White Rock in November 2018, apparently on the platform that high rise buildings were not appropriate outside the Town Centre Plan Area. The Town Centre Plan developed in 2011 designated a specific area within central 'uptown' White Rock as the principal area for high rises.

In July 2018, the council at the time passed a resolution to issue the development permit for 1310 Johnston Road to G.S.R. Group, authorizing the construction of a 30-unit, 12- storey residential building to replace the existing two-storey structure. Following the election of a new mayor and council in November 2018, the new council passed a number of resolutions, one of which was aimed at amending a bylaw to reduce the permitted maximum height of any building at the G.S.R. site from 12 to six storeys.

These resolutions resulted in amendments to the Official community plan (OCP) and the zoning bylaw affecting the area in question. The city notified the company of the resolutions and invited it to make submissions, based on the changes being considered.

G.S.R. followed through with a building permit application in January 2019, at the 12-storey building height. The city withheld the building permit on the grounds that the permit application conflicted with the OCP and zoning bylaw amendments under consideration. Following a public hearing in March, and a special meeting to approve the amendments, the city notified the developer that the 12-storey building was no longer permitted.

The developer then took court action alleging that the developer should be able to proceed with the development, and also sought orders to quash the new bylaws and resolutions. The company held that the issuance of the development permit provided a degree of certainty to proceed with the development as planned and claimed that the decision to withhold the building permit was unreasonable.

The city responded by arguing that a council's decision to issue a development permit was not a general approval of all aspects of a development and that it had acted reasonably and fairly.

In her ruling, B.C. Supreme Court Justice Carla Forth found the city's decision to adopt the bylaws to be reasonable and lawful, and declined to grant the orders sought by the developer.

On March 31, 2020, the B.C. Supreme Court sided with the City of White Rock to not permit the approval of a 12-storey building, even with a development permit approved.

Questions:

1. Was the decision reasonable under the circumstances?
2. How does the City of Vancouver's charter regard a development permit?
3. As the developer, how would you change this process to your favour?

Community Benefits Get Richer

As you move closer to final approvals (third and fourth readings of the bylaws by council or regional directors), the basket of community amenities could get richer based on demands from councillors and staff. The real estate industry relates to this as a 'late hit'. Even though the later requests appear out of order and unfair, these requests can mean the difference between continuity and indefinite deferral. Investors and financiers don't want to hear about it, and it needs to be dealt with immediately and decisively.

There should always be a strategy for how to deal with the mayor and council in any municipality. This is a complex process of first understanding their biases and motivations, and then determining if they will support the project. In order to get approvals, there will have to be some give and take. Be prepared to give, even towards the end when things appear to be done. It will be a close vote if there are any controversies, and there may be additional conditions added by council which, while sometimes not well-informed, are generally well-intentioned. Other times you may be fortunate enough to experience a constant growth in support from the community. If this occurs, there may be a unanimous vote in favour by mayor and council. I prefer this scenario and tell my clients this unanimous vote should be their goal, otherwise high risk stakes could delay the project indefinitely and, as I've mentioned, it could all be because of just one vote. Make no mistake, it takes hard work to build necessary support for a project and it's best to remember that the deal is not done until the ink is dry. In other words, do not assume completion of approvals until the development agreement is signed by all parties.

The Late Hit

I would like to share with you a number of incidents that are worth remembering as you work with mayors, councils, and staff on your development proposals. A close friend and developer colleague told me of an incident that is jaw-dropping, though it is the exception, not the rule. A project approval he'd been working on had gone on for years and finally, with the support of the community, the municipality negotiated a deal they thought could work. However, this deal required the developer to give up 67 percent of the land for open space and agriculture, leaving only the remaining 33 percent for residences. Then, at the last minute, my colleague and his partners were called to the city manager's office and it was announced that the residential portion would be reduced to only 25 percent. When asked what the rationale for the sudden change was, the city manager responded, "I promised it to someone."

The choice at that moment was to pull the staff report and defer the vote scheduled for council that evening, which obviously sets up a long-term delay; or, to acquiesce and go with the reduced 25 percent residential allocation. My colleague chose the latter, and the project was approved with 8 percent less housing to support the 75 percent of undeveloped land. There are many reasons this was an unfair process, but the main one is because it was requested at the last minute and so gave the developer little choice, and no time to deliberate. The power, as we discuss elsewhere, was in the hands of the municipality and it was wielded in an autocratic way. This is an unfortunate situation, but such things can certainly happen. You must expect the unexpected.

Mayor is King

Let me now describe another case of politics affecting development. In this case, I will describe how working politicians to your advantage, but still respecting the powers that be, can be achieved. This situation happened to me.

Imagine that you have just finished a successful downtown plan—for example, the entire downtown for a mid-sized Vancouver Island municipality. You had the support of staff, and a glowing report is going to council outlining the extent of the outreach. Further, you had sent out 1,000 personal invitations to events, and had over 300 participants in two workshops alone. Your outreach has included personal interviews with business owners as well as a series of small group discussions, from which you have prepared a focused implementation playbook, outlining various initiatives, timing, and sources of funding. Everything appears clear, straightforward, and feasible. You think, *we have this one in the bag!* It will be cakewalk at council.

Then came the final presentation to council. Fortunately, I had probed senior staff and found out that that mayor was not in support of the project. He felt that the community had not been consulted enough, despite the 1,000 personal invitation letters. Maybe a faction of the business community did not feel adequately connected to the proposed plan, who knows? But the fact of the matter was that we had to act quickly in the next few days to either turn the tide, or ensure we secured the majority vote at council. I immediately went to work with senior staff and the city manager. I knew that it would be suicide for me to present the plan to a hostile mayor, because I was easily dispensable … the guy from out of town—what does he know?

My approach was to take a completely low profile and let staff, who supported my project, present the recommendations, with me just saying a few words at the end; that way, the mayor might listen, as it would be his own staff presenting all the facts regarding participation and support.

The city manager and staff jumped on it. Like me, they knew the majority of council were on board, especially a young councillor who had been highly engaged and impressed by the process. The stage was set, and on the evening of the council meeting, it started off as planned. Staff made the presentation, with endorsement of the city manager.

However, when it was the mayor's turn to speak in response to the presentation, he was not swayed. He thanked staff and the city manager, but then attempted to undermine the process and plan. As a former RCMP officer, he had a 'command and control' way about him reflective of his disciplined training and so at first I was concerned, as he was quite forceful in his presentation.

But then I carefully observed the other councillors. One councillor nodded periodically as he spoke, but no other councillor even smiled as the mayor went on and on. Then it was time for the rebuttal by the other councillors. Imagine my surprise when, one by one, they respectfully reduced the mayor's concerns to chatter, not substance.

Following the discussion, the mayor announced a brief break in the proceedings. As he passed me, he said, and I will never forget this, "You have your agenda and I have mine." Then, after the break, there was a call to order, followed by a vote on the project. To my surprise the project was unanimously approved! The Mayor got his say, and we got the vote.

I learned four things that day:

- Never assume victory, even if you have the facts on your side.
- Design the presentation so it is staff and the city manager making the recommendations.
- Give the mayor and council their say and their 'wins'.
- Win on facts.

Community Influence and Trust

Starting early to build community trust is critical to approvals, especially if there is rezoning involved. In June of 2020 I had an experience where a marketing specialist phoned me in a panic. It was literally 22 days until the public hearing, and she wanted to know if I could help build community support for the project. After almost two years in a rezoning process, they had left only 22 days to build support, after a council vote of 4 to 3 at the first and second readings!

Upon further investigation, I learned from the municipality's director of development services that the developer had issued a statement to the community at the first public house that the development company had the right to build the building. Wrong! This was only partially incorrect. Although the official community plan's designation for the site supported the 4-storey development proposal, the zoning did not. Hence the requirement for a rezoning process involving public review. In the subsequent rezoning process, the adjoining property owners petitioned against the project.

The project was getting very little support on all fronts. With a three-storey apartment next door, and duplexes behind, the proposition sounded reasonable, but previous applications had failed. The overall support was not there because the applicant did not *build trust* with the community. As I have mentioned, never assume you can win support, especially at the last minute.

In the end, the developer felt he did not have to retain me to obtain approvals and his proposal, which was for a reasonable four-storey apartment building adjoining a three-storey building, was denied. It was unfortunate because it was a good proposal, complete with building step-backs at the fourth floor, an attractive central amenity space, and it would have been a good addition to the neighbourhood. Instead, it was deferred at the public hearing and then denied by city council. It is such a waste of time and resources when a building plan addresses affordability and diversity of housing in a community but no one is sympathetic to it; however, this situation could have been avoided if a sensitive and inclusive community engagement process had been implemented from the beginning.

First Nations

> *An informed acknowledgement is authentic, accurate, respectful, and spoken with heartfelt sincerity. It is not a platitude. The exercise of doing the research to find out on whose land a meeting or event is taking place is an opportunity to open hearts and minds to the past and make a commitment to contributing to a better future, which is the essence of reconciliation.*
>
> *—Bob Joseph and Cynthia F. Joseph, Indigenous Relations (2019)*

First Nations now have a legally reinforced seat at the development table. In November 2019, the provincial government passed legislation to implement the *United Nations Declaration on the Rights of Indigenous Peoples* (UNDRIP). The UN declaration emphasizes indigenous peoples' rights to live in dignity, to maintain and strengthen indigenous institutions, cultures and traditions and to pursue self-determined development in alignment with indigenous needs and aspirations.

The associated British Columbia *Declaration on the Rights of Indigenous People's Act* (Bill 41)[47] aims to create a pathway forward for human rights of indigenous peoples, while introducing better transparency and predictability in working together. The legislation sets out a process to align British Columbia laws with the UN declaration. It provides a framework for decision-making, flexibility for making agreements, and it has regular reporting requirements.

47 Government of British Columbia. November 2019.

John Ralston Saul notes in his book, *The Comeback:* "On June 25, 2014, the city council of Vancouver voted unanimously to acknowledge that the city sits on unceded aboriginal territory. This is not merely a politeness or a formality: Yes, it is a gesture of respect to the Musqueam, Squamish, and Tsleil-Waututh First Nations … these territories were never ceded through treaty, war or surrender."

A day later the Supreme Court of British Columbia ruled that full aboriginal title to land does exist. [48] These decisions, among others, have major implications on real estate development approvals across British Columbia. The extent is still to be determined. Again, these are sensitive issues with long histories. In this context, in all negotiations with First Nations, we should respond with empathy and compassion. First we must understand, and then be understood.

The trend toward joint ventures between First Nations and well-established developers is evident throughout the Lower Mainland of British Columbia. Many First Nations are taking an active role in partnerships, providing economic, cultural, and environmental benefits to their membership. These partnerships are across reserve lands, treaty lands, and First Nations territories.

The Senakw development is the most significant example of a partnership between a well-established developer—Westbank—and a First Nation, the Squamish Nation. Senakw is the largest First Nations development in Canada, featuring 6,000 homes in 11 towers. It is planned for the south foot of the Burrard Street Bridge in the city of Vancouver (see detailed description on next page).[49]

---

48 John Ralston Saul, *The Comeback*, 174-176.

49 Kevin Chan, Daily Hive, Vancouver Urbanized. November 5 and December 11, 2019, n.p.

GAME-CHANGER: SENAKW

Senakw is the traditional village site of the indigenous Squamish people.

The proposed Senakw Village development on 4.7 hectares (11.7 acres) is a game changer for the City of Vancouver and the Squamish Nation. The $3 billion project is the largest First Nations development in Canada. It was approved by Squamish Nation council members on December 10, 2019.

The proposed development at the south end of the Burrard Street Bridge includes 11 towers, each up to 56 stories, and will be implemented in five phases. Senakw will create 6,000 homes, with the majority dedicated to market rental housing. The redevelopment of reserve land is a 50/50 partnership with local developer Westbank, and each of the partners will realize up to $10 billion over the life of the project.

The proposed development has some significant implications, including:

1. The development does not have to go through the City of Vancouver's development review process, therefore the development, planning and design can be expedited under the jurisdiction of the Squamish Nation, with construction targeted to commence in 2021 and completion projected in five years.
2. The City of Vancouver is supportive of the development and has some influence in transit and infrastructure delivery to the site. The development aligns with the city's policy for reconciliation.
3. The project will deliver as much as 25 percent of the City of Vancouver's 10-year housing strategy, which promises to deliver 20,000 new secured market rental units.
4. The development will only provide parking for 10 percent of the housing units, relying instead on the project's strategic location close to transit and within walking/bicycle distance to downtown.
5. Density will be achieved by building taller towers, making space on the ground for parks and community spaces. Basketball and lacrosse courts are planned for underneath the Burrard Street Bridge, which will activate currently under-utilized space.
6. A potential district energy plant could reduce greenhouse gases by 70 to 75 percent, with estimates of only 1.5 tonnes per year as compared to 6.0 tonnes of greenhouse gas generated by conventional housing developments.
7. The development will be under the jurisdiction of the Squamish Nation.
8. The development could provide Squamish Nation economic security for generations to come, while providing between 150 and 200 homes to First Nation members at below market rates.
9. Between 70 and 90 percent of the units will be designated market rental units, while the remainder will be leasehold strata condominiums.

"This is truly a landmark moment in our Nation's history. The Senakw Project will transform the Squamish Nation by providing immense social, cultural and economic benefits to Squamish Nation members for generations to come." - Khelsilem, spokesperson and councillor for Squamish Nation.

The Situation Room: Decision-Makers and Influencers

To summarize this discussion, let us take a closer look at each of the approvals players to better understand their roles, responsibilities, and motivations for either approving or disapproving your application. The following depiction, Figure 4.4: *Project Heat Chart - Players, Influencers, and Decision-Makers,* provides a tool you can use to analyze your own projects and increase awareness as to who, and when, the players influence the review and approval of your project.

This chart will help inform you as to who has the power, and what the extent of influence is on the decision. It is important to first gain this understanding, so you know what each of the players needs to support your project. Often, this level of project power analysis is not completed and so a project plan ends in disappointment or delay, since the needs of the players have not been addressed properly or have been largely ignored.

Each project varies with degree of influence and, as each municipality and regional district is permitted to vary their approval processes, decision is controlled by specific parties. The titles of the players may also change depending on the size and maturity of the municipality or regional district.

Player	**Role** (Review; Approvals/App)	**Influence** (Low; Medium; High)	**Timing** (Beginning; Middle; End)	**Decision** (L=low; M=medium; H=high)
Mayor	Approvals	High	Middle - End	High
Council	Approvals	High	Middle- End	High
Community	Review +App	High	Beginning-End	High
Staff				
Director Development	Review + App	High	Middle- End	High
Director of Planning	Review +App	High	Middle- End	High
Director of Engineering	Review +App	High	Middle- End	High
Director of Parks	Review	Medium	Middle- End	Low
Fire Chief	Review	High	Middle-End	High
Police Chief	Review	High	Middle-End	High
Real Estate Services and Housing	Review	Medium	Beginning - End	Medium
Director of Social Services	Review	Medium	Beginning - End	Low
Development Planner	Review	Medium	Beginning - End	High
Parks Planner	Review	Medium	Beginning - End	Low
Engineer	Review	Medium	Beginning - End	Medium
Planning Advisory Commission	Review	Medium	Middle	Advisory
Advisory Design Panel	Review	Medium	Middle	Advisory
***First Nations Territory/Lands**	Consult	High	Beginning	Low/High
Circulated Agencies + Utilities + Crown Corporations				
Ministry of Transportation and Infrastructure	Review + App	High	Middle	High
Ministry of Environment and Climate Change Strategy	Review + App	High	Middle	High
Ministry of Forests, Lands, Natural Resource Operations and Rural Development	Review + App	High	Middle	High
Ministry of Municipal Affairs and Housing	Review + App	High	Middle	High
BC Hydro	Review + App	High	Middle	High
Railways (CP and CN)	Review + App	High	Middle	High
Other Utilities and Communications (BC Tel, BC Hydro, Cable, etc.)	Review + App	Medium	Middle	Low to High

Figure 4.4: Project Heat Chart - Players, Influencers and Decision-Makers

5. RISK AND ASSESSMENT

Real estate development is the art—perhaps someday it will be the science—of building real estate value by managing development risk.
—Richard B. Peiser, Professional Real Estate Development (2003)

Nothing gets done unless there is someone to lead a project and take the risks. However, these risks should be calculated ones that have been carefully evaluated, and their potential outcomes determined. Risk aversion varies with individuals and companies based on their experience, resources, and goals. Risks go well beyond the approvals part of development, but the approvals part of the process is central to success.

As I've mentioned, one risk faced by developers is that of support by the municipality or the community for the project. The community considers such things as the increase in traffic, noise, the loss of green space, decrease of property values, and quality of life when deciding whether a project is viable in their neighbourhood. The municipality, on the other hand, sees potential increased demand for community services, potable water, sewer upgrades and/or replacements, road widenings, requirements for more community amenities ... and the list goes on.

In addition to operational and functional risks, other indirect risks can affect approvals. From a staff standpoint, and the political side, the questions are, *will the developer follow through? Can they be trusted? Do they have the track record (covenant) to do what they say they are going to do?* An abandoned, partially-built building is not something anyone, including financers, want to take over. It is not their business. Their concerns, as well as perceived and real risks, should be considered early in the process. Their views count.

On a broad and inclusive basis, the following questions probe the full gamut of risk associated with real estate development projects. These questions bring home the need to ask macro questions before poking at details. These questions, in part, start the framework for what should be a structured and informed decision-making process shaped by discipline and focused intent.

Questions should include:

- How do we determine whether to proceed or not with the project?
- What are the key factors determining a 'go' or 'no go'?
- In classic economic terms, what is the opportunity cost of proceeding?
- What alternatives do we have that align with the 'go'?
- What is our exit strategy if our plans don't work out?

As we contemplate these questions, we might realize we have some fundamental choices to make. Normally, the lower the risk, the higher the cost of development. That is why, in some instances, some realtors will take a property through the rezoning process (if it is not onerously complex) in order to reap the premium value benefits associated with permissions for additional density and market focused land use.

In essence, developers build value where few see it, and manage risk in the process. A developer is willing to take risk, which includes convincing planners, politicians, and the community that their development is worth approving. Their arguments should be convincing and compelling in order to have the authorities and community support their proposition through the approvals process. The more support, the lower the risk; the less support, the higher the risk. That is one reason why your banker or your investment group want to know that you have had approvals from the municipality or regional districts before they advance funds for your project. Approvals matter in assessing risk and advancing funds.

This chapter explains the risk associated with different real estate types, and the associated challenges and opportunities as well. It also examines the critical importance of diagnostics (macro-analysis) and due diligence (micro-analysis) at both the general and detailed levels. The discussion then proceeds to preliminary financial analysis and the associated concept of determining residual land value, as well as an examination of how to leverage value to optimize return on investment. The chapter concludes with an introspective look at how developers make the decision to go, hold or sell real estate projects based on available information. As we will discover, knowing the 'project killers' early can save money, relationships, and the real estate business.

Risk and Real Estate Types

The old adage 'high risk, high return' can quickly turn into 'high risk, no return and extended liability' if a project goes sideways. It is important to consider risk as it relates to specific real estate types before we proceed further. Choosing what type of real estate development fits your risk profile should shape your investments. I will describe the various types of real estate in simple terms, since such fundamentals are often overlooked when it comes to decisions on investments and associated impacts on the approvals process. The illustrations I will provide are not exhaustive, but they will give you an indication of how risk ties to approvals.

I would like to start my discussion with a sobering reminder of the concept of 'ego real estate', which is directed by the heart and not the head. My first example is that of 666 Fifth Avenue in New York City (see case study on page 118). This example illustrates the risk of following your ego in property acquisitions. When considering a property for development, remember the axiom at the end of Chapter 2: Never fall in love with a piece of real estate. Always closely regard analytics, associated risks, and worst-case scenarios when acquiring real estate, especially in significant real estate ventures. Using more than one third party to help you with this due diligence task may be necessary. There are high risks, even for an established real estate company, when entering a higher-stakes real estate games that they have little experience playing. Even experienced people cannot assume the best outcomes.[50]

[50] Charles V. Bagli, Kate Kelly, *New York Times*, April 3, 2017 and August 3, 2018, n.p.

EGO REAL ESTATE: DANGEROUS AND RISK PRONE

The Kushner Companies bought the skyscraper at 666 Fifth Avenue in January 2007 for $1.8 billion—the most paid for any New York office building. Jared Kushner, the son of the owner, signed the deal on his birthday. The deal was supposed to symbolize a move to the 'big leagues' of Manhattan for Kushner, a move similar to that made by his father-in-law, Donald Trump, decades before. The company moved from Florham Park, New Jersey to the 15th floor of 666 Fifth Avenue in Manhattan.

The total paid for the building was not much more than the $1.72 billion paid for the MetLife Building, but while the price worked out to $600 a square foot with the Metlife building, the Kushners paid twice the price, at $1,200 a square foot, for 666 Fifth Avenue. At the time, although almost fully leased, the rent only covered two-thirds of the annual debt payments. This was a risky venture, especially in a declining market. Then, when the 2008 financial crisis set into the epicentre of New York the following year, rents declined.

In order to stem the bleeding, the Kushners decided to sell part of the building. The Carlyle Group and Crown Acquisitions bought the retail space for the remarkable price of $525 million, but the proceeds were used to pay off secondary loans, not the main mortgage. The interest-only loan of $1.2 billion eventually ballooned into $1.4 billion. Cash flow only covered 66 percent of the debt obligations, and vacancy hovered around 30 percent.

In 2016, the Kushners came up with another idea. They did not fill vacant space as it became available, because they decided to redevelop the site into a 1,400-foot-high luxury condominium, hotel and retail complex worth a projected $12 billion, with $7.5 billion in costs and a seven-year development timeframe. They would need to borrow a staggering $4.2 billion to make the deal work. Meanwhile, still in the shadow of the 2008 crash, the luxury market, fueled in part by foreign investors, had cooled drastically. Could the Kushners actually get the required approvals to proceed with such a development?

In 2018, Brookfield Asset Management, the manager of 275 office buildings worldwide, pre-purchased a 99-year lease on the building to relieve the debt load. Jared Kushner, by then a top White House advisor to his father-in-law, Donald Trump, was relieved of the $1.4 billion mortgage, although he placed his property interest in a family trust when he joined the White House.

Brookfield is betting on a turnaround based on several factors, including the building's premier location on Fifth Avenue near Rockefeller Centre and Central Park, and its proximity to public transportation. The company is investing $700 million to renovate the lobby, install new elevators, refurbish vacant offices, and attract new tenants. In retrospect, this pragmatic makeover should have been considered in the first place but was probably not viable based on the wall of debt that could not be serviced.

Below is a labyrinth diagram (Figure 5.1) for you to peruse. It is a tool you can use to evaluate risk factors as you move through your process. In a labyrinth, time and right decisions are part of the dynamic that increase or decrease risk as you move through twists and turns. One wrong move can create a dead end, or costly delays. Keep your eye focused on each decision, as they are all individually important in arriving fast and early at the end.

Figure 5.1: The Labyrinth of Sound Decision-Making
In the labyrinth above each decision affects the rest and so success is based on insight and foresight

Lower Risk

There is no such thing as low risk in today's market, or future markets, as things can go wrong even if the property and approvals appear sound. As we saw in 2008, and again with the pandemic, the tides can change overnight. This is why I use the term 'lower risk' as a relative term as opposed to 'low risk' which tends to presume no real risks.

Certainty is a dangerous word in deal-making and approvals, although ironically, a high degree of certainty is exactly what we are looking for in real estate deals and approvals. For example, just the other day, a former classmate of mine who is now a developer in North Carolina remarked that their tenants, including medical professionals, are asking for deferrals or decreases in rents due to the pandemic, which is affecting their income streams. Although lease agreements are in place, exceptional circumstances require exceptions. You have to be ready for the unexpected, even in lower risk situations.

In a lower risk situation, multiple factors play into its attractive, and more risk averse, profile. A well-located property that has a building and/or associated cash flow creates a situation where there is an immediate yield or return on invested capital. An example is when the building, group of buildings or parking lot provide cash flow. This cash flow can partially or fully amortize a loan on the property while development approvals proceed. It is what some savvy real estate investors call, 'a gift that keeps on giving', since the property will continue to support itself without an external cash call, while its capital value increases year after year in a normal market.

Another lower risk financing option is when the property owner seeks a joint venture partner who knows the labyrinth of local approvals processes and wants to remain in the game to seek higher potential gains; however, developers only go for this situation if the majority control rests with the developer and the continuing interest by the existing property owner is silent—in other words, if he or she has full control of the decision-making process without meddling from the property owner.

Property that is pre-zoned is also considered lower risk, as the approvals will not require the long public reviews associated with zoning. If zoning associated with a proposal meets current requirements under current zoning, it is referred to as an 'outright' application and it means land use and density are already accommodated for within the existing zone or OCP. If no public hearing is required, then approvals rest with staff and/or council, depending on the size and complexity of the proposal. However, as these approval processes tend to vary in each municipality or regional district, make sure you confirm the details of the approvals with staff people who knows all the requirements for your property. Do not allow a general 'gloss' over the details.

Another feature that can indicate a lower risk property is if there is an indication of a proven market and surplus demand based on adjoining property pre-sales.

Summary assessment of lower risk properties:

- Good location and proven market.
- Good cash flow that can help finance property.
- No rezoning.
- No public review.
- Fees are predictable and predetermined.
- No major physical or policy constraints, verified by trusted source.
- Ready to go to development permit and building permit approvals.

Medium Risk

A classic medium risk situation is when a property is located in a good location but there is no proven market demand for the prescribed use. For example, if a land assembly has five old houses on the property that are not providing significant income, and you would like to develop multiple-family residential housing. The official community plan has just been updated to allow this use and density on the property, but the increased building height and density are new to the community, and the current zoning needs to be changed to permit the density, height and building massing on the site.

You are breaking new ground in the community, and higher density residential and commercial mixed-use development will require rezoning. As well, there are community amenity contributions (CACs) to consider, and they are negotiated to be up to 80 percent of the calculated land lift that will be created by the change in use and density.

Further, since the development is a new type of development for the community, it will require an extensive public engagement process.

All of this combined is indicative of a medium risk property as the negotiated land price assumes a specific increased density that is not necessarily guaranteed. Add to this a development planner in charge of the file who is conservative, and you are working with a situation that could be dicey.

Summary assessment of medium risk properties:

- Good location but no proven market.
- Nominal cash flow.
- Rezoning requires extensive public review.
- Physical or policy constraints to be verified by third party.
- No real support or tested process.
- Community amenity contribution is unpredictable.
- More information and a reassessment of risks is required.

High Risk

Imagine a land assembly of 20 hectares (45 acres) in the suburbs that is essentially a 'greenfield' development; in other words, it has not been developed except, perhaps, for lots between two and four hectares (five to ten acres) in size, most of which are hobby farms. The existing zoning is 'rural residential' and the OCP designates the land as rural.

Any development will require both a rezoning and an OCP amendment as you will be breaking new ground here because there is no pattern of new development to follow, except for the large rural lot, single-family residential pattern adjoining the property. The price on the property demands at least some multiple-family residential density as part of the development.

There is also a fish-bearing stream running through the property, and setbacks according to provincial regulations are 30 metres on each side of the stream, greater than the 15-metre setback modification that was negotiated into the price of the land.

Council wants employment to be a top priority when it comes to development in the area, but your business is housing. Further, the planning department is interested in compact, affordable housing, while you are interested in detached, single-family homes. All of this combines to spell 'disaster' if not handled correctly.

Summary assessment of high-risk properties (Figure 5.2):

- Large lot rural land.
- No real competitive location, and no proven market.
- Some interim cash flow potential from renting houses, but not significant.
- Rezoning and OCP amendments are required.
- Public review by single-family residential landowners is required.
- No real staff or council support, or tested process.
- Community amenity contribution is unpredictable.
- More information and a reassessment of risks is required as it appears the opportunity cost is too high.

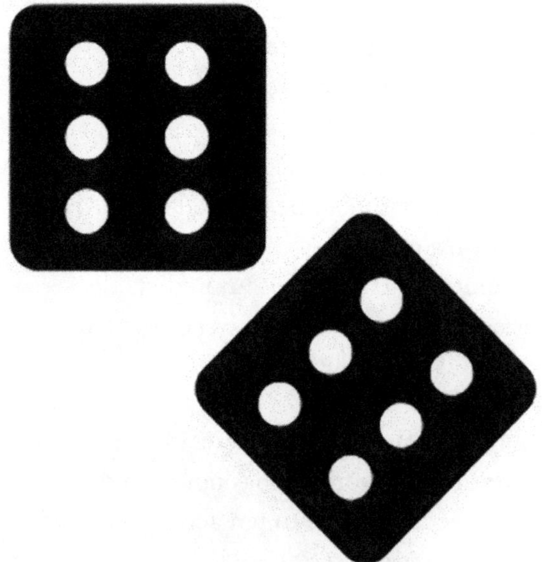

Figure 5.2: Risk and Dice

An informed investment does not involve a roll of the dice to determine outcome

The graph below (Figure 5.3) summarizes and further illustrates the increase in risk between an income property that is zoned, a zoned non-income property, and finally, raw land that does not have zoning. Note of the following:

Income Property and Zoned Sites: An income property, such as a shopping centre on part of the property that is generating significant income, can help fund property redevelopment, both in terms of collateral and actual cash flow.

There can also be a significant decrease in risk if you are working with zoned land that does not require any changes to policy.

Zoned Property: If a property is already zoned when it is acquired, it could save you significant time to get to the development stage, as you will not bear the burden of public review, which can extend approval times from two to five years. Also, as your property rights are already in place, you can build what you want to without a requirement for community amenity contributions, which is normally tied to increased density or change of use.

Raw Land: The graph below illustrates a steep increase in risk when considering raw land. This land normally requires rezoning for a proposed new use. For example, if you are proposing a suburban development in an area that is zoned rural, you will need to get appropriate zoning. This rezoning process is uncertain as it requires a public review, and there is always the possibility that the changes may not be approved. Remember, a successful rezoning is a privilege, not a right.

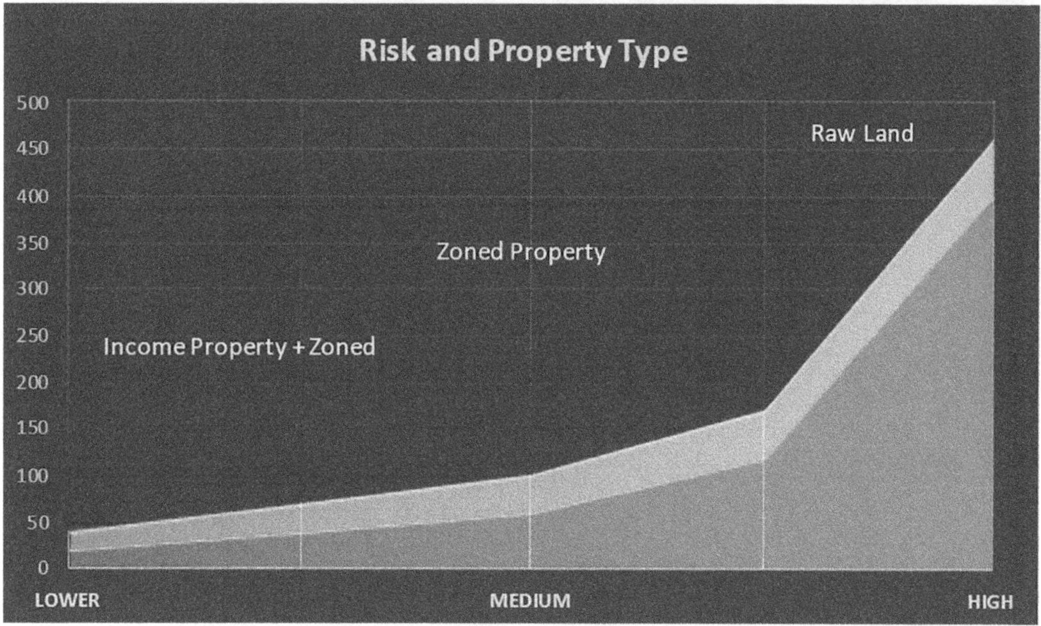

Figure 5.3: Risk and Property Type

There is normally a correlation between the level of risk and the sales price of a property. As previously illustrated, if a property is low risk and has appropriate zoning in place, then it follows that the value of it is higher. Conversely, if property is raw land and there are no guarantees about use and future use, then land will fetch a lower price.

So, if we compare an urban parcel of land that is zoned to a rural parcel that is not zoned, and both are the same size (but with the urban parcel in a prime location and the rural parcel in a suburban edge location), it is only logical that the urban property will fetch a higher, if not exponentially higher, price. Location, current zoning, demand, and less processing make the urban location the prime target, hence the premium price (Figure 5.4 below).

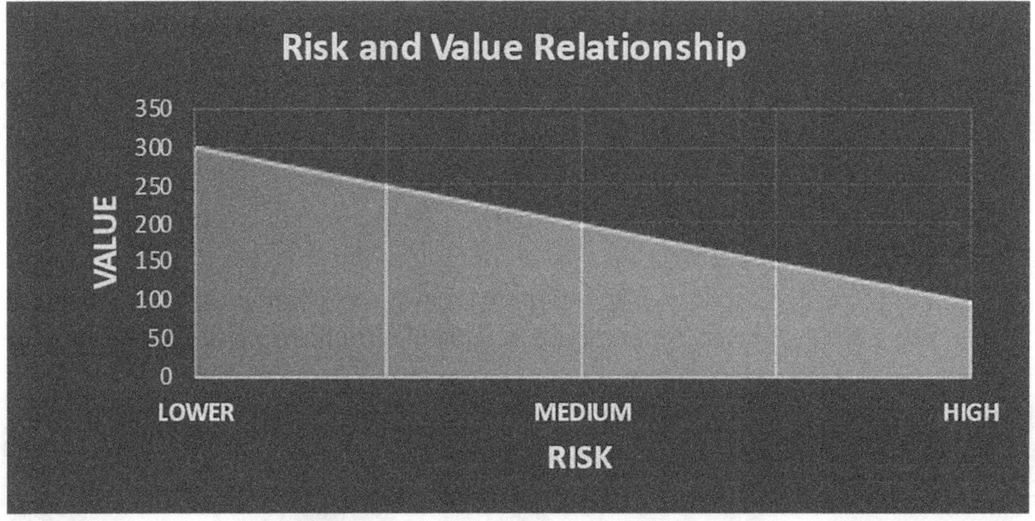

Figure 5.4: Risk and Value Relationship

Risk also decreases as development projects proceed through the project approvals process. For example, in a re-zoning scenario that requires applications, formal approvals, and a public hearing in front of council, if you are successful and receive your development permit, building permit, and move to construction, the risk further declines, as illustrated below (Figure 5.5).

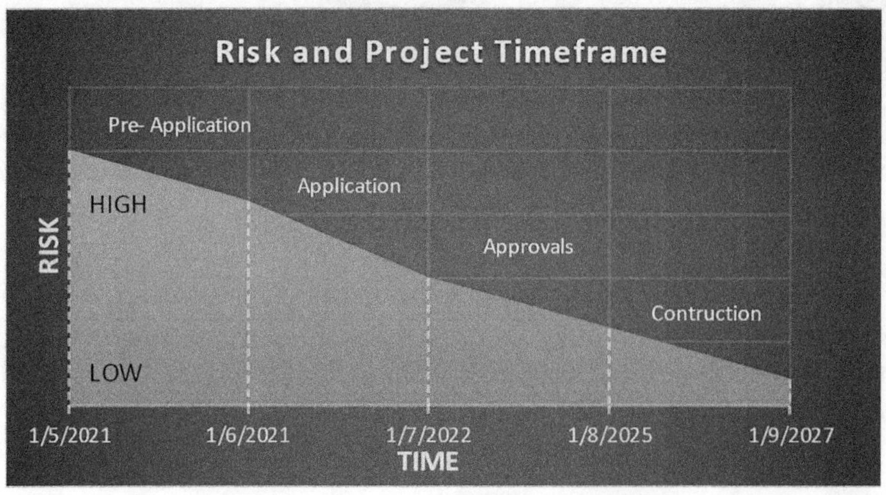

Figure 5.5: Risk and Project Timeframe

Diagnostics and Due Diligence

When you want to actually purchase a property, you have to dive deeply into understanding the property and its full potential. You must go beyond its general location and type, as we have just done, to truly understand what you are getting into. A life-long lesson is always a good way of emphasizing the importance of this due diligence. Here is an example of one.

A Mistake After 40 Years in the Business

I was on the way to a site on Vancouver Island a few years ago with a developer client and I lamented that a project had gone sideways because of a mislead client.

The engineer in the car piped up and said, "I run into that type of situation on almost a weekly basis, whether it is me or them."

Then the developer conceded, "I made a fatal error with due diligence last Friday, after more than 40 years in business."

I immediately asked in dismay, "What happened?"

He described how a realtor came into his office and presented a deal that he could not close himself, as there needed to be a certified cheque for $1 million submitted with an offer before the end of the day. My client reviewed the proposal, and the consultant's report on the property, over the next two hours and made the conclusion that the 38-townhouse yield was indeed achievable based on the recommendations in the report. He wrote the cheque and submitted the offer with the $1 million payment by the deadline. Congratulations were in store ... at least he thought they were.

The following Monday morning, after the weekend, upon further review he found out that the consultant did not consider the full implications of the building setback requirements from the stream on the property, and therefore the yield was reduced to 30 units. His profit was gone, and he was left to seek his $1 million through the courts. This developer missed a fundamental detail that additional due diligence would have uncovered. The lesson is, make no presumptions without expert review. After 40 years in the business, mistakes still happen, and they are potentially very costly, as per this example.

The Need for the Big and Small Pictures

There is a reason why I have combined the discussion of diagnostics with that of due diligence. I don't want you to miss the big stuff for the small stuff. This dual strategy combines the big picture analysis (diagnostics) with the details (due diligence). It is important to understand all factors relevant to developing a site. If, for example, the basic location and land use designation is wrong, why waste money on analyzing soil contamination. The big picture is as important as the small picture, but only paying attention to one can spell uncertainty and higher risk.

Normally in a site acquisition process a buyer has 30 to 60 days to do their due diligence before the deal is closed. This time is precious, and no big mistakes are acceptable. Keep the big picture in mind as you deep-dive into the small stuff so that you are aware of the canary in the coal mine. If the air is poisonous, no matter how much coal there is, it won't save the day.

Each property acquisition requires a careful eye to ensure there are no red flags that will undermine the project. Look for those red flags that are not obvious. These may include soil contamination, First Nation claims, significant stream setbacks, liens on title, environmental areas (wetlands or wildlife), and the list goes on. Use a rigorous process to ensure your property qualifies for development. Any of the considerations I mentioned, and others relevant to specific regional policies, could stop development or create approval delays, especially when external agencies (such as provincial ministries) become involved.

For example, when a site on the way to Whistler was being considered for development, the client spent significant money investigating potential contamination, since the property was adjacent to a former mining operation. Only traces of spotty contamination were found outside the intended development area and so the developer concluded that any further investment in investigating contaminants would just be futile, as there was no end in sight.

When dealing with government ministries in this way, it is best is to move from a studies approach to a management approach. In this case, that meant stopping further soil studies and meeting with the Ministry of Environment to confirm that best efforts had been made under the circumstances and offering to monitor further development to ensure no contamination was detected. In essence, the developer could create built-in safeguards in site construction, and propose a soil sample regimen, so that no further detailed soil contamination studies are required, and conditional approval could be given.

Diagnostics

The Age of Enlightenment was an 18th century movement that rejected established dogma in favour of rational inquiry. René Descartes, in his 1637 *Discourse on Method*, foreshadowed the Age of Enlightenment when he wrote, "The first precept was never to accept a thing as true until I knew it as such without a single doubt." [51]

With that in mind, there are six things a developer should do to ensure they have no doubt:

1. Don't rely on past policy to shape the future of approvals processes.
2. Ensure your available studies are current and that they reflect site conditions.
3. Review previous applications on the site and adjacent sites.
4. Be careful to not prejudge situations.
5. Get the facts.
6. Verify the facts—measure twice and cut once.

The big picture of a successful development, and what that looks like, is sometimes up to the senior vice president of development, while the vice president of acquisitions tries to 'sell' the property to the company. However, even though due diligence involves coming out 'clean', market price, community resistance and politics can, and should, play into the game. If you refer again to Figure 4.4 in Chapter 4, you will note that 'influencers' and 'decision-makers' should be on side to ensure there is confidence that they will support the application. Otherwise, you may need to end the operation right there. It's better to make an informed decision rather than one that comes back to haunt you during the subsequent approvals process from hell!

Fundamental diagnostics are:

- Market segmentation, inventory, absorption, price, and niches.
- Site history and potential.
- Success or failure of local development applications (public files).
- Residual land value analysis.
- Proforma optimistic, realistic, and pessimistic scenarios.
- Record of approvals in the planning department.
- Council cycle and support.
- Community profile and potential demands.
- Costs and fees.
- First Nations interests.

[51] Patricia Daniels et al, *Alamac of World History*, 210.

Due Diligence

Doing your homework is fundamental to success. It gives you clarity and order (Figure 5.6 below). Details make the deal and shape success. Online resources, contacts, trusted consultants, and 'boots on the ground' site visits with purpose are critical to success. I have developed two checklists. The first is a shorter one-page list included as Figure 5.7 on page 130 and the second is longer, entitled the *Acquisition Comprehensive Checklist* detailed in Appendix A. These checklists should give you a jumpstart in your investigation into the viability of your property for development, provide a method for either a 'snapshot', or a full deep investigative dive.

Figure 5.6: Due Diligence

Due diligence should give clarity and order to complex and confusing information

These lists detail all elements that will affect approvals, and include measures of timing, content, and outcomes. The short checklist focuses on the most important aspects of acquisition and should be used in determining whether to proceed with the sales offer or formalize the offer further with a letter of intent (LOI). It is not meant as a final evaluation. If a project is accepted under these considerations, further due diligence is required and then the *Acquisition Comprehensive Checklist* in Appendix A will be your guide and should be completed before proceeding further.

As mentioned earlier, each company should have fundamental investment criteria that directs qualification of properties. These could include:

1. Potential value and unique signature (e.g., can additional value be found to create a unique product).

2. Preferred location (e.g., Fraser Valley, Whistler corridor, Cambie Street corridor in Vancouver).
3. Return on investment (e.g., 15 to 20 percent on cost and development management fee).
4. Type of building/development (e.g., what type of land use, how to maximize variety for sale and income stream).
5. Price point (e.g., mid- to upper-end product).
6. Maximum development approvals timeline (e.g., two years).

The short form, the 'due diligence checklist' (pre-sale) should include the following project overview (below) and *Due Diligence Preliminary Short Checklist Analysis* following on the next page:

Project Overview

- Current use of land.
- Land conditions and context.
- Is there an income producing component that can be kept as an annuity?
- Size of property.
- Current taxation.

Due Diligence Preliminary Short Checklist Analysis

(Short form: see also Acquisition Comprehensive Checklist in Appendix A)

- What can we build under current or proposed policy?
- What is the current OCP designation and zoning, and what can we build under current policies?
  - o What rezoning are we seeking and what do we want to build?
  - o What is the possibility and support for rezoning the property (risks, First Nations interests, community opposition, and staff/council support)?
- Can we pursue (Yes or No)?
  - o Do we have the financial capability to execute?
  - o Do we have the human capacity to see this through?
  - o Are there any partnerships necessary for success?
- Market analysis (attach documentation and summary projections)
  - o Macro statistics – Local/regional population growth, employment health and projections, psychographics (who lives here, who wants to live here, what will the area look like in 10 years?).
  - o What is the regional market like? – Supply, demand, absorption, housing prices.
  - o What is the local market like? – Supply, demand, absorption, housing prices.
  - o What are the attitudes of the local area? – What type of person would live here?
  - o Is there a gap in the market? Where do we fit?
  - o Is there competition? – Are there other developments? Who are the developers? What are they building? What is their timing of delivery of planned development?
- Financial analysis (attach preliminary proforma)
  - o 1) Proforma: Build proforma with estimated price/sf (above) and cost/sf (for example: use Altus Group 2020 Canadian Construction Cost Guide as reference – (see Figure: 5.8) and complete sensitivity analysis of at least three scenarios – optimistic, realistic, and pessimistic (reviewing sales price, costs and timing, and financing options as part of variables analysis).
  - o 2) Residual land value analysis: Build proforma with 15 to 20 percent allocation for profit (profit on cost as minimum) and from this analysis find what we would pay for land. Use this analysis as a negotiation/partnership reference to work with landowner or vendor on land/deal price.
- Other development opportunities associated with property
  - o Are there things we can do other than housing? Income producing assets? Hotel? Retail/office spaces? Interim uses like parking or entertainment?
  - o SWOT (Strengths, Weaknesses, Opportunities, Threats) analysis summary of project and other potential opportunities.
  - o Pros and cons about this site.
  - o Exit strategy (various ways to exit projected development: sell interest, drop option to purchase, etc.).

Figure 5.7: Due Diligence Short Checklist.

Due Diligence Report

Following the purchase (or prior to the purchase of the property) a full due diligence report of the property is required for costing, financing, joint venture requirements (if any), development programming, and design development.

This report should be concise but comprehensive and you can use the *Acquisition Long Checklist* in Appendix A as a reference:

The contents should include the following as a minimum:

Executive Summary

Project Description

- Area, site description, and context
- Project description

Market Analysis

- Comparable projects
- Market positioning and branding

Policy Analysis

- Amendment(s) requirements, timing, potential success, process, and associated costs

Development

- Recommended development plan
- Phasing and sequencing
- Development details
- Project estimated timelines and milestones

Proforma Financial Analysis and Financing Structures

- Proforma assumptions with references
- Proforma summary and specific sensitivity analysis
- Financing structure and return on investment with potential options

Appendix

- Site survey
- Land appraisal
- Land use policy
- Legal information
- Environmental and geotechnical reports
- Transportation reports and other technical reports as necessary regarding heritage resources etc.
- Sources of Information

Preliminary Financial Analysis

Although this book is not intended to cover *all* the aspects of real estate development, I present some preliminary financial analysis because it is important to understand financial sensitivities and risk if you are to move your application forward through approvals.

The following 'back of the envelope' financial analysis tool is meant to help you estimate return on investments, and the impact of certain sensitivities on project performance, including revenue, costs, and ultimately profit measurement.

Here we are going to do a quick analysis on two projects to see if the fundamental 'return on investment' criteria are met. Return on investment is normally measured as profit of between 15 and 20 percent on cost or revenue. An estimation of return on investment will tell you if the project is viable or not. Of course, estimations are based on specific assumptions at specific points in time, so you must be mindful that variables in financial analysis can change; nevertheless, such an analysis provides a general sense of viability, as a starting point.

Quick analysis such as this is generally followed by a more detailed 'proforma' (cash flow) spreadsheet analysis that is projected to be over the life of the project on an annual basis, and it includes concept development, pre-sale, construction, and post-sales. The return on investment in a more complex analysis factors in financing over a number of years, or the 'dynamic cash flow' as well as more complex measurements of internal rate of return (IRR) and net present value (NPV). These are used to measure real returns on a present value and final sale basis.

Take care with financial analysis, as it is only one tool used to measure success. Analysis is only as good as its assumptions. You are estimating your numbers in a sea of change. Sales revenue, construction costs, soft costs, cost of money, and equity requirements can change with changing market conditions, and the economic forces of supply and demand. Such things are beyond your control, as we discussed in Chapter 1. Choose your assumptions carefully. The right assumptions at the right time lead to wise, informed decisions. As background for the financial analyses that will follow, for a sample townhouse project and a high-rise project, you should familiarize yourself with the following cost-based terminology.

Basic Terminology

1. *Land Cost:* The total cost to purchase the land.
2. *Floor Space Ratio (FSR or FAR):* The ratio of the building area to the site.

3. *Gross Building Area (GBA):* The total building area to the outside building envelope.
4. *Building Efficiency:* The percentage building area that is saleable.
5. *Saleable Area:* The net building area that is saleable (net of common areas).
6. *Hard Cost:* Construction costs.
7. *Soft Cost:* All other costs including consultants, finance, contingency, and management.
8. *Project Sales Revenue:* Total revenue from unit sales.
9. *Project Cost:* Total costs for the project.
10. *Gross Project Profit:* Revenue less costs equal profit.
11. *Profit as a Percentage of Cost:* Gross profit divided by total cost.

We will observe and reflect on potential construction costs as a component of our financial analysis by reviewing the excerpt from *Altus 2020 Canadian Construction Cost Guide* in Figure 5.8 on page 135. What do we observe between Vancouver and Calgary, and within the Vancouver metro area with regard to costing?

1. There are significant variations between Calgary and Vancouver.

2. There are urban and suburban revenues and costs as well as specific site variables (e.g., location, design, use, materials, soils, demolition, hydrology, slopes, and others).

3. Parking is separated as a specific line item that varies with type, location, and design specifications.

4. As we discussed earlier, there are higher values in prime locations.

5. There are variations within the same municipality, as well as in different suburban locations.

6. There are significant variations of fees and timing of application approvals that could indirectly affect revenue and cost advantages (the time/cost of money).

7. Revenue and cost estimates should be <u>local,</u> relating to the <u>current</u> local specific land use market and the local construction costs. *

8. In a multiple-year scenario, a cost escalation factor should be built into the assumptions and financial analysis that reflect the local market trends.

9. Any financial projections should be backed by a current set of assumptions reflected in the financial analysis, so that a reviewer (financier, bank, joint venture partner or finance committee) can analyze and comment.

10. These costs are constantly changing and adjusting with supply and demand for units and construction materials and trades.

11. The range of costs demands a contractor review of current costs and cost escalation trends based on local similar projects.

12. The proforma cash flow analysis will always be a working spreadsheet that is constantly being updated with new and refined data.

***Note:** The measure of 'highest and best use' normally determines the optimum economic purpose for the site, but largely ignores the *most appropriate use* for the site, that is influenced by policy, staff, council, and the community. A community would normally prefer building *community* rather than building *commodity*—or in other terms, they prefer quality of life over quantity of product. These different interests can splinter support and need to be reconciled for approvals.

Private Sector Price per Square Foot

	BUILDING TYPE	Vancouver	Calgary
RESIDENTIAL	CONDOMINIUMS/APARTMENTS		
	Up to 6 Storeys (Hybrid Construction)	220 - 325	185 - 255
	Up to 12 Storeys	230 - 335	220 - 265
	13-39 Storeys	240 - 340	230 - 265
	40-60 Storeys	260 - 350	235 - 270
	60+ Storeys	280 - 355	n/a - n/a
	Premium for High Quality	up to 220	up to 205
	WOOD FRAMED RESIDENTIAL (Dimensional Lumber)		
	Row Townhouse with Unfinished Basement	130 - 205	125 - 160
	Single Family Residential with Unfinished Basement	145 - 260	125 - 185
	3 Storey Stacked Townhouse	170 - 235	145 - 170
	Up to 4 Storey Wood Framed Condo	190 - 250	160 - 205
	5 to 6 Storey Wood Framed Condo	210 - 275	160 - 210
	Custom Built Single Family Residential	430 - 1,090	405 - 860
	SENIORS HOUSING		
	Independent / Supportive Living Residences	215 - 310	170 - 265
	Assisted Living Residences	245 - 335	205 - 275
	Complex Care Residences	290 - 390	275 - 375
COMMERCIAL	OFFICE BUILDINGS		
	Under 5 Storeys (Class B)	240 - 300	185 - 250
	5 - 30 Storeys (Class B)	240 - 280	185 - 255
	5 - 30 Storeys (Class A)	265 - 335	220 - 290
	31 - 60 Storeys (Class A)	280 - 400	240 - 335
	Interior Fitout (Class B)	55 - 115	50 - 85
	Interior Fitout (Class A)	110 - 210	85 - 160
	RETAIL		
	Strip Plaza	125 - 185	190 - 240
	Supermarket	190 - 240	170 - 205
	Big Box Store	180 - 240	165 - 205
	Enclosed Mall	265 - 360	215 - 285
	HOTELS		
	Budget	190 - 245	160 - 205
	Suite Hotel	310 - 360	235 - 295
	4 Star Full Service	315 - 390	250 - 310
	Premium for Luxury	up to 180	up to 150
	PARKING		
	Surface Parking	7 - 26	6 - 20
	Freestanding Parking Garages (Above Grade)	95 - 135	75 - 100
	Underground Parking Garages	120 - 180	120 - 160
	Underground Parking Garages (Single Level, Open Cut Excavation)	95 - 130	115 - 135
	Underground Parking Garages - Premium for Unusual Circumstances	up to 185	up to 120
INDUSTRIAL	INDUSTRIAL FACILITIES		
	Warehouse	100 - 140	80 - 110
	Urban Storage Facility	100 - 145	80 - 110
	Data Centre - Tier III	620 - 1,015	495 - 935
	Pharmaceutical Lab	580 - 820	415 - 630
	Manufacturing Facility	310 - 410	245 - 330

Figure 5.8: Private Sector Construction Costs

(Source: Altus Group, 2020 Canadian Construction Cost Guide)[52]

Townhouse and High-Rise Case Studies

The following are the assumptions and information that provide the foundation for a financial analysis. These financial projections are for illustrative purpose only, and the revenues and costs are not meant to be location- or time-specific, but simply a general

52 Altus Group, *Canadian Construction Cost Guide*, January 2020, 9.

demonstration of the structure and components of quick analysis to help determine initial viability of a project. The assumption is that project units will be sold prior to, or immediately following, construction commencement.

The two hypothetical projects are located on two different sites in suburban locations somewhere in the Fraser Valley, east of Vancouver. This relative location will provide a basis for cost and revenue estimates.

These are 'static' measurements (one year) and do not consider cost, revenue, and return implications over a longer time frame (i.e., discounted cash flow and net present value (NPV) or internal rate of return (IRR), both discussed earlier) that measure the time/cost of money over the years of the development, assuming a phased development.

In the case of rental property, such as commercial leased property or purpose-built rentals, a different calculation is used, as property value is based on income that is in turn capitalized to determine the value of the property.

This capitalization rate (Cap Rate) is determined by comparing a project's net operating income to the sales price of similar properties. The ratio between the comparative property value (say $20 million) and the net operating income (say $4 million) is the determined cap rate, which in this case is 5.0. Following this logic, if your property is projected to produce $2 million in net operating income, then using the cap rate of 5.0 results in a property value of $10 million dollars. There is an inverse relationship between cap rate and price—the lower the cap rate, the higher the value. Cap rates ranged from 3.5 to 4.1, depending on use, in the Metro Vancouver area in 2019 [53] (different land uses have different values in the marketplace).

1. All measurements are in imperial measurement; in some cases, numbers are rounded.

2. We know projections can't be absolutely accurate; the question is by how much? These tools are just a simple way to compare and contrast various investment opportunities.

3. Costs and revenue are based on current prices as of January 2020.

4. The format for the quick financial analysis was adopted from G.P. Rollo & Associates, with permission and review.[54]

53 Altus Group, *Canadian Construction Cost Guide*, 4.

54 G.P. Rollo and Associates, June 2020.

Townhome development preliminary analysis

Site Facts and Assumptions

Site area .... 43,560 sq. ft.
Floor space ratio 0.60
Gross building area .... 26,136 sq. ft.
Building efficiency 100%
Saleable area .... 26,136 sq. ft.
Number of units .... 17 units
Average unit size .... 1,537 sq. ft.
Land cost ($3,000,000) $176,470/unit
Construction cost (hard cost including parking) .... $160 per sq. ft.
Soft costs (30% of land and hard costs) 30%
Units sales price (revenue net of commissions) .... $430.00 per sq. ft.
$661,000/unit

Project Revenue

Sale revenue per sq. ft. $430.00
Adjust to per gross building area $430.00 (100%)

Project Cost

Total land cost $3,000,000
Total gross building area .... 26,136 square feet
Land cost .... $114.78 per sq. ft. gba
Hard cost .... $160.00 per sq. ft. gba
Total land and construction .... $274.78 per sq. ft. gba
Soft Costs (30%) .... $82.43 per sq. ft. gba
Total project cost .... $357.21 per sq. ft. gba

Profit

Total sales revenue .... $430.00 per sq. ft. gba
Total cost .... $357.21 per sq. ft. gba
Gross profit .... $72.79 per sq. ft. gba
Profit (% of cost) .... 20% per sq. ft. gba

-

Sensitivity analysis on revenue (can also be done on land and other costs to see impacts):

1. If the market is in an upswing two years down the road, after approvals are complete, we can possibly increase the revenue to $450/square foot, or from $661,000 to $692,000 per townhome unit, which correspondingly increases the return on cost (profit) to **26%** if costs remain constant.
2. Soft costs are calculated at 30 percent of land, and can vary from 30 to 60 percent based on variables like community amenity contributions (CACs), etc.
3. The market could move in the opposite direction, forcing us to decrease sales revenue to $400/square foot, or from $661,000 per townhouse unit to $615,000 per unit, thus decreasing our return on cost (profit) to **12%,** assuming all other costs remain equal.
4. Using our investment criteria (15% to 20% return on cost), our sales prices need to be in the $640,000 to $660,000 range to make the project viable, especially if costs escalate. More detailed analysis is required if we acquire the land.

High-rise condominium development preliminary analysis

Site Facts and Assumptions

Site area .... 43,560 sq. ft.
Floor space ratio 3.0
Gross building area .... 130,680 sq. ft.
Building efficiency 85%
Saleable area .... 111,078 sq. ft.
Number of units .... 140 units
Average unit size .... 800 sq. ft.
Land cost $8,400,000
Land cost by land area $192.84
Construction cost (hard cost including parking) .... $260.00 per sq. ft.
Soft costs (30% of land and hard costs) 30%
Units sales price (revenue) .... $600.00 per sq. ft.
$480,000.00/unit
Sales commission 3%

Project Revenue

Sale revenue per sq. ft. .... $600.00 per sq. ft.
Building efficiency 85%
Adjust to per gross building area .... $510.00 per sq. ft. gba
Less commissions at 3% .... $15.30 per sq. ft. gba
Net revenue .... $494.70 per sq. ft. gba

Project Cost

Land cost per sq. ft. $192.84
Convert $/sq. ft. divided by 3.0 FSR .... $64.28 per sq. ft. gba
Hard cost .... $260.00 per sq. ft. gba
Total land and construction costs .... $324.28 per sq. ft. gba
Soft costs (30%) .... $97.28 per sq. ft. gba
Total project cost .... $421.56 per sq. ft. gba

Profit

Total sales revenue .... $494.70 per sq. ft. gba
Total cost .... $421.56 per sq. ft. gba
Gross profit .... $73.14 per sq. ft. gba
Profit (% of cost) .... 17% per sq. ft. gba

Sensitivity analysis on costs (can also be done on revenue increases and decreases):

1. If you negotiate a land price reduction from $8,400,000 to $7,400,000, you increased the return on cost (profit) to **20%.**
2. On the other hand, if construction costs increase from $260 per square foot to $300 per square foot as you await your approvals (including parking), the return on cost is reduced to **4%** with the land price remaining the same.
3. The cost range in the Altus Costing 2020 range from $240 to $340 for hard costs excluding structured parking, so our estimate may be underpriced, even if the high-rise we are proposing is a lower high-rise.
4. We may want to reconsider our land price proposal further to better ensure a viable project. Land price is a fixed cost at the beginning of the project, so it is wise to achieve a price that is conservative and works for you, your investors, and your banker.
5. In contrast to land cost, the revenue side (unit sales) is a variable projected cost that may change up or down with market supply and demand. So compared to land cost it is uncertain.
6. Using our investment criteria (15% to 20% return on cost), it appears costs will need to be scrutinized further, as the downside could make our project not viable and there is a significant risk. Unlike townhomes, we cannot phase the high-rise building development into smaller increments if the market demand declines.

CONSTRUCTION COST CALCULATION QUESTIONS:

What is the construction cost per square foot on the following commercial (Class B) building?

GLA (Gross Liveable Area) = 40,000 square feet
Below Grade (parking) = 30,000 square feet
GFA (Gross Floor Area) = 70,000 square feet
Building Efficiency = 85% (net of common areas that are not leasable)
Net Saleable Area (NSA) = 34,000 square feet
Total Construction Cost = $12,000,000

Is the answer $300/square foot and why?
Is this a reasonable cost? Does this match the Altus Cost Guide (Figure 5.8)?
Would you prefer to build this building in a suburban location or is a less suburban location preferable?

Notes:

1. Unit costs should only apply to GLA.
2. Unit sales should only apply to NSA.
3. Parking should be calculated separately.

Residual Land Value Analysis

This quick financial analysis may also indicate that the asking price for the land is too high. If the return on cost is below the standard of 15 percent return on development cost, then a separate calculation of residual land value is required. To determine this, you must take the revenue amount and then subtract the hard and soft costs (without the land) and the profit. The resulting number is the residual, or what the asking price for the land should be. If the resulting number is *above* the asking price, then your return exceeds 15 percent; but, if the number is *below* the asking price, then your return is less than 15 percent. To use the previous high-rise development example, which determined the 17 percent return on cost, we simply restack the numbers to determine the land price as follows:

Net revenue .... $495.00 per sq. ft. gba
Less hard cost (less land) .... $260.00 per sq. ft. gba
*Less soft costs (30%) .... $97.00 per sq. ft. gba
Less profit (17% adjusted for land) .... $73.00 per sq. ft. gba
Total costs + profit .... $430.00 per sq. ft. gba
Residual Land Value .... $65.00 per sq. ft. gba

**Note: The 30% soft costs implicitly take into account the unsolved for land value as does the profit of 17%.*

We can see by this example that there is a relatively slim margin of safety to meet our 15 percent return benchmark. Further, the risk associated with the high-rise development more than compensates for the land price subsidy. However, there is extensive risk in process and details, which could easily erode the two percent buffer and, in fact, since the base range is between 15 and 20 percent, 17 percent is in the minimum sweet spot for return on cost. Lower return on investments could be considered, based on corporate goals and other benefits, including accrued market demand, increasing land prices, location, and the interest cost of borrowing funds.

Something to keep in mind is that mixed use does not always add value to land, as additional requirements (like a concrete slab above the commercial component, and underground parking at up to $40,000 to $60,000 per stall) can tip the scale toward loss, not gain. In the case of development of the Willoughby Town Centre in Langley, the residential component above commercial did not contribute an additional increment to land value.

Again, these are initial snapshots of what the future holds. These numbers need much more refinement as the project progresses, so that these fifteen or so lines of numerical analysis transform to hundreds of lines in the detailed *Proforma* (cash flow) model that should be developed with more market and cost information at a local level. In this refinement process we move from a class D cost level, through the development permit process with class C or B costs, to the final class A tender costs. Each level requires much more detail and verification as you proceed through the application and approvals processes. As you move into the development permit and building permit stages, financial commitments are required based on cost, so this work has multiple benefits.

Positive and Negative Leverage

Now that we have looked at a simplified, quick analysis to assess preliminary financial viability of a project, let's review a method to possibly increase return on our investment.

In the previous example, regarding the townhome and high-rise developments, we assumed that we used only our own money. However, the normal way to finance a project is to borrow from others, similar to securing a home-based mortgage. When we finance a project in this way, we don't use all our valuable cash, and so we can distribute cash to more than one development opportunity and, in so doing, spread our risk. This is what is referred to as 'leveraging' money to increase returns on equity investment.

One of the popular terms in the early 1980s was 'leverage is the name of the game'.[55] The old adage 'never use your own money' is related to this way of thinking. You can use other people's money to increase your profit. Simply speaking, you borrow money at a lower rate than what you anticipate you will make in profit.

For example, assume you pay 100 percent of the development costs for a project and the return on the project is 18 percent. Alternatively, you borrowed 80 percent of the development costs, and after servicing the debt cost, the project return on the project increases to 70 percent—hence *positive leverage,* as illustrated below (Figure 5.9 below).

POSITIVE LEVERAGE: Projected revenue is *above* cost

	100% EQUITY	**80% LEVERAGE**
Total Revenue	118.00	118.00
Project Cost	100.00	100.00
Interest Cost	-	4.00
Total Cost	100.00	104.00
PROFIT	18.00	14.00
Debt	-	80.00
Equity	100	20.00
Return on Equity (ROE)	**18%**	**70%**

Figure 5.9: Positive Leverage

55 Suzanne Goldenberg, *Men of Property*, 14.

I want to explain this example in more detail. Leverage can work with you, or against you. Let's say the total revenue on a development project is $118 million and your project cost is $100 million. You can choose to fund the entire project (which is rather unlikely since you do not have the equity) or you can borrow 80 percent of the cost ($80 million) at a rate of 5 percent, with a resulting debt service of approximately $4 million. The no leverage yields, as we saw before, 18 percent on the $100 million in equity, or 70 percent fully leveraged after debt service.

This leverage concept really sounds good, let's review the advantages:

1. I only have to use 20 percent of my money (equity) on a construction loan (normally this is 50 to 60 percent on a land loan);
2. I can use the other 80 percent on other projects and spread out my risk;
3. I can increase my return on my equity from 18 to 70 percent; and
4. There is opportunity to increase the 70 percent return on my equity if sales revenue increases above $118 million.

Now, let's assume that the revenue projection did not meet expectations and sales revenues were $89 million instead of $118 million—a shortfall of $29 million. The project cost remains the same at $100 million, and the debt service cost remains constant at $4 million. If you had used your own money, the result would be a loss of 11 percent, but the *leveraged* result is an astounding loss of 72 percent (Figure 5.10 below).

As we can observe, the concept of leverage can work *for* you in an up-market but be detrimental in a down-market. If your project revenue is significantly less than projected, this situation can create significant *negative leverage.*

NEGATIVE LEVERAGE: Projected revenue is *below* cost

	100% EQUITY	**80% LEVERAGE**
Total Revenue	89.00	89.00
Project Cost	100.00	100.00
Interest Cost	-	4.00
Total Cost	100.00	104.00
PROFIT	-11.00	-15.00
Debt	-	80.00
Equity	100	20.80 *
Return on Equity (ROE)	**-11%**	**-72%**

**Equity on 80% leverage = 100 (project cost) + 4 (interest cost) = 104 x 20% = 20.80*

Figure 5.10: Negative Leverage

We have just reviewed type of risk as it relates to land type and land value. Due diligence to determine the level of risk; preliminary financial analysis to determine the level of economic viability; residual land value analysis; and finally, the merits of borrowing money to increase the return on our money (leverage) all affect the price we pay for the property.

These are all methods of risk assessment and measurement against conservative benchmarks. But what do we do now with this information?

Go, Sell or Hold

What have we learned in this chapter and how can this knowledge inform your future decisions? We must now make the decision to go, sell or hold.

A presentation by the well-respected Altus Group on November 15, 2019 was entitled, *Owning land in a soft market: build, hold, sell?* [56] This presentation was a reminder that we were in a soft market well before the pandemic hit our shores. We have learned the following to help us on our new pathways to success:

1. The *type of property* is important in short-, medium-, and long-term thinking, as are your corporate goals. The type of property is related to its acquisition price and associated level of risk:

    a. *Income Property and Zoned Site:* An income property with significant cash flow, and existing development rights on the vacant portion, that fits your future program will probably be the most expensive property, as it possibly has the least risk, and the income can maintain the property and leverage your equity financing in the future project.

    b. *Zoned Property:* The zoned property may not have income, but it does not require what could be a risky, time-consuming public process to approve a new land use or increased density. At the same time, you may be able to exercise an option on the property, and terms of sale may be more to your advantage with a mid-range price.

    c. *Raw Land:* Raw land is at the top of the chart in terms of risk but may be offered at very favourable prices and terms. On the other hand, there is significant risk in the rezoning process, and, with that, land financing may

---

[56] David Eger and Christopher Mullins, *Vancouver State of the Market*, Altus Group, November 15, 2019.

be a significant barrier as financial institutions and investors often withdraw their appetite during soft times (similar to the financial crisis in 2008).

2. The depth and breadth of *diagnostics and due diligence* are critical in unearthing the questions regarding a 'use searching for a site' or a 'site searching for a use'. Let no stone remain unturned. Let no extra conversation about ground-proofing the data be left outstanding. Even after all the reviews, balance the feasibility with a third-party impartial review (your trusted banker or experienced mentor)—and your own intuition.

3. Finally, we looked at *quick financial analysis, residual land value* and *leverage* analysis to quantify our due diligence and measure potential returns. These measurements provide further substance and comparison to other options and investments. But these measurements are preliminary and need more work.

In the end, after visiting a number of sites, doing due diligence, and completing numerous financial analyses, we have come to realize that all sites are different, yet require a similar level of attention to minimize risk.

Testing Due Diligence
Test Your Knowledge: Ask Questions and More Questions

CASE STUDY:

6.77 hectares (16.73 acres) in Surrey, British Columbia, asking price $22,900,000 (Frontline Realty, January 22, 2020)

Top 10 Questions?

1. Can we afford to pay for this property? It is $1.369 million a gross acre!
2. Can we even get a land loan, and at what cost?
3. How many units can be built based on the net developable area?
4. The use is specified as duplex/townhouse: Is this current zoning or does it have to be rezoned? What is the net development area? (see Figure 5.11 below)
5. Is there a market for this use and design specifics?
6. What is the competition, both immediate and longer term?
7. Are there any limitations on this site?
8. Financial requirements: DCCs, CACs, off-sites
9. How long will approvals take?
10. Adjacencies and context?

PART 3: TRANSFORMATIONS

6. CHANGING APPROACHES

New opportunities rarely fit the way an industry has always approached the market, defined it, or organized to serve it.

—Peter Druker, The Discipline of Innovation, Harvard Business Review (1985)

The Seeds of Innovation

We may not be in a boom market right now, but given the right factors, it may rebound at any time. It is a new market, and we need new ways of looking at it to minimize risk and maximize return. It is a market, at least in the near term, that is conservative, risk-averse, and has positioned the buyer in the driver's seat. We must remind ourselves again that, even before the pandemic, B.C.'s real estate market had cooled and softened. At the same time, we must be cognizant of the fact that in any development cycle, the market goes down and eventually recovers, as we discussed in the previous chapter. In these interim periods of stagnation—and decline, to some degree—how do we innovate, not only to survive, but to thrive?

Where do the seeds of innovation come from and how do we find that path? We have survived so far, so why change? Peter Druker, the iconic management guru, certainly had something to say about it and in his view, it does not rest alone in an entrepreneurial context. Instead, he believes it rests in seven components. According to Druker, inside a company exists four opportunity areas: unexpected occurrences, incongruities, process needs, and industry and market changes. Three external opportunities he mentions include demographic changes, changes in perception, and new knowledge.

We can easily see that these conditions apply to our current crisis and provide entrepreneurial opportunities:

1. *Unexpected occurrences:* The pandemic and associated impacts.
2. *Incongruities:* Ever-expanding approvals timelines, and increased community benefits.
3. *Process needs:* Variable and unpredictable approvals processes.
4. *Market changes:* Market decline, affordability challenges, and rising development costs.
5. *Demographic changes:* Rise of single households and growth of seniors, within the context of rising immigration trends.

6. *Changes in perception:* The era of the single-family house is waning and the new single-family is the townhouse—quality of place trumps quantity of space.
7. *New knowledge:* Access to real-time data and the era of 'big data' brings more intelligence to the developer and more refined consumer fingertips.

Druker says, "What all the successful entrepreneurs I have met have in common is not a certain kind of personality, but a commitment to the systematic practice of innovation. Innovation is the specific function of entrepreneurship, whether in an existing business, a public service, institution, or a new venture started by a lone individual in the family kitchen. It is the means by which the entrepreneur either creates new wealth-producing resources or endows existing resources with enhanced potential for creating wealth." [57]

In this context of innovation, let's imagine a new and refreshing process approach. This process is neither 'top-down' nor 'bottom-up'. Noted urban planner Joe Berridge speaks about these processes in his recent book, *Perfect City.*[58] In simple terms, it means that the approvals process is not forced unilaterally by staff, council and/or developer (top-down) without reasonable consultation with the other interests, normally the community that has to bear the brunt of the development. Opposite to the top-down approach is the bottom-up approach that is rooted in the community and drives the process from the bottom to the developer, staff, politicians, and other stakeholders. The *Approvals+* approach in this book seeks to balance these two extremes.

Robert Moses, of New York infrastructure fame (1920 to 1970), completed amazing infrastructure projects with great ingenuity and craft, but many argue that they were at extensive social expense. Especially during his latter tenure, he tried, sometimes successfully, to ram expressways through established neighbourhoods without real consultation, which is a perfect example of a top-down process.[59] Vancouver tried a similar initiative in the late 1960s, through downtown and along Burrard Inlet, but it was successfully resisted. [60]

On the opposite end of this spectrum is community activist hero Jane Jacobs. She went head-to-head with Robert Moses on occasion and actively pursued the bottom-up, grassroots approach, first in New York and then in Toronto. As a journalist and writer, she was effective in gaining community support against projects that did not include local public interest.[61]

57 Peter F. Druker, Harvard Business Review, *Breakthrough Thinking*, 144-145.

58 Joe Berridge, *Perfect City*, 8-21.

59 Robert Caro, *The Power Broker*, n.p.

60 Mike Harcourt and Ken Cameron, *City Making in Paradise,*43-49.

61 Jane Jacobs, *The Life and Death of Great American Cities*, n.p.

In contrast, the *Approvals+* process I have outlined later in this book is neither bottom-up nor top-down, but firmly in the middle. The *Approvals+* approach attempts to address public interest *and* private interest, not as polar opposites, but as mutually supportive pillars early in the process. *Approvals+* introduces three levels of even-status engagement—an energized and widely supported third alternative between the poles (Figure 6.1 below).

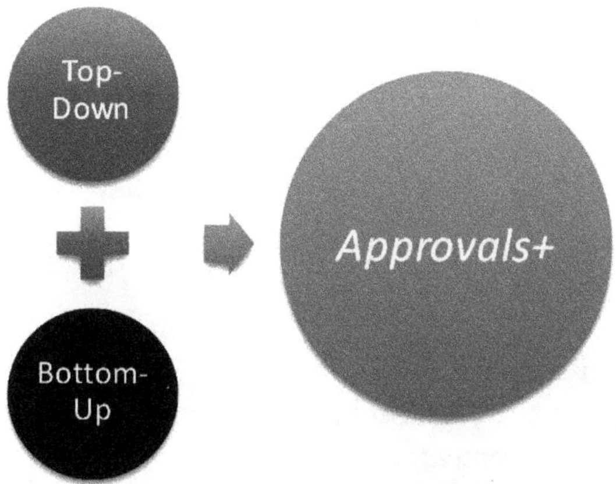

Figure 6.1: Approvals+ Process

The combination of "top-down" and "bottom-up" processes = APPROVALS+

Nine Distinct Characteristics

> *People often resent change when they have no involvement in how it should be implemented. So contrary to popular belief, people don't resist change – they resist being controlled.*
>
> *- Ken Blanchard, Leading at the Higher Level (2007)*

So now let's look at the foundation blocks for this innovative *Approvals+* process and define *how* this process is different.

There are nine distinct characteristics of this enlightened process.

1. Approvals+ is defined by three interacting elements, as well as:
2. Consideration of a third alternative;
3. A dynamic interactive process;
4. Specific rules of engagement;
5. Front end due diligence;
6. Engagement from the beginning;
7. Three levels of engagement;
8. Proactive community benefits; and
9. Agile thinking.

There are subtleties in their execution, and aggressive, alternative strategies can be used when the timing is right.

The premise of *Approvals+* is to 'go slow to go fast'. In other words, if we obtain a firm, mutual understanding of what is needed and expected (often two different things) at the beginning of a process, then the balance of the process becomes fulfilling those requirements, exploring viable alternatives, and actively managing relationships to ensure the right delivery.

1. *Three Intersecting Elements:* The overlap and interaction of diagnostics, due diligence, and engagement (on three levels—community, council, and staff), and applications/approvals are important throughout the *Approvals+* process. There is always the check-back and confirmation, from concept to detailed plan, to ensure all parties are in line as the dynamic process continues. Alignment of common interest is essential to success, and when there are differences, they are confirmed and approved as part of the plan (Figure 6.2 below).

    Cautions and Coaching: These are truly intersecting elements. One without the other creates imbalance and project intelligence deficiencies. It is not always easy to engage early, and often each party can be distracted by self-interested 'business', and not building trust and one team through inter-relationships.

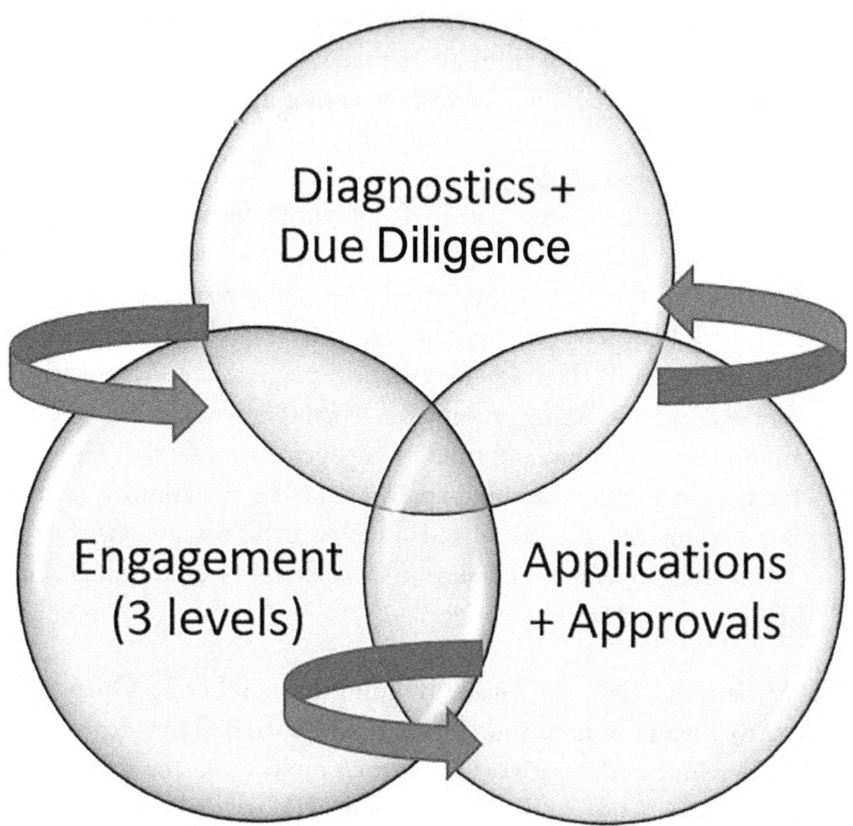

Figure 6.2: Three Intersecting Elements
The interaction between the three intersecting elements is important throughout the process

2. *Open to the third alternative:* There are normally at least two alternatives to a plan—the developer's plan and the community's/municipality's plan. The developer 'needs' the 100 housing units, and the community and municipality want only 50 units with significant park space. The developer normally illustrates more than they need so they can compromise with 75 units in the eventual negotiations.[62]

   But what if we changed the game? What if we sat down together and first defined our principles, goals, and vision for the property? Then, using that framework, we defined programs for the property including a variety of housing—townhomes, duplexes, and single-family homes, with rights of first refusal on the purchase of some of the housing units by local community members. Valuable central park space is shaped, significant trees become part of a linear park system and valuable trail connections to adjoining neighbourhoods

[62] Stephen R. Covey, *The 3rd Alternative*, 337.

are created. The collaboration results in 110 units, 35 more than anticipated. The result is the winning third alternative defined by common interests with everyone including the community benefitting in the collective thinking and process.

Cautions and Coaching: Some, if not most, developers are apprehensive about active community engagement. There is a perception, although it is largely declining, that community members are stealing their land rights and should not have the right to dictate land use and density. This view is understandable if there are no realistic expectations and framework laid out for the decision-making process. But when there is a clear set of expectations from the community, and rules of engagement, then there is a framework for the developer, the municipality, and the community to know what is a reasonable ask and what is outside their discussions. See *Appendix B: Building Agreement Through a Consensus Process* for further details on achieving the third alternative.[63]

3. *The Static versus Dynamic Model:* Building on number 2, 'Open to the third alternative', we now have four interactive elements. This *Approvals+* process is then dynamic and iterative, in that each project and the four core elements interact—diagnostics and due diligence (DD), early engagement (EE), applications and approvals (AA), and the third alternative (3rd Alt.). They are integrated into each step. In simple terms, in each 'wheel' or phase (as illustrated in the second *Dynamic and Interactive Model*, Figure 6.4 below), elements work together, then proceed to the next step. Each phase then interacts forward and backward to ensure one phase builds on the other.

   In contrast (as illustrated in the first *Static Linear Model* (Figure 6.3 below), the static linear model moves from one phase to the next without regard for all the elements in the process. For example, as illustrated in Figure 6.3, effective engagement does not take place until the second phase, and the third alternative is not really considered until the third and final phase. The phases are not iterative in that they don't work interactively and build on information before, or alter earlier information to address new ideas or issues. The results of the static linear model can create limited flexibility, higher design costs (as no alternatives are considered until the end), significant delays in approvals, and significant misunderstandings in expectations at the staff and community levels.

   Cautions and Coaching: Leaving engagement and the consideration of the 3rd Alt. to later in the process can spell disapprovals and delays.

63 Sylvia Holland and Michael von Hausen, *Public Process Playbook*, 83.

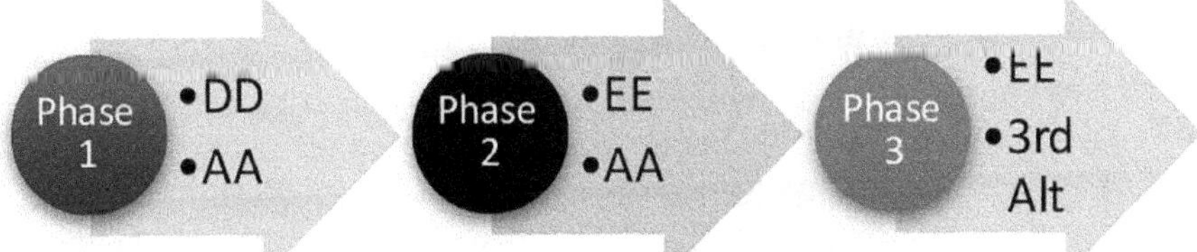

Figure 6.3: Static Linear Model
DD= diagnostics and due diligence; AA= Applications + Approvals; EE= Early Engagement; 3rd Alt = Third Alternative

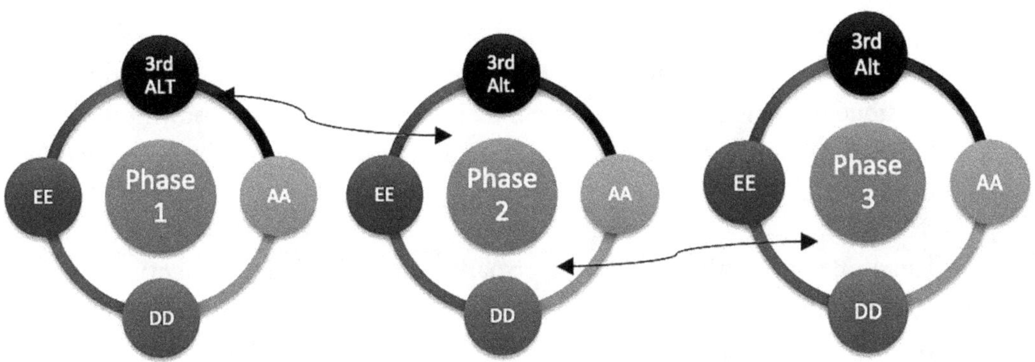

Figure 6.4: Dynamic and Interactive Model
DD= diagnostics and due diligence; AA= Applications + Approvals; EE= Early Engagement; 3rd Alt = Third Alternative

4. *Rules of Engagement:* Defining rules and expectations is paramount to a common understanding of how approvals will work. Without rules, and the understanding of those rules, misunderstandings become the undoing of the process.

   For example, one engagement rule could be that the project's municipal development engineer and planner be at every meeting concerning infrastructure to ensure that technical and community concerns are addressed. Minutes of those meetings will be circulated to the delegated development team members so that all know the progress. The basis to this rule is that the principal project team members are at the meeting and the rest of the project team is informed of the results.

   An early meeting with the municipality and the developer is tantamount to breaking the ice. Clarity of roles and responsibilities are important in supporting a process where multiple views are heard and included in the development plan. It will be a successful joint process by design.

Cautions and Coaching: Normally each municipality or regional district have their own processes and protocols, but it is always helpful to organize and confirm the goals, principles, and vision of the process and project at the beginning. It is an opportunity to define expectations early and provide a method to resolve conflicts before these conflicts undermine the rest of the process.

5. *Front-end loaded:* Due diligence, early engagement, and broad concepts should be initiated early in the process so important information about, for example, opportunities and challenges is included in the conversation. Late discoveries are not acceptable, though they will emerge sometimes. Be prepared to leave no stone unturned and have someone on your project team and the staff team be responsible for the detailed information so nothing is lost, misplaced, or overlooked.

   I had one close call with late information in Halifax, Nova Scotia when the local architect discovered a view cone (no-build area) through the property after we had started site design! Fortunately, it was early enough to make height and building adjustments. This late information did not please the developer, but we adjusted the site design to make sure the project was not only viable, but broadly supported by the community.

   Cautions and Coaching: Sometimes a developer proceeds with extensive architectural drawings, assuming that the inspiring concept and associated detail will gain approval when fundamental land use and density have not been established; or sometimes the developer presumes that the additional density will be accepted in the rezoning, when in fact, it is an erroneous assumption, and it leads to substantial wasteful expenditures.

   I was brought into a process in South Surrey where exactly that had happened. The local community was up in arms after a developer presented the preliminary architectural plans for a seniors housing complex when they had never spoken about use, density, and appropriateness. It was too late to 'bring the patient back to life' when I got to the scene. The damage was done, and the municipality was not on side. Game over.

6. *Engagement from the beginning:* Traditionally, the engagement piece of the puzzle was the community, and it was left until toward the end of the process. Many

municipalities and regional districts are now requiring an earlier, more proactive approach to engagement. Earlier engagement enables both the developer and the jurisdiction to get a sense of the scope of the application and identify where challenges remain. When challenges are addressed, then support is more likely. The active engagement of staff and council is also part of the engagement puzzle. Leaving one out, or overlooking their importance, can spell doom, both from a political and an application point of view. Early, informal meetings to establish expectations, a familiar relationship, and a sense of trust with both staff and council are important (Figure 6.5).

Thinking you can bully staff or council is shortsighted. One developer, a prominent lawyer in Vancouver, without my support, attempted to disqualify a director of planning from an application due to a perceived conflict of interest. He eventually phoned me and admitted it did not work and that he would 'eat crow'.

> *Cautions and Coaching*: A communications and engagement plan requires a formal approach on multiple levels from the beginning so that all are aware of your application and are contacted at the right time. To go top side prematurely to the mayor because of resistance from staff on density or land use can undo trust. On the other hand, having periodic meetings with various councillors and the mayor to keep them updated can be very helpful, as long as the meetings are open and transparent.

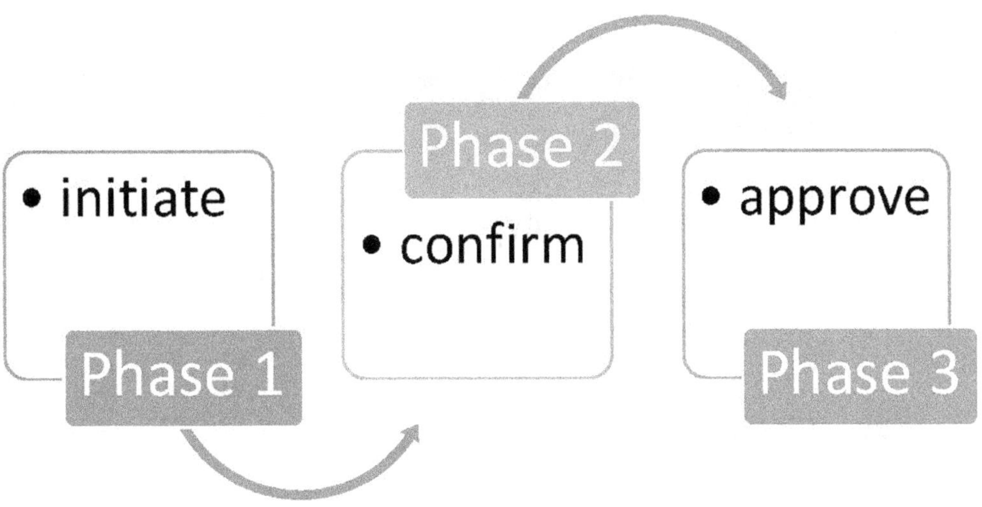

Figure 6.5: Early Engagement

Early engagement can create confirmation early and support at the end

7. *Three levels of engagement:* There are three levels of engagement that need to be recognized, engagement with staff, with council and with the community, not necessarily in that order. Engaging with each of these groups requires a communications strategy that keeps all of them updated on progress with meetings, workshops, and open houses (which are venues to keep all informed). Early meetings can actually be informal, such as pre-application meetings with staff, or a coffee meeting with the president of the residential association (Figure 6.6).

   It is always good to build your community engagement plan with staff, as they normally have experience in various areas of their municipality or regional district. They can also direct you to the key players in the community. It is also good to have a staff member refer you to neighbourhood leaders so your eventual phone call to the community member is not without reference and support (Figures 6.7, 6.8, 6.9a, 6.9b below).

   > *Cautions and Coaching:* Be careful who you meet early on in the process and verify your contacts with staff to avoid confusion and unnecessary hostility or misunderstanding. Ensure that you are talking to the right person, whether it be staff or a community member. Go slow and be cautious at the beginning, and ensure support for meeting formats and timing, otherwise good intentions can end in an unruly meeting. Sometimes a small workshop discussion might be a better choice than an open house.

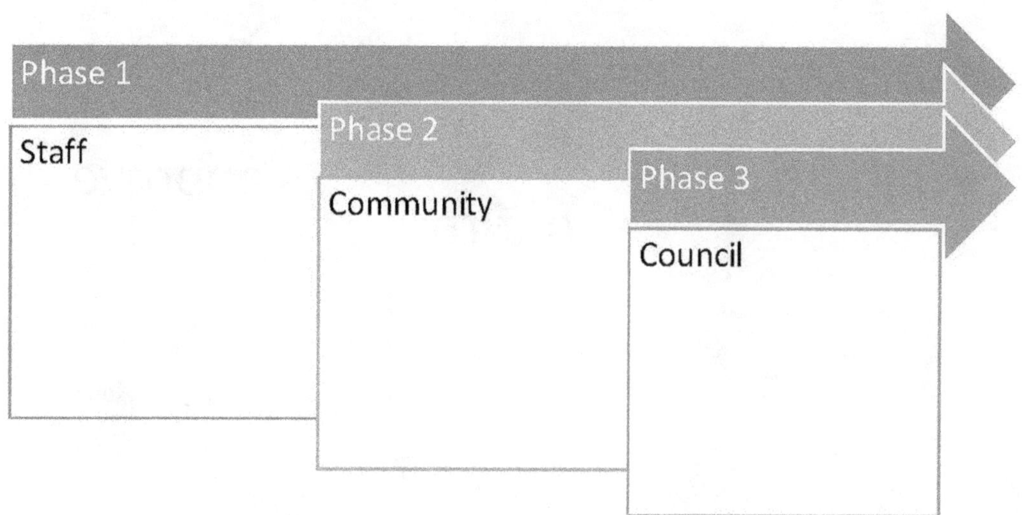

<u>Figure 6.6: Three Levels of Engagement</u>
Think of the three levels of engagement as acting together

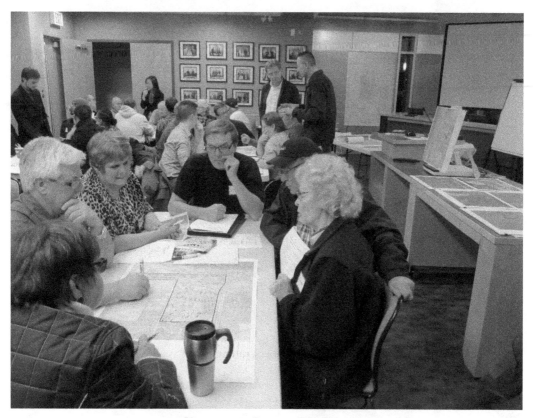

Figure 6.7: Project Workshop
Interactive Workshop with landowners

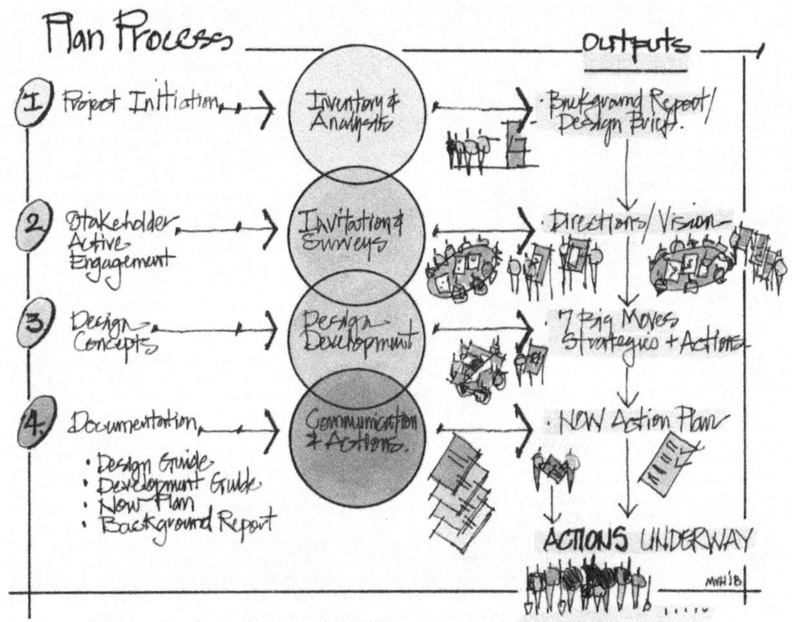

Figure 6.8: Public Engagement Process
Community engagement process plan example

IAP2 SPECTRUM OF PUBLIC PARTICIPATION

INCREASING LEVEL OF PUBLIC IMPACT →

	INFORM	**CONSULT**	**INVOLVE**	**COLLABORATE**	**EMPOWER**
PUBLIC PARTICIPATION GOAL	To provide the public with balanced and objective information to assist them in understanding the problem, alternatives, opportunities and/or solutions.	To obtain public feedback on analysis, alternatives and/or decisions.	To work directly with the public throughout the process to ensure that public concerns and aspirations are consistently understood and considered.	To partner with the public in each aspect of the decision including the development of alternatives and the identification of the preferred solution.	To place final decision-making in the hands of the public.
PROMISE TO THE PUBLIC	We will keep you informed.	We will keep you informed, listen to and acknowledge concerns and aspirations, and provide feedback on how public input influenced the decision.	We will work with you to ensure that your concerns and aspirations are directly reflected in the alternatives developed and provide feedback on how public input influenced the decision.	We will look to you for advice and innovation in formulating solutions and incorporate your advice and recommendations into the decisions to the maximum extent possible.	We will implement what you decide.
EXAMPLE TECHNIQUES	• Fact sheets • Web sites • Open houses	• Public comment • Focus groups • Surveys • Public meetings	• Workshops • Deliberative polling	• Citizen advisory committees • Consensus-building • Participatory decision-making	• Citizen juries • Ballots • Delegated decision

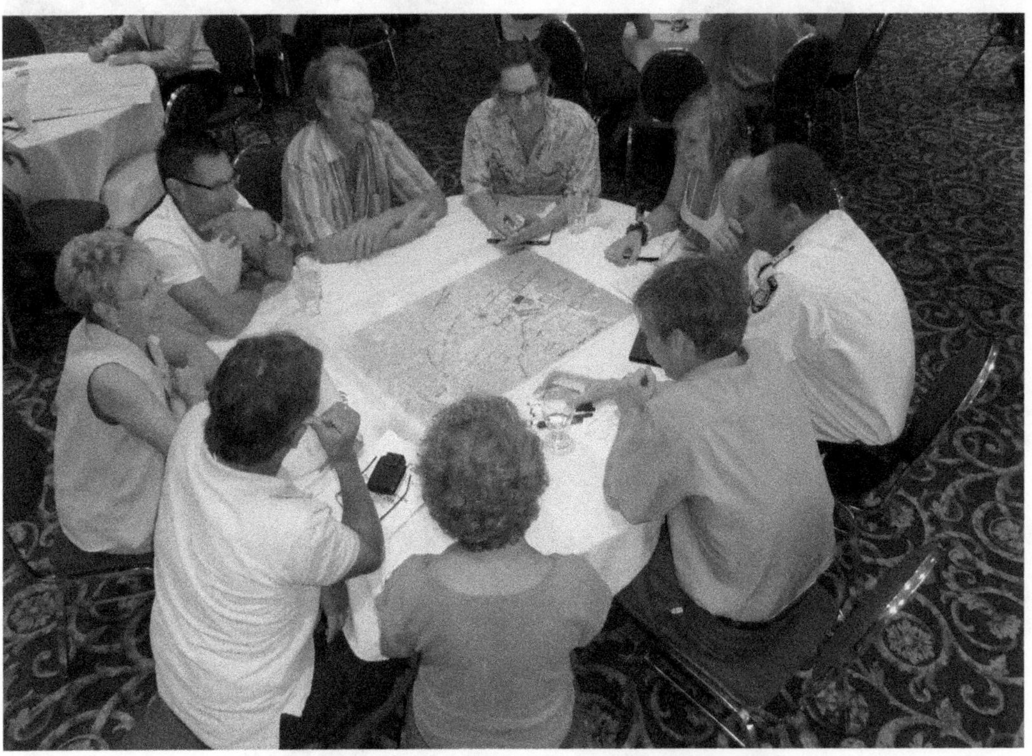

__Figures 6.9a, 6.9b, Spectrum of Public impact__
The International Association for Public Participation (IAP2) has a spectrum of public impact

8. *Community Benefits:* Put yourself into a situation where a new development is proposed behind your house in an area that has essentially been park and green space since you moved in 10 years before. How would you feel if suddenly there was a sign erected at the entrance saying a rezoning of the property was underway? You receive a flyer in the mail inviting you to an open house to review the plans. There is no mention of saving the trails and significant trees, or even conserving part of it as a community park. Opportunity lost!

   On the other hand, if there was a community workshop where you were allowed to discuss what was important, and what neighbourhood features should be saved, before a plan was produced, do you think your response to the development would be different and more supportive? Further, if the eventual plan that evolves from this workshop incorporates community benefits defined at your workshop, don't you think your response would be even *more* positive?

   > *Cautions and Coaching*: Be careful to promise only what you can, and will, deliver. Too many times, there are loose promises made by development interests early in the process. They cannot be delivered due to cost, ownership, or regulations, yet in the heat of the moment—to gain support of the community, staff, or council—certain overtures are made that can be, and will be, interpreted as promises.

9. *Agile and responsive:* Certainty and flexibility come from knowing where you can be responsive and where you are not flexible. That means that the potential 'gives' have to be predetermined. If there is an additional 'get' for the 'give', all the better. Some ideas from staff, the community, and council can be good, such as value-added ideas of location adjustment, but if the number of units or site construction is affected, then costs increase to the developer, and this is a sensitive point.

   I remember clearly a situation where my consulting team was doing a stakeholder workshop for a 400-hectare (1,000 acre) development plan for Gasoline Alley – the major commercial area in Red Deer County, Alberta. One of the landowners whose property adjoined the proposed high school site indicated that the potential noise and nuisance associated with the school use would affect his quality of life.

   Don Wuori, my landscape architect, listened carefully to the landowner, confirmed his location and asked, "What if we were to shift the high school further east? Would that work?" The landowner responded, "That would be great." That kind of agility pays off, as the audience then knew we were flexible and responsive. Support for the plan became self-evident, and an open discussion of further potential refinements ensued.

> *Cautions and Coaching:* Be careful before making split-second decisions. It is always important to carefully consider any changes to a plan from the perspective of staff, council, and the community, as well as the developer and financing interests. Take time to consider any changes and confirm their viability with all key stakeholders before making a firm commitment.

Working with Multiple Interests

Eris is the Greek goddess of disagreement, and she is also known as the temptress who instigated the Trojan War. The clash of personalities in real estate approvals processes is a wicked problem that deserves examination. In every disagreement, there are not only two parties involved, but often multiple parties with multiple interests. It is important that we further understand the motivations and kinds of people in real estate development, not to mention the players on the approvals side that hold the real power, before we can fully propose a solution that works.

On one side you normally have the aggressive developer, on the other side you have municipal staff whose obligation it is to protect public interests, and on the outside of the process we have the community. There are many conflicting interests, and each party can change their bias as the process evolves.

Developer: On the development side are many tough, inward-looking individuals with big egos—termed Type A in the lexicon of personality types. Adding more outward-looking individuals to the development team may better balance this chemistry. If we understand real estate types, men like Donald Trump and other such business moguls, then we may understand why paradigm shifts can be difficult or impossible. The traditional lone, alpha male, wolf types rarely change, and it is difficult to teach them new tricks. Among them are also highly skilled professionals, and sometimes less skilled professionals, who use bravado rather than strategic thinking and understanding to advance their applications.

Staff: On the municipal or regional district side, you also often have experienced and skilled development approval professionals who have responsibilities to affirm the existing policies and regulations. These are their bibles and inform their basis for rational decision. Any deviations from the intent and substance of these regulation and policies could be risky for them. These staff members in turn serve their managers, directors, and council. They are there to protect the health, safety, and public welfare of their constituents, serve their masters and protect their jobs.

Mayor and Council: Mayor and council are supposedly at the top of the pyramid, and they have the delegated authority to approve, or disapprove, applications. Count on any controversial application to come before them and know that they have the final say in any significant application, unless delegated to the approving officer in an outright application that doesn't need to come before them for decision.

When it comes to naysayers who are informed and skilled, Mayor and council can be highly volatile. Given the 'right' facts from community representatives, Mayor and council can simply defer an application to save face and do so almost indefinitely. The tipping point for swaying them is sensitive and should not be left to the public hearing. When there is doubt and question, gamble is normally a flip of the coin and is unlikely to be in the developer's favour.

Community: Finally, many communities feel that they are footnotes in the process. Sometimes, they do not hear about the plans for development, or redevelopment, in their neighbourhoods until a rezoning sign is erected on the site. Communities are made of many different stakeholders, with many different interests and goals. First Nations, residents' associations, and special interest groups are all players in the game and need to be heard. They often believe a development proposal is a done deal, and that the process of workshops or open houses is simply to pacify community members, and not to genuinely hear their ideas or concerns. They are sometimes right, as no one really wants to work with them—which is unfortunate, but true. I believe the people of the community are the local experts, and are there for the long-term health of the community. You should listen and actively engage early with community members, and I will outline the rewards of this approach in the suggested *Approvals+* process outlined in this book.

We can now see how the developer, the public officials, and the community can be worlds apart in their motivations and intentions. Somehow, the developer has to make his real estate development profitable, while public sector staffers have to ensure it fits the plans and regulations, with community support. This is a tall order and success, both financially and politically, is a common goal if seeded properly and presented astutely to the public.

Misunderstanding and Relationship Building: Let's look briefly at the development process and understand its character and mood in a high stakes game. Just like with the rest of the development process, misunderstanding can lead to pre-judgment and unnecessary delay and so relationship building is a 'must'.

The development process is often regarded as being somewhat like the gladiator tradition of Roman times, a contact sport where the last person standing wins. Endurance, abuse, and misunderstanding is generally part of this process. Brains and brawn are necessary as the applicant, community, and municipality battle things out through the media, in community centres, and in council chambers. The good and liberal intentions of democracy become pitched skirmishes of self-interest.

Developers normally follow the status quo to be successful. Doing something different, in product or process, spells suspicion, risk, and uncertainty for both community and decision-makers. In the end, it is council, as the delegated representative of the community, who must make the final decision. They are sometimes caught in the centre, trying to please their voters while trying to do what may be the right thing for the community (Figure 6.10 below).

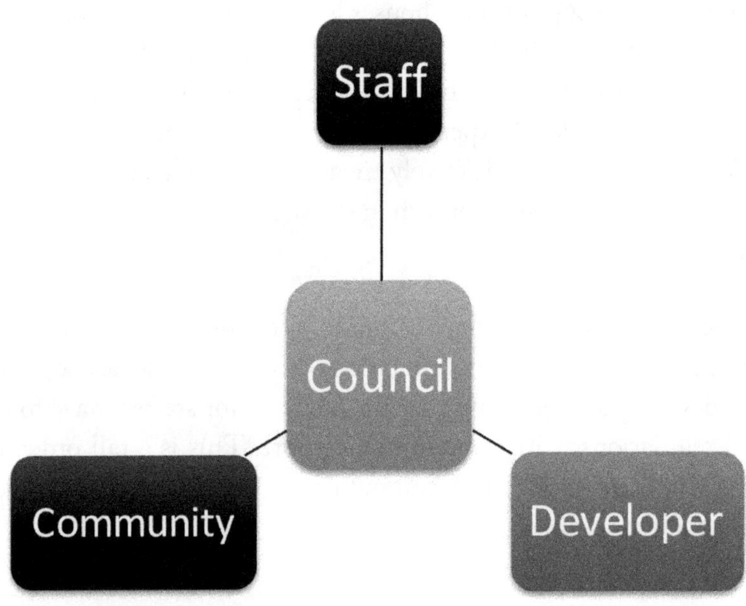

<u>Figure 6.10: Council as Final Decision-Maker</u>
All roads lead to council in major applications for final decisions

Seasoned developers know that relationships ultimately win approvals. I know in my own proactive practice that my 'soft, genuine hands' often win the day. Being heavy handed in the era of political-correctness, and amid the rise of the gender-balanced team, simply does not work and is unacceptable to the point where certain individuals who act in this way are not invited to meetings.

I remember one senior development manager who was describing his challenging relationship with the City of Calgary. He was literally red-faced, very animated, and spitting anger at what seemed to be one inch from my face—and I had just met him. I responded, "Mark, nice to meet you at last, and it is good that you are getting your feelings out right now, because when you walk into City Hall the next time you will be able to calm down and actually function in the meeting."

Emotion gets us nowhere except into trouble. If we are trained to bully people through a process, or use aggressive tactics, how do we change that behaviour to achieve different and more effective results?

Finding Our Pathway and Approvals' Culture

Do we take the normal pathway, or the one less travelled (Figure 6.11 below)? We want to reduce risk as much as possible, so we go normally with 'their' (the municipality's or regional district's) process as described in their approvals handbook, or the process described on their website. These tools are very helpful for creating a starting point for negotiations, but by no means should be considered an end point, the so-called 'ticking the boxes', as each project is unique in its own way.

Figure 6.11: Choosing the Best Pathway

Do we choose our own pathway, a mutual pathway or one that is unpredictable?

As the process evolves, further discussions, or maybe even pre-application meetings, soon teach us that each step is not that straightforward, and the requirements for review and approvals are not predictable. Staff, with all good intentions, are sometimes not willing to pinpoint target dates, which can leave your project in limbo. Meetings can continue without really moving our projects forward. Although we have a good relationship with the planning director, and director of development services, perhaps we decide to go 'topside' and speak to the Mayor, or the local councillor. Now everything churns to a stop. What happened?

What happened is that we didn't attempt to understand the needs and requirements of the particular municipality we are working with. Instead, we got confused, impatient, and started pointing fingers rather than seeking clarification and defining the specific project pathway together with our public service colleagues. The director of planning and director of development services felt betrayed when you went to the mayor, and his or her position was largely compromised. Essentially, you must put on the shoes of these people and walking their walk, or, as negotiation experts Roger Fisher and William Ury say, "Go to the balcony," and see the situation from a different and more distant perspective. Instead, we simply think that 'they' are wrong, and we are right.[64]

Going topside to the Mayor or councillor can, in many cases, betray trust and undermine the approval process, because politics and influence starts entering the process when it is in fact a technical matter that needs time to resolve.

If you do this, your good intentions will often dissolve into distrust and you will have to rebuild the trust bridge that has been destroyed. Your file could move from the priority pile to the secondary pile, set aside until the political aspect is resolved. You have landed back in the same place where you started! You did not understand the municipality's culture and their motivations.

Do you change your project manager, or the planning consultant, to get the results you want? Do you revisit the director of planning and apologize for your premature actions? Do you withdraw your application and reposition the product to better match the supported policies? Do you sell the property?

Before jumping to drastic conclusions or actions, I suggest moving to a new way of looking at the approvals process that is enlightened and rational. This paradigm shift in how you relate to other players in the process, and how you act, will not be easy but is certainly worth trying, so you can achieve consistent and successful results.

---

64 William Ury, *Getting Past No*, 37-39.

Shifting Paradigms

We have to look at approval pathway options to find the sweet spot for each project, even though we may have a standard process for development tuned over years. The way we approach each project and the context can determine success or failure, regardless of its economic viability.

A paradigm is a pattern or model of thinking that influences how we behave. It is how we view the world.[65] Take, for example, the environmentalist and the developer. They are from two different worlds. The environmentalist sees a forest as an untouchable natural asset, while the developer commonly sees the forest more as a commodity—valuable timber and land to be developed for some land use that is in demand. These differing views used to be common, but they are not so much anymore as smart developers look at the forest as an asset when at least partially retained. Even if they don't have a choice in this, they understand that forests can be enhanced as an amenity for the future community.

These views are extremes, but they still tend to be commonplace in large land developments, particularly in new areas that have not been developed before. These are termed 'greenfield development', and they constantly come under community scrutiny. This clash of values tends to lead to compromises that do not satisfy either party.

A mini paradigm change happened to me on my road bike recently. I was on the last leg of my tour de White Rock circuit and needed to shift into the turning lane to make a left-hand turn on my bike. I set out my left hand to signal a shift to the left lane across oncoming traffic. With a glance behind me, I quickly shifted lanes and moved to the left turn lane. The driver behind me continued in the through lane and stopped at the stop sign, with his window rolled down. I glanced over to expect some cursing driver full of road rage, but instead, I experienced a courteous driver actually looking out for my safety. He simply said calmly, "Next time, leave me a bit more room. You came across my lane rather suddenly."

I said, "Thank you," twice, actually, and then made my turn. I was dumbfounded as I realized that driver was thinking of my safety.

A similar parallel can be drawn in a development process where everyone is generally suspect of others' motives. The fact is, we all have a common interest in developing an outstanding community—we just have to leave a bit more distance between 'us and them' to first understand, rather than pre-judge, the other's behaviour.

---

65 Stephen R. Covey, *The 3rd Alternative*, 10.

So, the game repeats itself and further resentments and misunderstandings are built into the processes that follow. The anger and resentment eventually spill over into public hearings or community meetings. Communities feel they have no voice and that they will become the losers in the development game, their quality of life eroded by insensitive development. Conversely, the development applicant is dismissive, thinking the community ignorant and unaware of the responsibilities and risks associated with development. Meanwhile, municipal or district staff are left to pick up the pieces and mend broken fences caused by misunderstandings, or worse, misrepresentations. No listening ear is to be found, and participants leave frustrated or disillusioned with a less than inclusive process. Alienation is the norm rather than the democratic public discourse that is a valuable contributor to informed decision-making for councils or district directors.

How do we change this situation for the benefit of all the players? Do we actually see the other person or party, and recognize them? Do we have compassion and empathy for their interests? Or do we simply dismiss them?

If we don't change our views and associated pre-judgements, we will end up in the same place as the example above. So how do we change the results? Well, we have to change the process. But rather than treating superficial symptoms, we should examine the core of the problem. We have to dig deeper and find out why we are not hitting the target, or at least optimizing approvals processes.

To actually change our performance, let's look at Steven Covey's *The 3rd Alternative*. I believe we have to prepare and consciously move to that new place, not by simply changing our process, but by changing ourselves. To solve our difficult problems, Covey says we have to change our thinking to find a higher way and better solutions than we've thought of so far. It takes more than one person to define a third alternative that addresses multiple interests, is owned by all, and is resilient. This is what will work, because it is thoughtful for the greater good; it is multi-dimensional and greater serving.[66]

This idea of a paradigm shift is deeply rooted in who we are and in what motivates us. That is why we need a broadly-based development team, with various roles, so we can work both the community, staff, and council in a proactive and positive way.

To begin with, let's think of a paradigm shift in real estate development where we change our vocabulary so that it is progressive and inclusive, rather than self-serving and exclusive. We have to be careful to believe in the words 'walk the talk', otherwise our efforts will be seen as disingenuous and manipulative. Some of this transformative process is happening already, but it is the exception rather than the rule.

---

66 Stephen R. Covey, *The 3rd Alternative*, 8.

Below is a chart that illustrates self-serving developer language under 'Community Liability' in the left column, followed by the transformative and positive language of 'Community Asset' in the centre column. Common wealth is created by word changes. This chart is simply different words, but as you see in the right column, these words can create a 'Net Gain' to the greater community. A lifeless commodity is turned into a living thing that has meaning and value to all involved. The paradigm has changed from one of 'I' to the collective 'we' (Figures 6.12, 6.13 below).

Community Liability	Community Asset	Net Gain
I	We	Exclusive to inclusive
Woodlot	Community Forest	Environmental asset
Connector path	Community Greenway	Environmental asset
Stormwater Pond	Environmental Restoration Area	Environmental asset
Roads	Local Streets	People oriented and safer
Elementary School	Community School	Universal use at night
Buffer	Neighbourhood Linear Park	Multi-functional and connected
Watercourse	Watershed Protection Area	Environmental asset
Traffic calming feature	Street safety management	Safety and traffic management
Housing	Variety and choice of homes	Inclusive of demand locally
Ditches	Bio-swales	Environmental asset
Commercial	Neighbourhood Services	Local use

Figure 6.12: Vocabulary Training from Negative to Positive

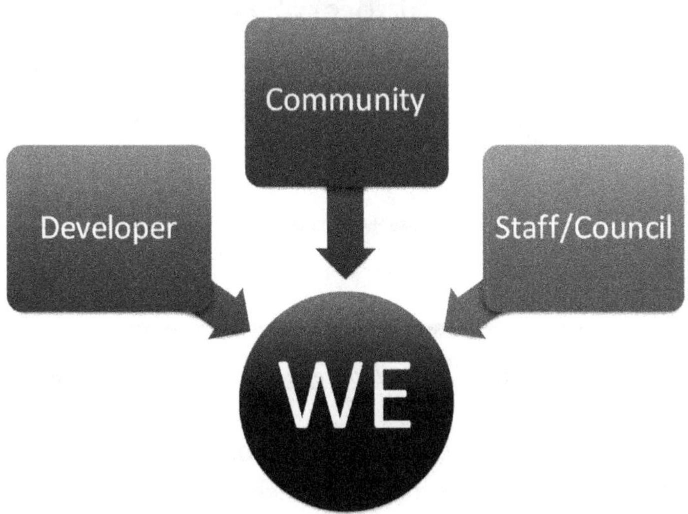

Figure 6.13: Common Centre
Moving from self-Interest to community Interest

7. NEW PATHWAYS FRAMEWORK

We are what we repeatedly do. Excellence, then, is not an act, but a habit.
—Aristotle

Provincial Review

As mentioned before, in 2019 the British Columbia Ministry of Municipal Affairs and Housing undertook a study entitled *Development Approvals Process Review (DAPR)*, and engaged the development, municipal, regional district, and other stakeholders in a conversation around the issue of the approvals process. As illustrated in the diagram below reproduced from the study, several elements affect development approval reviews, including the developer, land use planning tools, development approval tools, financial tools, enforcement tools and public process (Figure 7.1 below).

Figure 7.1: Elements of Development Approvals Process Review

The DAPR report addresses the challenges, and opportunities for improvement, in the current development approvals process and seeks to eliminate barriers to affordable housing and accelerate the construction of much-needed homes. The first three phases of the process involved stakeholder consultation throughout the province, which informed potential changes to the local government development approvals process.

The top six challenges and opportunities, as ranked through the discussions, were the following:

1. *Local government application processes,* including variations across municipalities, and developer applications.
2. *Local government approval processes,* including delegation of authority on land use permits, and the requirements for public input.
3. *Development finance tools,* including the use of development cost charges and community amenity contributions.
4. *Subdivisions,* including the role of the approving officers, the use of preliminary layout (PLAs), approvals, and requirements of parkland dedications.
5. *Provincial referrals* and regulatory requirements from provincial ministries, Crown corporations, and major utilities.
6. *Training and research* to improve the broad understanding of development approvals.[67]

Phase 4 of the DAPR, the final phase, is underway. It seeks to initiate solutions and include a longer-term process of evaluating and acting on opportunities for updating local government development processes in British Columbia.

This chapter strives to improve the process of approvals through the suggested *Approvals+* approach. It addresses the sixth point (training and research) above, in that it provides the basis for training and informed research that will improve broad understanding of development approvals.

These new pathways are based on experience and case studies. In many cases, developers follow the municipality's, or regional district's, approvals process without their own, making well intended, prescribed steps into a generic process that does not fit project needs. Unfortunately, this municipal process is often not modified based on the specific project, context, and worse, sometimes it is modified due to political motivation. We want a predictable process and structure that can be customized to individual projects. Let's examine this idea further.

[67] Ministry of Municipal Affairs and Housing, *Development Approvals Process Review*, 4.

Approvals+ Process Path Overview

> *The path means the way to adjust to the situation and establish victory – find this and you survive, lose this and you perish.*
>
> — *Sun Tzu, The Art of War*

The power of common clarity in approval processes is crucial, especially when approvals are so difficult to understand, and have so many layers. Since each jurisdiction has their own processes and applications, I have tried to generalize about what this path is, yet still be as specific as possible, so the method for getting through them that I am laying out is comprehensive and comprehensible. In this way, hopefully you can customize the steps to the needs of your own project.

This *Approvals+* process is intended to add value in each step (hence the 'plus' addition), so even in the unfortunate situation where you have to pull the parachute and exit the process, you will still have a relatively valuable asset that you can sell at a profit, rather than a loss. The process is supplemented by specific alternative strategies laid out in Chapter 8 (following). With this information, you can modify specific elements to give a boost to value and, at the same time, stay in the game all the way through to final approval by council, and eventually construction.

Changing Our View of the Path

You might not see a new pathway, because you have always followed that one trail up the mountain and it has worked for you. The timing, level of difficulty, and experience is the same and predictable. You see the picture from only one vantage point.

In general, people tend to oversimplify things and, in so doing, not understand the full complexity of the problem and how to solve it. We don't want to try a new path—it takes energy and raises concern about the unknown. Our comfort level is affected. What if this new pathway leads to a dead end, or a more dangerous route fraught with unseen challenges?

Let's look at the picture from multiple vantage points so we can see the possibility of an improved and enlightened process on a different path. Just like your existing approach, after practicing the new path a number of times it will become instinctive, more effective, and the natural way to go. The same applies to pre-conceived attitudes to a new approvals process. Remember, you don't need to remember all this analysis or the components, but they are worthy of review before, during, and at the end of your process so you can structure, observe, evaluate and improve each time. Think of this as a reference when you get into a corner where you believe there is no way out. There is always a way out, you just have to find the appropriate pathway!

The Approvals+ Framework

The *Approvals+* framework consists of three components (Figure 7.2 below):

1. *Pre-Conditions*
   The intent is to mechanically and psychologically change the foundational structure of the existing process. Pre-conditions for doing so include:

   - Leadership and personal approach
   - A diverse team and third eye
   - Trust-building partnerships
   - Site feasibility
   - Timing
   - Policies
   - Community-building
   - Process structure and fruits

2. *Systemic Operating Elements*
   Systemic operating elements include trust, agility, and persistence. They are continuing touchstones throughout the process; hence they are referred to as systemic elements.

3. *Core Process*
   The three phases of the core process include pre-application, application, and approvals.

This chapter will go through each of these three components and explain each one in more detail.

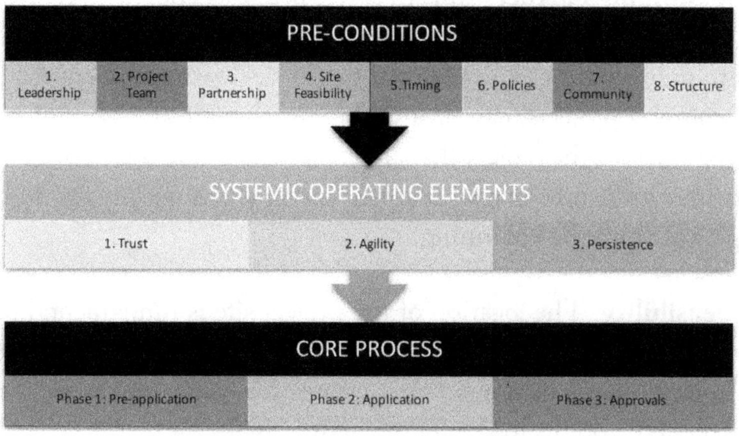

Figure 7.2: Approvals+ Framework

Pre-Conditions for Success

There are eight fundamental pre-conditions to finding new pathways to approvals. These shape the foundation for the eleven process steps that follow, as well as inform the strategies and tactics. Without these game-changers in place as part of the corporate belief system, the process of approvals—and the results—will revert back to the same old pitched battle that is more a gamble than a winning approach with consistent results. Real estate will always be a gamble to some degree, but the degree changes if you strip away as much risk as possible.

1. **Leadership and Personal Approach:** It all starts in the home boardroom with good leadership. If the development attitude is to act like a bully to get things done, then the result of this warrior approach will produce only winners and losers. On the other hand, if a structured and agreed-upon process is developed internally and then molded with the jurisdiction in a compassionate way, common interests and objectives come into play with a mutually supportive spirit will guide the process. Adjustments can be made as the process proceeds, and everybody wins.

2. **A Diverse Project Team and Third Eye:** Multiple perspectives are necessary to bring insights from different points of view that cover all the bases. If all the players on a team are pitchers, then there's no coverage at home plate, on the bases and outfield. The roles and responsibilities of the players, and their ability to speak out without repercussions, is important. An additional 'third eye', meaning external support, is also important. It can bring outside intelligence to the table at different milestones in the planned process, helping the project on the appropriate path.

3. **Trust-Building Partnership:** An active listening approach, first to understand and then to be understood, is music to the ears of planning and development staff in municipalities and regional districts. A workshop approach, especially with complex projects, can be a way to develop a framework of principles and guiding rules for the project that all parties, including the community, can agree on. In an active and engaged process, staff and community can be supporters of the project from the beginning.

4. **Site Feasibility:** The location of the project site is fundamental to the success of the project. The adage of 'location, location, and location' still commands the front runner position in real estate. Location means many things, but fundamentally points to the following merits:

- *Physical location*: includes access, infrastructure, visibility, environment, views.
- *Economic viability:* includes the measure of market demand for the land use; the supply of competitors in the marketplace; and the revenue/cost ration to yield 15 to 20 percent return on cash. If a 'development and hold, then sell', scenario is preferred, then the capitalization value of the property should be there to build the capital value of the asset; and
- *Social support:* includes support from the surrounding neighourhood and larger community, as this has influence on the outcome of the approvals process. This is of rising importance.

5. **Timing:** Timing is not always considered, but it is crucial from a funding and development delivery perspective.

   Entering development formal approvals in an election year is not a good idea as formal approvals largely shut down during what is termed 'silly season'. No politician wants to make a potentially controversial decision within four to six months of an election.

   Similarly, if the official community plan (OCP) or zoning bylaw is being updated, or going through an entire overhaul then, while applications in stream normally continue, new applications are stayed until the formal approval of the new bylaw(s) is complete. That said, it is important to ensure that your interests in land use designations and zoning are either protected in the process, or amended to include your projected land use and density. Appropriate development permit guidelines are also an element to carefully examine, and mold, as necessary.

6. **Policies:** Simply assuming that approved land uses, and associated policies and regulations, can change in your favour can be a fatal error. If a rezoning and an OCP amendment are required for your project, then prepare for a whole public process that tends to complicate matters. Staff may say that the rezoning and OCP can be parallel-tracked—meaning they can be aligned in approvals, rather than going through one by one—but it still brings further, necessary scrutiny to the application, whether this be from external agencies or the greater community.

7. **Community-Building:** One of the first questions I ask developers when I enter an approvals process is, "What are the community benefits?" At the core, this means I am asking how the development is going to improve the community, what I refer to as 'net community gain'.

A community benefits package is important for gaining community support, and the community should be actively engaged in shaping it. If they do, chances are the eventual public hearing will be populated by community supporters instead of badge-wearing nay-sayers.

This package can contain a number of items that are beyond community amenity contributions, or it can commit the community amenity contributions (CACs) to specific projects, like a new recreation centre, an enhanced trail system, or a street tree enhancement program. Local space for community non-government organizations (NGOs) is another sought-after community benefit. Be careful, though, not to commit to tenant improvements and a long-term lease if it affects the long-term viability of the property. Sometimes it is simply better to make a direct contribution to community organizations, without complicated commitments.

8. **Process Structure and Fruits:** In the end, we come back to the process structure and organization that connects all the foregoing in a clear, comprehensible, and achievable process. The rigour of the process determines the quality of the product. The process tree diagram below (Figure 7.3) reveals that the 'soil and farming' methods determine the quality of fruit from season to season. Without a rich soil (location, policies, and regional structure) and robust public engagement, policy framework, and urban design principles, the fruits of the process (the resulting community development) will be largely unpredictable and could vary largely.

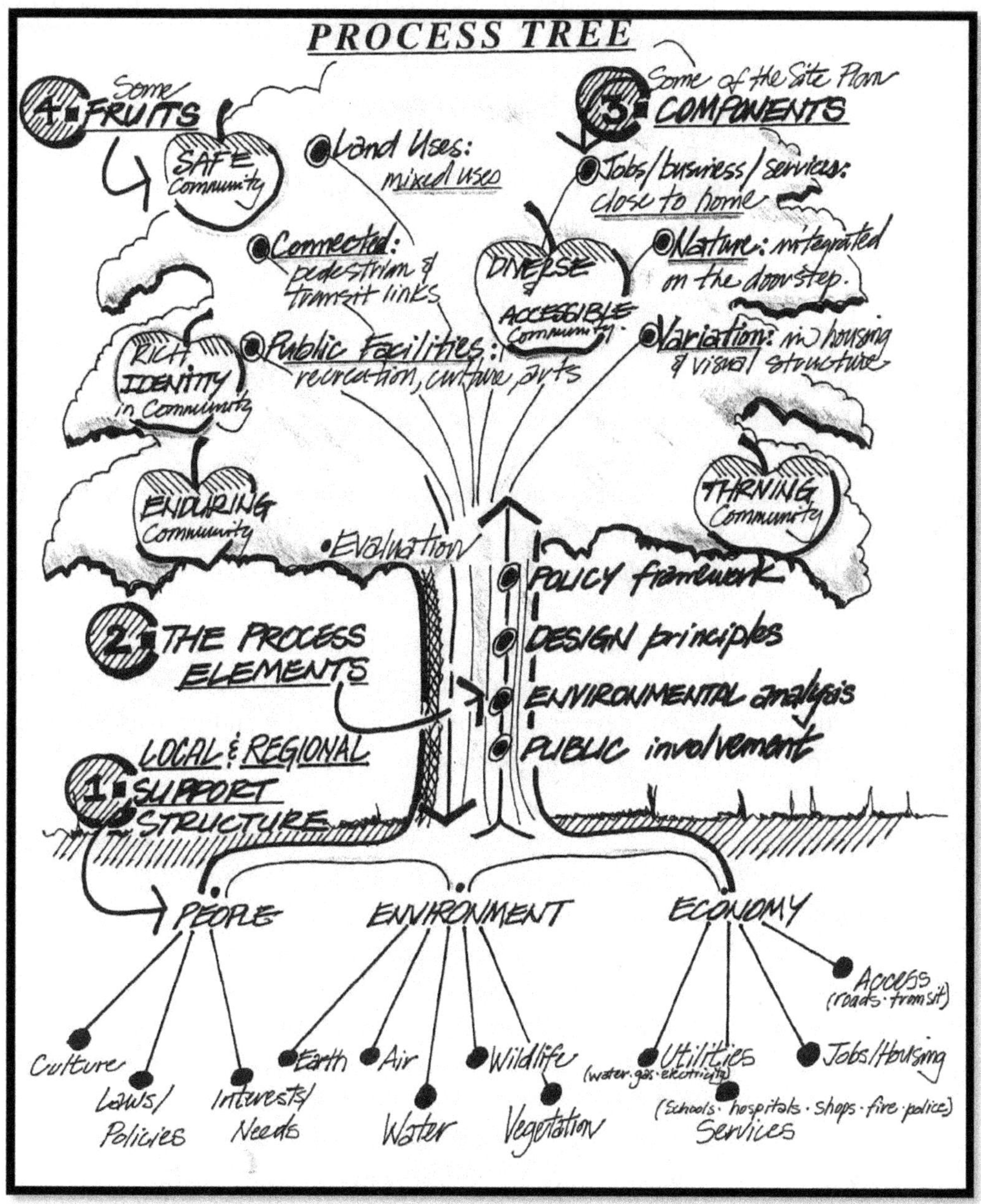

Figure 7.3: MVH Process Tree[68]

68 Michael von Hausen, *Dynamic Urban Design*, 98.

Systemic Operating Elements

Beyond the pre-conditions for success that we just discussed, and before we explore the *Core Approvals+* process, I would like to examine three systemic operating elements (SOEs) that will help the effective operation of the *Approvals+* process.

To understand this concept of SOEs further, especially in comparison with the pre-conditions, think of the pre-conditions for a car: You need an engine, wheels, car frame, motor, outer body, and other hardware. But without the proper gasoline, and/or electricity, oil, and lubricants, the actual *operation* of the vehicle is impossible. You have all the parts (pre-conditions), but nothing to fuel the system. The three SOEs, trust, agility, and persistence, are necessary for running your 'car'. Like gasoline, electricity, and oil, they ensure the successful operation of your process. As you will see, these elements help lubricate and fire the system, and make it run efficiently and effectively. Without them, nothing happens, and the process becomes sluggish or dysfunctional.

Trust: Trust is the first SOE. Trust can never be assumed; it is earned. Trust is necessary for any partnership, or for mutual respect, to develop. It is essential, and it is central backbone (or lubricant) of the *Approvals+* process. Without it, all parts grind to a halt.

Trust is crucial in multi-party plans. Once trust is established in an open and transparent way, the process of building a strategy together with other parties becomes so much easier. Over the years, I have developed a methodology for building trust between parties. Once trust is established, the negotiations become much easier.[69]

Figure 7.4 that follows illustrates the 'four Cs' of trust building that lead to a cooperative venture. The 4Cs— *cooperation, collaboration, communication, and coordination*—are key to the four foundational elements below:

- *Understanding.* Before any project proceeds, it is important to first understand the other parties' views and opinions.
- *Equity.* Creating a sense of fairness in the deliberations allows everyone to express their opinions.
- *Openness.* Being sincere in each gesture and comment builds trust.
- *Respect.* Showing genuine understanding toward other parties' views and comments makes others feel valued. Treat others as you expect to be treated.

These fundamental elements must be established at the beginning of each meeting. Without understanding, equity, openness, and respect, parties cannot work effectively together.

---

69 Michael von Hausen, *Small Is Big*, 126-127.

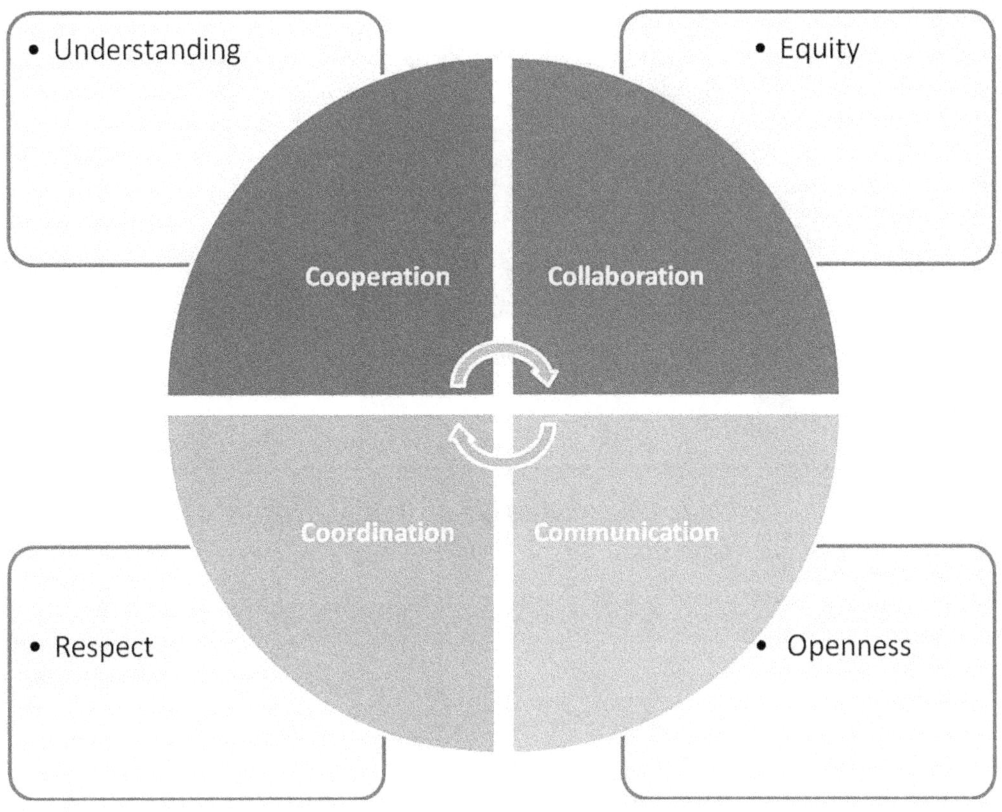

Figure 7.4: 4Cs Wheel of Trust

I developed the two diagrams below for my major growth management negotiation projects. They illustrate the importance of identifying common interests—challenges and opportunities as well as facts and perceptions. Once common interests have been established between parties, strategies and options can be developed that have a common mission (Figures 7.5, 7.6).

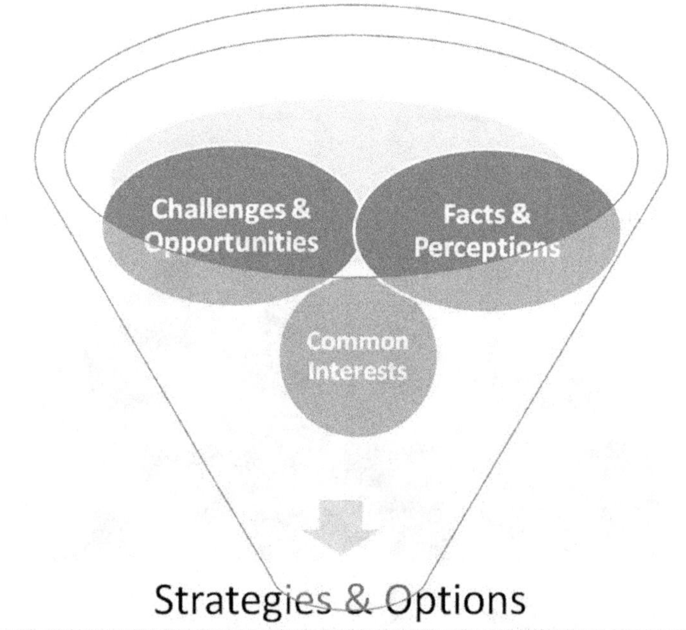

Figure 7.5: Negotiation of Difficult Differences

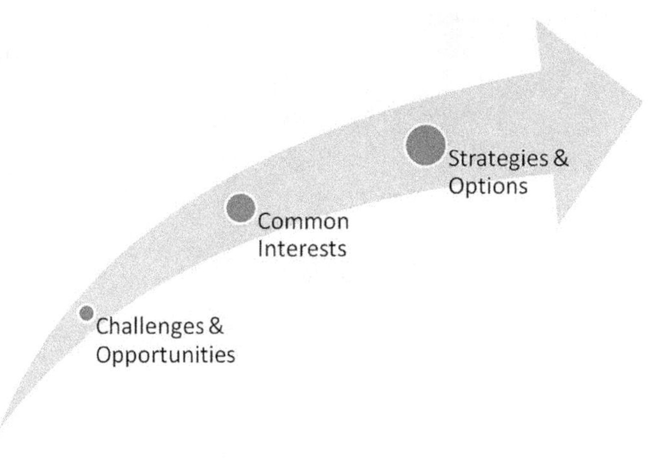

Figure 7.6: Conflict Resolution Process
Getting more than expected

Agility: Agility is the second SOE. The ability to adopt to new situations, and use them to your advantage, is a necessary element in development approvals. That is what agility brings to the process (Figure 7.7 below).

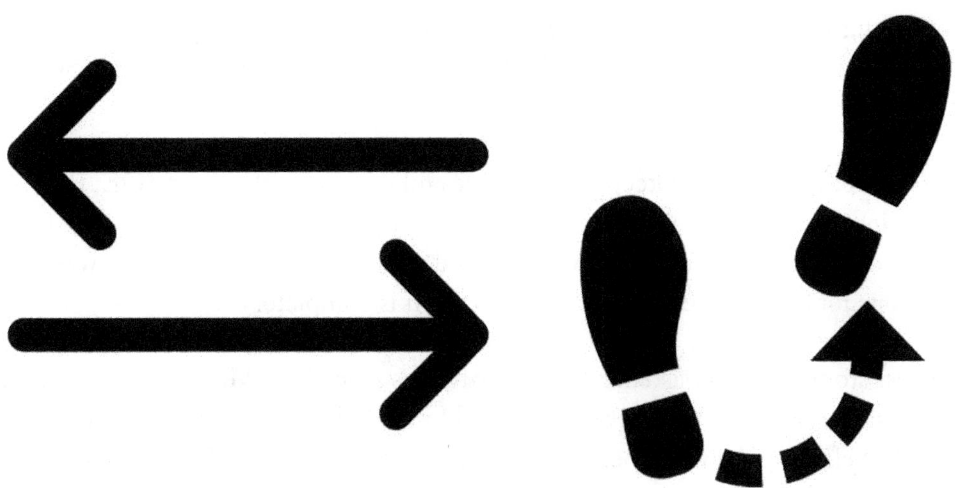

Figure 7.7: Agility is the ability to change direction or alter the pathway.

Think of the development process, including approvals, as a complex game of chess—or better still, a Rubik's cube. Each part of the process impacts the other, with no obvious pattern of success and closure. It takes training and repetition to understand the patterning and predictable results. It is definitely not like the simpler game of checkers, where rewards or consequences of moves and responses are often more predictable. Development approvals are an ever-changing game, where time and rule changes come seemingly out of the blue, or behaviour factors in as part of the play. It has the prime characteristics of the Rubik's cube twists and turns. Expect the unexpected and plan for unforeseen challenges in development approvals.

Part of the problem is that, unlike the production of a dowel, for example, approvals are not completed in a controlled environment; in fact, it's absolutely the opposite, as staff decisions are not made in isolation. Even between different municipal departments, such as engineering, planning, parks, and the police, there can be diametrically opposed views based on different standards, policies, and training. Other unpredictable components include the opinions and goals of council, the community and provincial or federal agencies that have jurisdiction that can trump local views. That is why we need a coherent process to systematically organize and cluster various components in the process, so they can be comprehensively dealt with, yet work iteratively with other parts of the process.

The 'agile operation method', evolved from the rapidly changing face of software systems, is a spiral, iterative process that produces partial functionality at each step in the process. One of the key features to this method is that it provides full visibility and allows for the participation of all stakeholders throughout the process.[70] The agile method has been adapted to other disciplines, including manufacturing. Other companies adapted the 'private public partnerships' (3P) framework for complex relationship management, outsourcing contracts where the needs of the client are constantly changing, and the contract framework needs to adapt. In Europe this is now defined by the ISO 44001 standard.

Persistence: The ability to keep the desirable end in mind is the third SOE. Persistence brings closure to each detail in the development process. No loose ends are left undone. The agreements are complete, reviewed, and executed. All parties are aware of the conditions for development, and communication is complete.

The best story about persistence I have heard was from Eric Martin, former executive vice-president with BOSA developments. He shared with our Urban Development Institute School of Development class his experiences in San Diego. He was having challenges with approvals at the City of San Diego for various high-rise developments that BOSA was proposing. He simply went into the office where approvals were given and sat there until he received the approvals. Day in and day out he sat there until he received the approvals he needed for his development permit, and subsequent building permit permissions. This is persistence personified. It worked and to his credit, the elegant and successful towers now adorn the San Diego downtown landscape. As they say, 'the squeaky wheel gets the grease'. This still holds true in some circumstances, providing your persistence is executed in a respectful and timely way.

When we blend trust, agility, and persistence throughout our process, we build support, can adjust to changing variables, and are able to keep our eye on the goal with determination. With the eight pre-conditions in place and the three systemic operating elements to constantly grease the wheels, let's now look at the three-phased *Approvals+* process itself.

So to summarize, when combining trust and agility with this last element of persistence, three foundation elements collectively help drive the process. Each is a lubricant and fuel to keep the process on track and moving forward that can adjust to changing conditions without losing momentum or focus.

---

[70] Daniel Brosseau et al, *The Journey of an Agile Organization*, McKinsey and Company, May 2019, 1-22.

Approvals⁺ Process

Figure 7.8 below summarizes the *Approvals+* Method. It outlines a 3-phase - 11-step process that can be adopted (agile) to respond to different conditions and provides various strategies and tactics for further modifying responses or restructuring the process to address particular challenges. Each step will be described in detail, to bring clarity to the step and its necessity. Each step and its sub-components are intrinsically connected. They feed on each other and together build a robust, agile process with a core discipline focused on success for all parties.

Phase 1: Pre-Application
(Diagnostics and Due Diligence)

1. Right type of property
2. Staff and right policy/regulations, or the will to change
3. Council's/regional board's temperature and right cycle
4. Community and adjoining neighbours' support and needs acknowledged

Phase 2: Applications and Review

1. Right local support team
2. Proactive engagement with community, staff, and council/regional board
3. Focus on the most important elements from staff's perspective
4. Precision development response and design elements are in place

Phase 3: Final Approvals

1. Closing with staff and agencies
2. Finalize support
3. Final development agreement

Figure 7.8: Approvals⁺ Process

The content of the *Approvals+* three phases is outlined for easy reference and use. The process consists of three phases, 11 steps, and 53 tasks. Each phase has sub-components that each have a rule, key questions, tasks, and strategy summary. With this structure, these phases can be referenced quickly to ensure you do not miss a critical element, especially when you are considering a new project or want to review an existing project.

<u>**Phase 1: Pre-Application** (Diagnostics and Due Diligence)</u>

What is emerging in the development applications process is the need to do more work earlier in the process, not only normal due diligence work, but more detailed political, staff, and community diagnostics to determine non-technical feasibility and support for the project. This non-technical feasibility can be a continuing challenge, as it is not straightforward nor is it certain. It varies with the time and place.

Remember, with this *Approach+* process, that developing your vision, goals, and principles along with site design concepts, and sharing them with the community and staff, is important for building trust and ownership of the plan. The old 'decide, announce, defend' (DAD) approach described earlier will probably not gain you much support for your project, as when the community, staff and council don't have the opportunity for genuine input, they will not be sympathetic to your plans.

1. Right type of property

Rule: Don't fall in love with any real estate unless you are willing to be heartbroken!

Questions
With the excitement of discovering a potential development project comes the necessity of analyzing what barriers and potential risks could exist. (See Appendix A for an extensive checklist of questions). Some of the questions include:

1. Are there any liens or encumbrances on the property title?
2. What physical limitations are there on the property?
3. What can be built on the property under existing policy, and what potential is there?
4. What is the macro and micro market potential, and what economic fundamentals are at play?
5. What is the property history, and associated development efforts in the past?
6. Does the property fit with company goals and strategies?

Task 1: Due diligence
As we discussed in Chapter 5, the need for diagnostics (big picture) and due diligence (small picture) are both critical in analyzing your site. You can use the short list (snapshot) method described in Chapter 5 to accomplish this, and/or the comprehensive due diligence checklist in Appendix A to review the property.

Normally a purchaser has 30 to 60 days to review a property before a commitment has to be made. Alternatively, an 'option' can be made on the property. An option costs a specified amount, but it extends the purchase period, depending on the value and status of the property, and gives the party right of first refusal to purchase the property.

In a hot market, there are no options and instead you might experience a bidding war for the property, and the property may be sold above asking price. This situation happened frequently in the Vancouver housing market a few years ago, when the market was overheated, and demand pushed prices well above appraised value and asking price.

In the current, emerging market, post pandemic, we could have the opposite situation, where the market is unstable as employment and business recover, and in-migration remains relatively static for the short term. In this type of market, you will have to work extraordinarily hard to capture buyers who remain or are emerging. They have to be incented to buy your product.

Task 2: Verification

Be careful to ensure that you have done your due diligence and verify your sources of information. Make phone calls to substantiate claims and double-check with other reliable sources. Otherwise, like my good friend who had 40 years in the real estate business, you might end up holding a dead duck rather than a golden goose.

Especially in a prime location where land is not developed, or is under-developed, I always ask the question, "What is wrong with this property or the policy?" If the price appears too good to be true and does not compare with similar properties, then I know I am looking at a red flag of caution. Now, like all good developers, if I can solve or negate that barrier to purchase, then I might create a viable deal for myself; seasoned developers find a way to make it work for them, whereas ultra conservative developers drop the option and move on.

Task 3: Criteria Based Decisions

Always use criteria to measure your decisions so they are well-informed rather than ill-advised and regrettable. At the same time, form an acquisition team that consists of both conservative and aggressive team members who can bring vision and fundamental economic viability (proforma cash flow) to the process. The short form for due diligence presented in Chapter 5 is a good place to start, as it probes the fundamental questions that should direct a logical and grounded avenue of inquiry. It is in the middle that you find the sweet spot that both anchors the 'what if something goes wrong' conservative variable and the 'what if' of the upside. Balancing rose-coloured glasses with realistic insight helps shape informed, grounded decisions.

Task 4: Third Party Backstop

Verify your deal assumptions and viability through a trusted third party. When I started out in real estate, I used to use my regional controller to bounce ideas and scenarios off of. Grounded in Saskatchewan conservatism and accounting, I gave my colleague,

Bill Berezan, the straightforward perspective of the deal, with no frills. His ultra-conservative lens always gave me a true test of project viability.

Also remember that emotion can get in the way of your normally good judgement if you fall in love with the piece of real estate. From my venture capital experience, I learned that a basic industry rule is to look for at least at 20 deals before closing a deal. This reference is a sobering thought; it is a reminder of how important it is to find the right deal to fit your company's criteria. Patience, and an eagle eye, is critical to decision-making.

Strategy Review

- Do not make a sudden decision without a reasonable third-party opinion.
- Use an alternative third-party to double-check.
- Wait longer if the deal is bothering you and you can't figure out why.
- Counter with a lower bid to see how hungry the vendor is.
- Restructure the deal so that it works for you and the vendor.
- Otherwise, move on to the next property as there is more land in the world.

2. Staff and right policy/regulations or will to change:

Rule: Three martinis with your director of planning are worth three current planning policy reports.

Questions:

There are seven questions, among others, to answer through key staff members in charge of approvals (approving officer) and their lieutenants, who run the development review process:

1. Who on your team has an established relationship with staff and can probe sensitive elements of the application?
2. What is the official community plan (OCP) designation?
3. What is the zoning for the property?
4. If the OCP or zoning is not in alignment with your development program, will they support the change?
5. Will there need to be regional policy amendment?
6. What is the past regulatory history and process/application for the property and adjoining properties?
7. What is the exact process, as well as the financial and regulatory conditions, required for them to support those changes?

Task 1: Requirements

Define the explicit requirements for approvals. As we are discussing generally complex real estate developments that involve rezoning to multiple uses and/or higher densities, the securing of these new property rights is fundamental to the viability of the real estate transaction. To review, site proposals that conform to both the OCP and the zoning bylaw generally do not require a protracted process, such as public review and public hearing.

Keep in mind that there are always exceptions, and that you will require verification as to what process, support, and conditions apply to your property. Also ensure that those permissions are relatively secure, by considering timing and electoral inclinations. Consider the pessimistic scenario and play that out to see if lower density and alternative land uses are viable or supportable.

Task 2: Process

Understand fully the process you are going to undertake, otherwise—if you are required to conform to discretionary conditions under current zoning or require a rezoning—you can expect a less certain, longer process. I can't emphasize enough that once an application comes under public and council scrutiny, lack of certainty can be characterized as exponential.

Task 3: Support

Determine the level of support for your application. I have heard the same statement numerous times when I enter a development conversation: "Don't worry Michael, we will be able to get the rezoning. I talked to staff, and they don't seem to have a problem with it." It still echoes regretfully in my head, as if a solemn reminder of pie in the sky. Statements like this make me reflect on how careful you must be when choosing clients. It is one thing to be optimistic, another to not understand the ocean you're swimming in, and still another to misrepresent the truth.

Task 4: Conditions

Define the conditions for approvals. Some people just don't want to hear about barriers to success. There are always conditions and requirements to project approvals which can render your project viable, or not. Face the truth early. A single presumption of success without scrutiny of the not so obvious facts has broken many developments, and only after multiple owners and right timing has the development proposal in a whole new form been able to proceed. So how do we do that with integrity?

Task 5: Confirmation

Be sure to confirm these conditions in writing, or via email, if possible. Alternatively, document what you heard at meetings and relay it back to the municipal staff to confirm. That way you have an agreed-upon process—and confirmation—that your proposal *could* be supported under specific conditions. Be as direct as possible and use explicit wording so there is little or no possibility for misinterpretation.

Strategy Review:

- Ensure that you probe key staff members to obtain backstories on the properties by having a number of coffee table conversations (if possible), where staff are comfortable discussing not only the regulations, but other factors that may affect development.
- Talk to other developers or realtors regarding realistic expectations.
- Walk the property with staff, if possible.
- Put yourself in the shoes of staff and understand their views.
- Listen to staff views carefully, and with understanding, before judging.
- Consider the third alternative from the beginning—the option that staff would prefer.

3. Council's/regional board members' temperature and right cycle

Rule: Find and respect the source of power and count your votes at the right time.

Questions

1. Who on your team has an established relationship with a member of council/board of directors, and can probe sensitive elements of the application?
2. Who leads city council, or the regional board of directors?
3. Who are the veterans and who are the rookies?
4. Who leads the local interests around your site?
5. How have they regarded other similar applications in the area?
6. Are we within six months of the next election?
7. What is the position of council on the neighbourhood and the community?
8. What are their interests in the election cycle and what are their hot buttons?
9. Will they consider an OCP or rezoning amendment for the site?
10. What are their conditions to approve an OCP or rezoning for the property?

Task 1: Political Temperature Check

It is always astute to alert mayor and councillors (or regional board chair and board members) of an impending application on a property to gauge their initial reaction and, most importantly, their concerns. If there are any significant perceived or real issues, don't ignore or downplay them, but listen carefully and let the councillor or board member define them fully. Acknowledge their validity and fill your notebook up with notes from the meeting or informal chat.

In some cases, councillors or regional directors will resist meeting alone because of perceived conflict of interest (or because of their location, perhaps in a different city). What sometimes works more effectively for them is to have a staff member join them. This approach is one way to keep staff fully aware of what is being said and to ensure current policy and facts are brought to the conversation. On the other hand, private and informal conversations with higher-placed public servants brings further details or subtleties to the conversation that would not be shared in a more formal meeting or in meetings where they have sent a proxy. I find a combination of formal and informal meetings provides the most information about the level of support, or non-support, for the potential application.

Task 2: Political Cycle Check

Timing of your application can be detrimental to outcomes. As mentioned earlier, within four to six months of an election (now a four-year cycle in British Columbia), there are generally no important development decisions made, as councillors and regional directors are out in the community working on re-election. That is why this period is called 'silly season'. In silly season, elected officials can be more risk averse than usual, their votes self-interested in an exaggerated way. Councillors and board members favour positive public interest when they mine for additional votes in upcoming elections.

Task 3: Councillor or Director Check

Defining who has the power of the vote is important in approvals. Whether it be the mayor and influential veteran councillors/area directors, or simply the local councillor or area director, these people's opinions will affect support for your application. In the regional districts of British Columbia, the number of votes is determined by the local area population.

Task 4: Community Amenity Contributions and Benefits

In many municipalities, there are required and emerging community amenity contributions that can sometimes tip a final vote in your favour, especially if an application is somewhat controversial. In return for a change in use or higher density for your project, office space for a non-profit at below market value, affordable non-market housing (on-site or financial contribution), replacement housing, and other contributions can be considered. Be careful of what is discussed and acknowledged in the early part of the process since, as mentioned earlier, these implied or explicit contributions will live long in the memories of council and others.

Task 5: Confirmation and Closing the Loop
Always document formal meetings and ensure that if something is said in an informal meeting that needs confirmation, it is confirmed by email. This closes the loop and provides a paper trail that builds through the approvals process.

Strategy Review:
- Informal discussions are important to build support over the length of the process.
- Formal meetings are also good, with staff support.
- Be supportive and understanding of council's/area directors' views.
- Invite the councillors/regional board members to walk the property or take a tour.
- Listen to alternatives from the beginning, and address the option that council would prefer, though it may be different from staff or the community views.
- Be careful of the potential for real or perceived conflicts of interests.
- Document, where possible, how to build a mutually supported understanding of expectations.

4. Community and adjoining neighbours' support and needs

Rule: Community is the expert and will tip the vote.

Questions
1. Who are the community leaders?
2. Who are the community organizations interested in the project?
3. Who are the neighbours?
4. What are the key challenges and opportunities?
5. How do they want to work with us?
6. What are their interests and needs?
7. Do First Nations have interests, claims or history?
8. Are there other stakeholders who should be included (e.g., provincial or federal government ministries)?

Task 1: Requirements
Requirements for community meetings, workshops, and open houses vary from municipality to municipality but all municipalities must follow the *Local Government Act* (LGA), except the City of Vancouver which is governed by the Vancouver Charter. Find out from municipal staff what the expectations are regarding community meetings. These requirements will be important for developing a comprehensive communication and engagement plan that includes not only the community and adjoining neighbours, but staff and council. All are connected.

Task 2: Process

Contact community leaders to define the process of engagement with the community. Informal conversations can confirm their level of support for outreach ideas and engagement. With staff's support a communication and engagement plan, with components including schedule of deliverables, can be finalized.

Task 3: Process support group

Consider developing a 'community leaders' group to be your eyes and ears in the community. These community representatives can ensure events and process are clearly communicated to community members. Regular meetings with the community leaders' group will build trust and support for the project.

Task 4: Needs and Wants

Define early what is negotiable and what is not negotiable, in other words, what can be discussed that is directly relevant to the project, and what is not relevant.

Carefully examine community benefits to ensure they contribute to the community. These could be different than what staff or the council/regional board needs and wants. There may be projects in the community that are underway, or already complete, which could make yours 'overkill'. It is good to compare your ideas with other projects in the area before developing the potential package. Not to do so may impact the viability of your project.

Be inclusive in your process. Research what special interest groups are active in your community and be proactive in contacting them. The same goes when dealing with First Nations; make contact early and engage, as appropriate, with support from the municipality/regional district. Developing trust and understanding sometimes takes many meetings, so start early.

Task 5: Rules of Engagement

Develop a uniform method of communication, documentation, and protocol regarding engagement with the community leaders, or your community leaders' group if you have established one. These standards should become self-reinforcing as the process progresses. In other words, the rules of the game become accepted and help discipline meetings and interactions. Be personable, but professional.

Task 6: Personal Touch

Creating trusted relationships in the community is important and should be done through existing contacts if possible. At the same time, a safe distance (COVID and otherwise) is important so as not to introduce perceived or real conflicts of interest or undue health risks.

Strategy Review:

- Confirm the statutory requirements of process and outreach.
- Define the process and customize it for the community and other key stakeholders.
- Develop a comprehensive community engagement and communications plan in liaison with municipal or district staff.
- Consider the creation of a community leaders' group that will ensure that information is appropriately disseminated within the community.
- Understand the needs and wants of the community, and how they could relate to the eventual proactive community amenity package you have coordinated with staff and council.
- Always remember to build trust in the process by doing what you say, not saying what you do.

Phase 2: Applications and Review

Moving into the formal application and review process can be overwhelming, as what seemed to be a straightforward site feasibility study process can turn into what seems to be a never-ending request for further information and clarification. Working closely with municipal or regional district staff from the beginning, and understanding the scope of requirements in explicit terms, is part of the formula to obtaining closure.

Official community plan (OCP) and zoning bylaw amendment (ZBA) applications, as well the development permit application, can be relatively straightforward forms requiring such things as information about the requested change in use and density, the current OCP designation or zone, verification of ownership, and, depending on the complexity and size of the application, a fee. They may also require representation authority if a party other than the owner is managing the application and approvals.

The supporting information for these applications helps determine the feasibility of the proposal. More and more, the level of detailed information, including architectural drawings, detailed landscape plans, and other engineering work, is required at the rezoning stage—well ahead of final development permit (DP) and building permit (BP) consideration.

In many cases OCP and ZBA approval can be combined to save time. Most often, the OCP and ZBA amendments are combined in parallel processes, which are followed in quick step by the DP and finally the BP approvals. Each stage of development requires further detailed information and resources, until finally construction drawings and final cost estimates support the issuance of a building permit which allows building construction to commence.

The detailed vision, principles, and goals for the project, as well as the design concepts and plans, will evolve in this Phase 2. Meetings, workshops, and design workshops with staff and the community can help shape and inform the evolving designs.[71] Aspects such as building height, intensity of development, architectural form and massing, sun and shade impact analysis, public amenities, park and open space, community facilities, active transportation, and buffering/transitions to adjoining uses all play into a comprehensive site plan evolution.

---

71 Social media and online interactive platforms should be used to engage the public, staff as well as council more comprehensively. These tools proved effective during the pandemic and should be used on an ongoing basis, especially in challenging situations where weather conditions, access, and inclusion of various age groups and cultures limit participation.

In this phase, it is important to cover all the requirements in detail and to the satisfaction of the approving officer.

5. Right local support team

Rule: You are only as good as your weakest link.

The local support team is critical to the success of the project. If you have the wrong consultants, chances are you will end up with the wrong result and wasted time just based on bid price alone. Select the right consultants, who are familiar with the site area, have worked with the local staff before and have a trust relationship with them, and know the issues. In addition, it is important to have the right consultant for specific tasks. Ensure that he or she is a recognized, respected consultant in the area of expertise required to solve the issue.

Questions

1. Who are the trusted professional consultants that you need for this specific project?
2. Who knows the local area and staff professionals?
3. What are the most important site and context issues?
4. How do you solve them?
5. What resources will it take to resolve the issues?
6. Who needs to be involved in the decision-making process?
7. How do you make the decisions, and who are the decision-makers (e.g., local department and/or provincial or federal ministries)?

Task 1: Formal application requirements
Familiarize yourself with the requirements for the official community plan amendment, rezoning, development permit, and building permit. Next, clarify the terms of reference for the study requirements, and then the associated drawings and the review (and sign-off/review) requirements. Normally, there is a development handbook or guide that explains in detail the steps and targeted timeframes for approvals.

Task 2: Selection of prime consultant
Carefully select the prime consultant who will manage the sub-consultants and oversee the project. The prime consultant should have a tested success rate with the municipality or regional district. He or she should be a trusted and established consultant who knows the area and the approval authorities. The prime consultant will have skill in helping manage the process and be part of the inside brain trust to advise on difficult situations.

Be specific on this person's scope of duties and responsibilities. Their responsibilities, for instance, may not include formally lobbying for support through council, but rather building support through studies and positive staff interactions. Separating these two functions is important so you can retain the trust of staff and the community while reducing risk of conflict of interest, or possible ethical misconduct (as per professional organization guidelines).

Task 3: Request for proposals and selection of consulting team

Formulate a terms of reference document for the project, and then have the prime consultant request proposals from qualified consultants who have local experience. The list of consultants should relate directly to the study requirements for the project. These include, but are not limited to, consultants who specialize in environmental, transportation, archaeological, soils, climate, flooding, railway, trees, and other concerns. The decision to select the consultant team should be cooperative between the prime consultant and development manager to ensure the right chemistry and competencies, not to mention a competitive price.

Task 4: Confirmation of issues and opportunities

Define and confirm important issues with the consulting team to ensure everything is covered to the greatest extent possible. To understate the importance of one issue could be a death blow to a project. Be realistic, and represent each issue or opportunity in a fair and balanced way to staff, council, and the community. At the same time, do not sound unnecessary alarm bells if the issue can be remedied through construction or sound monitoring processes.

Task 5: Management structure

Develop a project management standard process regarding budgets, invoice submission, recording of meeting minutes, and communications. This common regimen, co-directed by the prime consultant and the development manager, will help track progress and determine milestones for each study, and for the deliverables expected from each consultant.

Task 6: Confirmation meeting and start-up

Establishing a team approach and connections at the first formal municipal or regional district meeting is important. A structured agenda confirmed by the municipality will provide an ordered approach to the project and will create a professional tone for each meeting.

The first meeting should be positive, so ensure the meeting is structured with an upbeat tone in mind. At this meeting you should deal with such things as roles and responsibilities, timelines, and deliverables. Respect each other and establish rules of engagement for moving forward. Difficult situations will arise, so you have to be prepared to work together to arrive at mutually supported solutions or agreements.

Strategy review:

- Confirm the application requirements and complete the application if you are going to proceed.
- Select the prime and sub-consultants.
- Review the issues and opportunities.
- Define the management structure.
- Organize and execute the start-up meeting with staff, and define roles and responsibilities, targeted timeline, and management structure.

6. Proactive engagement with community, staff, and council/regional directors

Rule: Manage expectations and issues early in the process.

Proactive engagement means reaching out to the community, staff, and council before they reach out to you. You want to hear any bad news before it's a problem and manage the messages early in the process, otherwise the rumour mill might blur or distort facts in favour of the self-interest of those who might not want development, no matter what the proposed benefits.

Questions

1. What is the vision for the community?
2. What is missing and what is needed?
3. What are the key messages for the development?
4. Who is the spokesperson for the development?
5. How does the community want to engage?
6. How does staff want to engage with the community?
7. How does council want to engage and with the community?

Task 1: Meet with staff to confirm engagement and communication
Finalize and confirm support for the community communication and engagement strategy. Involve staff in crafting and refining the strategy. Confirm their roles and responsibilities in the engagement process. They normally like to attend and at least monitor any meetings or workshops, and sometimes they will actively facilitate and lead the discussion, depending on the application.

Respect sensitivities, no matter what staff perception of the project is. Sometimes, staff have to follow recommendations from their superiors, and their own views might be different. This type of situation is not in their control, and the viewpoint they are purveying may simply be based on experiences the municipality has had with similar projects in their community. Do not take it personally. Managing risk on staff's end is important. They don't want to be seen as supporting a project that is somehow flawed.

Task 2: Engage with the community.
As suggested in Phase 1 (stage 3, task 2), use a community leaders' group if possible, and meet with them as representatives of the greater community to confirm your engagement strategy. Refine the strategy with them so they take ownership of the steps moving forward.

Be careful not to overemphasize the process community leaders' group role in the actual engagement and be clear with them on their roles and responsibilities. You don't want the group, or anyone, finding an excuse to hijack your process in favour of their own agenda.

A community discovery workshop can be an initial event to kick off the process, especially if it is supported by an active, online engagement process that includes survey topic groups, and 'kitchen table' group discussions. In small projects, a small workshop might be the best tool to engage the neighbours and concerned citizens. For larger projects, a sequence of meetings, workshops, and open houses should be planned and scheduled early in the process, both to adhere to statutory requirements of the *Local Government Act* (LGA), and to suit particular requests from neighbours and the community.

Normally, an open and interactive dialogue, supported by the local 'support group' or residential association, provides the necessary transparency to first build understanding, and then build a development plan. The reverse results largely in community uproar. Check to ensure that your community leaders' group is representing the various perspectives of the community. The group is in place to ensure that communications are valid and inclusive. Support for the project should come with time, with proper validations.

Task 3: Meet with mayor and councillors (regional board chair and board members)
Arrange meetings with the mayor and councillors who are interested in the project. Start with the person at the top—the mayor, as he or she is normally the leader of the decision-making process.

There may be a hierarchy of councillors, based on experience, yet it may be some of the rookie councillors who are most active and engaged with the community. Select and meet with all the councillors, if possible, to get their views on the potential project. Ensure you listen carefully to the common themes and note potential red flags that might signal critical approval, or disproval criteria.

Keep everyone informed of the communication and engagement process as it progresses and listen to them for additional suggestions or refinements.

Task 4: Explore the project potential and alternatives
Listen for suggested modifications, or alternatives sites that may be more viable and supportable for your project. These alternatives may be pet projects of councillors or the mayor, or they could encompass a vision that may, in some form, be incorporated into an early development concept and then become further shaped over time. Take care to not deny suggestions early in the process, as they could undermine your site development potential and, more importantly, your credibility as an active listener in the community.

Strategy review:

- Meet with staff to confirm and refine engagement strategy.
- Engage the community through a community leaders, group mechanism to refine strategy and reaffirm the steps forward.
- Keep in mind that the community leaders' group is an option, and may not be appropriate for your project.
- Meet with mayor and councillors (regional board chair and board members) to obtain an early reading on support, engagement, and suggested refinements.
- Be open to ideas and suggestions, as these are part of effective, active listening, and feedback can help you develop inclusive, key messages that will open the gateway for moving forward toward approvals.

7. Focus on the most important elements from staff's perspective

Rule: Current policy largely determines staff support for the project.

Staff support is critical to the overall success of the project. If staff do not support the project on a regional or local policy level, these are grounds to reconsider the project. In many municipalities or regional districts, staff policies are fundamental to the decision-making process. To alter a major regional or local policy can be seen as a seismic and precedent-setting decision.

Take, for instance, a proposal to develop a cluster of residential developments adjoining, but not in, a designated rural village centre in a regional district. This change may be seen as the 'thin edge of the wedge'—a precedent-setting decision that could open the gates for growth in any part of a regional district, not just in village centres. Further, the planning department must circulate your application to other departments and agencies for review and comment. This circulation could result in a whole additional series of comments, and standard and non-standard conditions that require a formal response.

Questions

1. What are the local and regional policies that affect your property?
2. What is staff's interpretation of the policies?

3. What are other department and agency concerns?
4. What are the design panel and planning commission concerns?
5. Are the policies going through a review? If so, what are the chances for change?
6. How do they affect the value and potential of your property?
7. What are ranges of changes (density and land use) that may be considered?
8. What are the conditions for change and trade-offs?
9. What are the optimistic, realistic, and pessimistic development scenarios?
10. What are staff's recommendations?

Task 1: Policy direction
Remember that personal views have little to do with policy directions. Policies are normally adopted by council through bylaws that require adherence. Policies are the benchmarks for reviewing development projects. Any change or modification requires a strong rationale and/or site-specific zoning.

Task 2: Staff's view on modification
Probe staff's view on changing policy, and their support for amendments. If there is significant resistance, then determine potential conditions under which they might reconsider their non-support, or consider a modified development scheme that they would support under new conditions.

Task 3: Accepted application and circulation
Following review and acceptance of the development application, the planning department will circulate the application to other departments and outside agencies for review and comment. The planning department will then write a summary report and submit the report to the design panel (where applicable), and/or the planning advisory commission for review and comment. The recommendations might include further information or design modifications before they can make final recommendations. Monitor and evaluate comments received from the circulation of the application to municipal and district departments, and outside agencies, as the process ensues.

Task 4: Council/regional board of directors' review
Await council's review of the application. Following further design panel and/or planning commission review, the application is sent to council. Council will review the design panel and/or planning commission's recommendations, including conditions. They may deny the application at that stage, or they recommend it move forward, with council directing staff to prepare a bylaw. It will then proceed to first reading of that bylaw.

Strategy review:
- Review all the important policies that relate to your property.
- Confirm staff's interpretation and rationale for those policies.

- Consider staff's conditions, and those to potentially change or modify policy.
- Prepare and present to the design panel and planning commission.
- Review and respond to agency comments as required.
- Review and respond to design panel and planning commission as required.
- Await and respond to council/regional board of directors' review.

8. Precision development response and design elements

Rule: Precise responses to specific design and planning conditions wins.

A complete application with all required studies, and a master or site plan report, has to be accepted as complete by staff before it can proceed to formal review and approvals from council. Before an application proceeds to the official community plan amendment, rezoning or development permit level of formal approvals, staff review all the required items to determine whether they are complete and, if they are, they will allow the application to proceed.

For example, in a rezoning application, a number of items could be deemed incomplete or inconclusive. These could include a soils contamination review (site profile, stage 1) that requires further examination (stage 2) before the site clean-up plan can be determined. In rural areas, the Ministry of Transportation and Infrastructure might want the transportation consultant to do more transportation modeling based on growth scenarios to determine the potential extent of transportation improvements on and off site. In turn, the results of these examinations could change the site planning and architecture for the site.

Not until staff are satisfied that these situations have been dealt with to their satisfaction will the application proceed to formal approvals.

As a final point, keep the community and council informed of any significant modifications due to further studies such as noted above. This could help moderate staff's position on specific conditions. In normal circumstances, these are technical requirements that refine the design and planning of the site, and off-site improvement requirements.

Questions

1. Have the design and planning feasibility reports answered all the questions to the satisfaction of the approving officer?
2. If not, what further work needs to be completed?
3. Can you use a monitoring method (e.g., soil contamination) to determine further measures without delaying the application?
4. Which staff members are in control of the decision?

5. How can we work together to resolve the issues?
6. What additional resources are required?

Task 1: Rezoning and/or development permit conditions
Conditions that are standard, general conditions, or specific design or planning requirements, are referred to as 'prior-to-approval' terms. These are conditions that need to be satisfied before the issuance of approval and/or a development permit. They require further documentation, guarantees—financial or otherwise—and changes to design, development, architectural and landscape drawings, as well as other specific or non-specific features applicable to the site.

Task 2: Further site examinations
Complete further studies of the site to determine other impacts or conditions. These can include further studies on environmental, archaeological, transportation, soils, geotechnical, and servicing concerns, among others. Unfortunately, in some cases, a third party may be required to replace or verify an earlier study.

Task 3: Design and planning refinements or changes
Make adjustments to the site planning, engineering, landscape architecture, and architecture as required to meet the conditions, or negotiate a better solution that is efficient and yields the same (or more) units/space, and increases the value of the development.

Task 4: Development cost charges and other off-site improvement costs
Confirm the development cost charges (DCCs) for your site, including water, stormwater, and sanitary sewer improvements as a result of the development. These DCCs can include park acquisition, in accordance with the LGA. In addition, there may be a request to contribute to an affordable housing fund, or on-site affordable (non-market rate) rental, or owned, housing.

Task 5: Community amenity package
Finalize the community amenity contributions (CACs) that are required by the municipality or regional district. These contributions are used for various improvements or additions to the community, including general public realm improvements, daycare facilities, community centres, and others. The municipality may have a specific per square meter charge for CACs, or they could be determined by a negotiated percentage of the land lift as a result of rezoning. See chapter 3 for further details about CACs.

Task 6: Communications and updates
Update the community and council/board of directors on the progress of the application.

Strategy Review:

- Fulfill the rezoning and/or development permit conditions.
- Complete further site examinations as required.
- Make the required design and planning documentation amendments.
- Confirm the DCCs for the site and other potential requirements.
- Finalize the CACs for the site.
- Update council/board of directors and the community on progress and status.

Phase 3: Final Approvals

This phase of the process covers formal approvals by council/regional board of directors and the eventual phased development agreement, which confirms all the aspects and guarantees for the development so it can be constructed. This phase can and does overlay with Phase 2, as council provides a total of four readings as the application information becomes more detailed (as explained Chapter 3).

The formal council approval and finalization of the development agreement have been separated to highlight the importance of council's roles in approvals. In this section, we will cover closing with staff and agencies, confirming council and community support, and final development agreement. These coincide with three readings to finalize support, and the final reading to confirm legal agreements.

Keep in mind that there are normally review and/or approval filters between staff and council which can include design panel review and/or planning commission review. In the case of the City of Vancouver, there is also a development permit board that reviews and formally approves applications. Design panels and planning advisory commissions are advisory in nature. They make recommendations but are not decision-making authorities. Their influence varies from municipality to municipality.

9. Closing with staff and agencies

Rule: Obtain all the required approvals in writing as early as possible.

There are nearly always outstanding issues that linger through the process, and emerge toward the end, that need to be dealt with. They must be taken care of or they can undermine development approval momentum and formal approvals, especially at council. Remember, there is no incentive for council to approve an application when there are outstanding items that need closure to *their* satisfaction.

Questions

1. What are the outstanding items that need to be addressed?
2. What are the expectations of the municipality, or the provincial or federal agency?
3. How do we resolve the issues?
4. Who needs to be involved?
5. What agreements need to be completed?

Task 1: Outstanding municipal or regional district requirements
Identify the final outstanding items required by the municipality or the regional district. These could include costing landscape improvements, or the letter of credits involved

with guaranteeing performance; or, tree retention and replacement documentation, such as detailed demolition and restoration plans. Other legal aspects could be requirements confirming easements and rights-of-ways regarding infrastructure, public access, and open space.

Task 2: Outstanding provincial and federal agreements
Towards the end of the process, other provincial and federal agencies will submit a letter confirmation or will require formal agreements to protect their interests and lands that either border or transect the property. An example is Section 219 of the *Land Title Act*, covenants respecting riparian areas and streamside protection measures, as well as other elements that protect the municipality and agencies from non-performance.

If a rail or public utility runs through or borders the property, CN or CP Rail also needs to confirm their approval of suggested crossings, or related improvements.

Task 3: DCCs and other levies/costs including CACs
Finalize the development cost charge (DCC) agreements and other site development costs, both on-site and off-site, including community amenity contributions (CACs).

Strategy Review:

- Complete outstanding municipal and district items.
- Complete outstanding provincial, federal, and other agency approvals.
- Finalize DCC, CAC and other cost charges as part of development.

10. Finalize support

Rule: Give them your victory.

When have you heard that the winners criticize the others? Rarely ever. Therefore, always credit others before yourself, especially council, staff, and the community. Community and council support should be regarded as a work in progress throughout the approvals process. To do otherwise can lead to disapproval at any stage, especially at the public hearing when the community has the opportunity to express their views.

There are so many variables that can tip the scale one way or the other, some external to the specifics of the project. An example is a change in building height policy that is more political than site-specific. It is critical to address outstanding concerns of the advisory planning commission, the design panel or, in the case of the City of Vancouver, the development permit board, as they influence council's decision.

Confirming support of key community members, associations and councillors well in advance of public hearings is advantageous. In many instances, their stance is not firm and can shift, even at the public hearing. It is critical to have supporters attend and tip the vote with measured, fact-based material supported by written submissions, if possible. It is best to have more supporters than nay-sayers, but sometimes the turn-out is hard to predict.

Controlling the key messages to the community, council, and the media through a planned and orchestrated set of press releases, and updates on social media (including a project website), is especially important.

Questions

1. Are the mayor and councillors supporting your projects and if not, why?
2. Can you meet with all of them to confirm their vote?
3. Can the non-supporters be convinced to support your project, conditional on additional elements?
4. Who are the community nay-sayers, and can they be convinced otherwise?
5. Who are your strong community supporters?
6. What changes to project messaging are required to increase support?

Task 1: Planning commission and design panel support

Develop concise and compelling presentations to the planning commission and/or advisory design panel. Read their reports and recommendations. Although these commissions and design panels may not have the final approval jurisdiction, they can extend significant influence on the final decision by council.

In larger municipalities, the design panels consist of design professionals such as architects, landscape architects, and others, including police, who are have 'crime prevention though environmental design' (CPTED) considerations. Planning commissions are broader in scope and include members from mandated organizations, and citizens at large.

Design review is part of the staff review process. It comes before the planning commission review. Each has its own merit and both influence staff and council support for the project. Experienced professionals and interested community members look at the applications in detail and make recommendations, which are considered in approvals reports from staff, and/or in the deliberations by council.

Task 2: Community support

Continue to work on the non-supporters of the project. They may disagree on some elements of the project, but that does not necessarily mean overall support for the project is in jeopardy. Even go door to door, at least with the neighbours, to ensure their concerns are heard and voices of support are heard at the public hearing. Help supporters to get to the public hearing and document their support. Submit their written letters of support to mayor and council.

Task 3: Broader community support

Ensure that support organizations, including the Chamber of Commerce, the Business Improvement Association, and others (as applicable) represent themselves at public hearings, and document their support for your project. The greater community of business associations, environmental organizations, community groups (trail organizations) can also be substantial influencers in the final decision.

Task 4: General council/regional board of directors' support

Continue to work with council on their concerns, so that concerns transform into opportunities and an affirmative vote. The final vote is not until the fourth and final reading of the application and associated bylaws, but the public hearing has a significant bearing on the vote direction of council.

Task 5: Formal council/regional board of directors' support

Seek formal council support. The application comes to council with a staff report that documents design review and planning commission comments and recommendations, as well as departmental and outside agency review. Staff has also formalized the development bylaw. The first reading of the development application by council is confirmation that the application has been accepted and is complete. Second reading follows first reading and asserts that the application is proceeding, and that a public hearing date has been set by council. The public hearing provides the public with the opportunity to express their views on the application. Following the public hearing, the application can be denied by a council vote, deferred until another date, or approved for a third reading.

Task 6: Communications and updates

Provide refined key messages on the project website in social media, and written media, that resonate with the community, staff, and council. Select your spokespersons carefully; ensure you have people you can trust to deliver a consistent, positive message that inspires trust.

Strategy Review:

- Listen to the design panel and planning commissions.
- Build community support in anticipation of the public hearing.
- Include community organizations in your support network.
- Continue to build support with mayor and council.
- Continue to affirm key messages that resonate with the community.

11. Final Development Agreement

Rule: The deal is not done until the ink is dry.

The final stage in the approvals process is the development agreement that comes with the fourth and final reading before council. The development agreement combines many aspects of the proposed development and confirms obligations, guarantees, covenants, roles, and responsibilities regarding the staging and execution of the project. It is a legally binding contract that is scribed by lawyers representing both parties.

There are, however, many more approvals and permits required before construction begins, but these do not require council approvals and public scrutiny. For example, subdivision of lands in a phased development may require additional permits, include the building permit, tree removal permits, excavation permit, environmental permit (if applicable), and others that enable construction processes on the site. Subdivision divides the land into separate parcels (or consolidates parcels) to permit a phased development scheme, with areas built in stages on separate parcels of land. It also allows for the sale of separate parcels to different purchasers.

Questions

1. What are the unique aspects of this development that need confirmation and clarification?
2. Who is responsible for various parts of the construction, and what are their obligations?
3. What are the financial obligations of the applicant, and when are they paid?

Task 1: Development agreement components
Confirm unique components of agreement and finalize terms.

Task 2: Legal drafting of terms
Draft agreement, associated covenants, easements, rights-of-ways, and details of execution.

Task 3: Financial obligations
Finalize financial obligations, timing, and guarantees.

Task 4: Council/regional board of directors' approval
Approve agreement at council (fourth reading of application and associated bylaw).

Strategy Review:

- Draft development agreement.
- Legalize agreement.

- Finalize financial obligations.
- Approval of development agreement by council/regional board (fourth reading).

This chapter has built a robust *Approvals+* process, complete with pre-conditions for success and systemic operating elements that flow with each of the three phases and associated tasks. It is both straightforward and complex. Each of the eleven steps have supportive rules, questions, and a detailed task list to help you customize your own project management structure for your specific project (or projects). Bear in mind that each project will have its own nuances that require a modified approach.

The next chapter provides nine different 'strategy driver' cases as ideas for your *own* project's direction. It is often specific, community-based strategies that create the menu for support and success.

8. SUCCESSFUL STRATEGY DRIVERS

You won't make your town a success by making it into a wax museum.
—Bruce Hayden, Mark Holland, and Bruce Irvine, Urban Magnets (2020)

Great places are not fabricated but are created by people. They evolve over time and it takes an intimate understanding of the place you are working in, and the people who make it great, to capture the right alchemy of the future.

I want to share with you some successful strategy drivers that I was involved with. It is curious that when I reflect back on these case studies, four common strategy drivers emerge:

1. Committed leadership from the beginning, whether it be bottom-up or top-down.
2. A "driver" that enabled success, or a catalyst for success.
3. An emphasis on the unique qualities of the site, and associated opportunities.
4. A sensitive and responsive design that excites staff, community, and council.

Each of these case studies provides ideas for innovation in your processes, especially when the process is stopped or running into resistance. It is then time to reinvent, or jump-start, the process with alternative actions. These case studies provide tools to spawn unique and effective approaches to help unlock dysfunctional situations. Each of the nine strategy drivers have a common, short structure so that you can focus on the details that interest you. They begin with a synopsis, then explain the underlying details of the strategy, and finish with pearls of wisdom.

First Principles Driven

Synopsis

My first experience immersed me in the front-end planning and design of the significant Brentwood Town Centre redevelopment in Burnaby, British Columbia (referred to also as *'Amazing Brentwood'*). Here the development framework was a result of a carefully crafted collaborative effort between Burnaby staff and the Shape Properties development and consulting team (lead by Darren Kwiatkowski, Executive Vice-President for Shape Properties).

After an effort to deliver site development concepts, without discussion, which received at best a lukewarm response, Darren and his deputy, Mike Nygren, decided to reinvent the process with a different approach. The Shape Team then worked arm-in-arm with the City of Burnaby planning staff to develop principles and tenets that would be the foundation for the project. This process opened the gateway for a trust and support, which carried through to the development application and approvals that followed.

Underlying details

Sometime in 2010, I received the call from a stranger. "It is Mike Nygren from Shape Properties," said an engaging voice at the other end of the line.

"Who the heck is Shape Properties", I thought silently as I quickly scanned my neurological rolodex. Nothing registered, but I decided I was willing to listen—at least for a few minutes. At that time, Shape Properties was just emerging as a major player in the Vancouver real estate market. Little did I know how significant they would eventually be! What developed from that phone call was an ongoing relationship with Shape Properties, with me supporting their efforts to reshape properties into outstanding destinations and meaningful places.

After that phone call, and following meetings with Darren and Mike, it was decided we needed to develop a different process for Brentwood, one that built a common vision. I would help facilitate that process.

Brentwood was part of one of the four town centres in the City of Burnaby that was directly adjoining the Brentwood Skytrain station, so significant redevelopment was anticipated; the question was what, and how.

The long-term Mayor of Burnaby, Derek Corrigan, was set on developing Burnaby as the next 'creative city' based on the best-selling book of the same name. The Shape team embraced the idea, but the challenge we had was to develop a *new* 'creative city' on the 11.5-hectare (28.4-acre) site of the Brentwood shopping centre, while retaining its valuable income stream during construction. In other words, retaining the goose that laid the golden eggs, while creating an elaborate underground parking structure to support the expansion into office and residential uses.

The Shape team met with the City of Burnaby and in conjunction with them, they determined it was best to start with 'first principles' to lay the groundwork for this complex redevelopment project. We set up a series of workshops with the City of Burnaby planning department to discuss components that would shape the site, from an extended pedestrian-oriented street, to integration with the multi-modal hub, and 'creative' places that could nurture idea generation.

The principles, tenets, and associated sketches provided the framework for a detailed master plan concept, and the development plans that followed:

Tenets

Tenets are universal goals and are non-site specific.

A. Strengthen the surrounding community.
B. Integrate exceptional urban design and architecture.
C. Create a diverse and inclusive community.
D. Encourage sustainable development.
E. Contribute to developing a creative city.
F. Create a livable community.

Principle Themes

Principle themes are grouped under the following common themes, and guide future site planning and design. Principles are the guiding rules for development, and touchstones for measuring performance. They are:

1. Edges and connections.
2. Site circulation and movement.
3. Transit oriented development.
4. The heart and public realm.
5. Diversity and integration
6. Sophisticated design.
7. Design evolution.

Each of these principal themes were further detailed to describe their meaning and site application, with site plan concepts, sketch illustrations, and photographs incorporating them. The subsequent detailed master plan and approvals proceeded smoothly from this first step. These common principles and tenets became references points for the ongoing development review and approvals process.

Pearls of Wisdom

- If the process stops, reinvent it in collaboration with the approval authority.
- True collaboration builds trust and cooperation.
- Detail the principles and tenets so they apply to the unique site.
- Be patient and be methodical in building a sense of common vision.
- Actively listen to the details and wording of the municipal staff.
- Municipal staff want the same great 'creative' city.
- Municipal staff know the barriers to, and opportunities with, approvals.
- Municipal staff will help you if you help them.
- Go slow first to go fast.

Vision, Goals and Values Driven

Synopsis

My second experience involved the former Canadian Military Forces base at Chilliwack. I found out that a neighbourhood without a clear vision simply doesn't know where it is going. Add to this vision directed goals and values and you have a solid recipe for success. Garrison Crossing does exactly that. It builds on 60 years of history at the former Canadian Armed Forces base in Chilliwack, located approximately 60 miles (100 kilometres) east of the city of Vancouver. I was fortunate to be part of the development consulting team.

The foundation blocks of an outstanding neighbourhood and a complete community were already in place before redevelopment planning began—walkable streets, a variety of housing, active and passive parks, indoor recreation facilities, a grand boulevard, mature trees, conveniently located schools, and adjacent shopping.

Former military personnel and their families helped shape the vision for the neighbourhood as part of an integrated neighbourhood planning process. As a result, sensitive vision and associated values emerged. The project embraces the overall theme of 'coming home', as former military personnel, through focus group discussions, indicated that this was the essence of CFB Chilliwack. The site was not cleared of the valuable landscapes and the 450 'permanent married quarters'; instead, a careful and precise surgical process not only retained its character but quadrupled its density with diversity and housing choices.

Addressing the rental housing on the property from the onset helped deal with local concerns of residents that they would be uprooted and pushed out of their homes. As the development would be phased over ten years, Canada Lands created a $500 relocation subsidy to aid in moving residents who needed immediate replacement housing, provided elsewhere on the base. This gesture of good faith helped build community support for the project.

The official community plan amendment and rezoning were approved unanimously by council within 12 months, and construction began shortly thereafter. Much of the first phases were pre-sold at up to 15 percent above market sales prices. The development won the UDI's Master Planned Community of the Year, among numerous other awards. Garrison Crossing is one of the first certified Leadership Through Energy and Environmental Design for Neighbourhoods (LEED) developments in Canada.

The plan quadrupled the number of homes on the property from approximately 450 units to 1,750 units, or a 4 to 1 increase in density. A legacy walk for veterans was developed; the Cheam Centre for recreation was refurbished and expanded, and a host of local parks were revitalized and restored.

Underlying Details

Here is the vision that guided development of the former military base:

> *Garrison Crossing is a unique, diverse, and thriving neighbourhood that complements its surroundings, contributes to the healthy growth of Chilliwack, and builds on its rich military past. Garrison Crossing is a model of responsible development that seeks to respect the natural environment, connect to its neighbours, provide for housing choice, and reuse the existing built and natural assets where possible.*

The project had the following goals, which included sustainable and new urbanism goals:

- *Adaptive reuse.* Use the significant natural and built resources of the site in redevelopment, including buildings, roadways, and trees where possible, to create an exceptional and unique neighbourhood.
- *Environmental sensitivity.* Respect, conserve, and enhance the significant and valued natural assets of the site.
- *Legacy.* Incorporate the rich military history of the site as an important central theme in redevelopment.
- *Diversity.* Provide for a range of types and styles of homes, local services, and associated amenities that include all age groups and complement adjoining land uses.
- *Connection.* Ensure that future redevelopment continues to provide activities and facilities for the surrounding neighbourhoods and the greater Chilliwack community.
- *Innovation.* Explore new and proven urban forms that create a more pedestrian, compact, green, and complete neighborhood that is more efficient, healthy, safe, and livable.
- *Value.* Build an outstanding neighbourhood that adds value to the greater community.

Great neighbourhoods are a result of good plans, great intentions, and a commitment to carry out the plan with the original intentions. The implementation plans go beyond the neighbourhood plan document. In addition to the neighbourhood plan document, the following continue to support the additional necessary detail for the design and building approvals process:

- *Site development design guidelines.* These guidelines specify site use regulations, public and private realm site planning, and landscape standards, as well as architectural standards that apply to subareas. These guidelines are registered on title to ensure that future landowners are aware of their permitted uses and design regulations.
- *CD-10 zone.* This comprehensive development zone specifies the regulations and standards for each of the subareas within Garrison Crossing, including setbacks, density ranges, and other use or site development restrictions. This zone permits the flexibility to retain existing houses, trees, and other elements associated with neighbourhood character, and respond to changing market demands and customized development standards in the longer term.
- *Customized engineering standards.* Specific technical drawings will address the specific road and utilities standards for Garrison Crossing.

Pearls of Wisdom

- Be proactive in responding to opportunities, and challenges, in the community.
- Develop a vision and goals that are rooted in the community.
- Create a strong, genuine brand that speaks of place and meaning.
- Conserve and enhance natural and historic features in the community.
- Be special in your site development response, based on the uniqueness of the site.
- Invite former and existing residents to help shape the plan.
- Illustrate how density, done well, can provide a necessary diversity and choice of housing.

Joint Agreement Driven

Synopsis

My third experience involves the design of a new community called Cambrian Crossing, in Strathcona County, east of Edmonton, Alberta. Through a joint planning initiative (JPI) structure, our development team worked closely with Strathcona County to develop a sustainable community plan and associated design for the land (Figure 8.1 below).

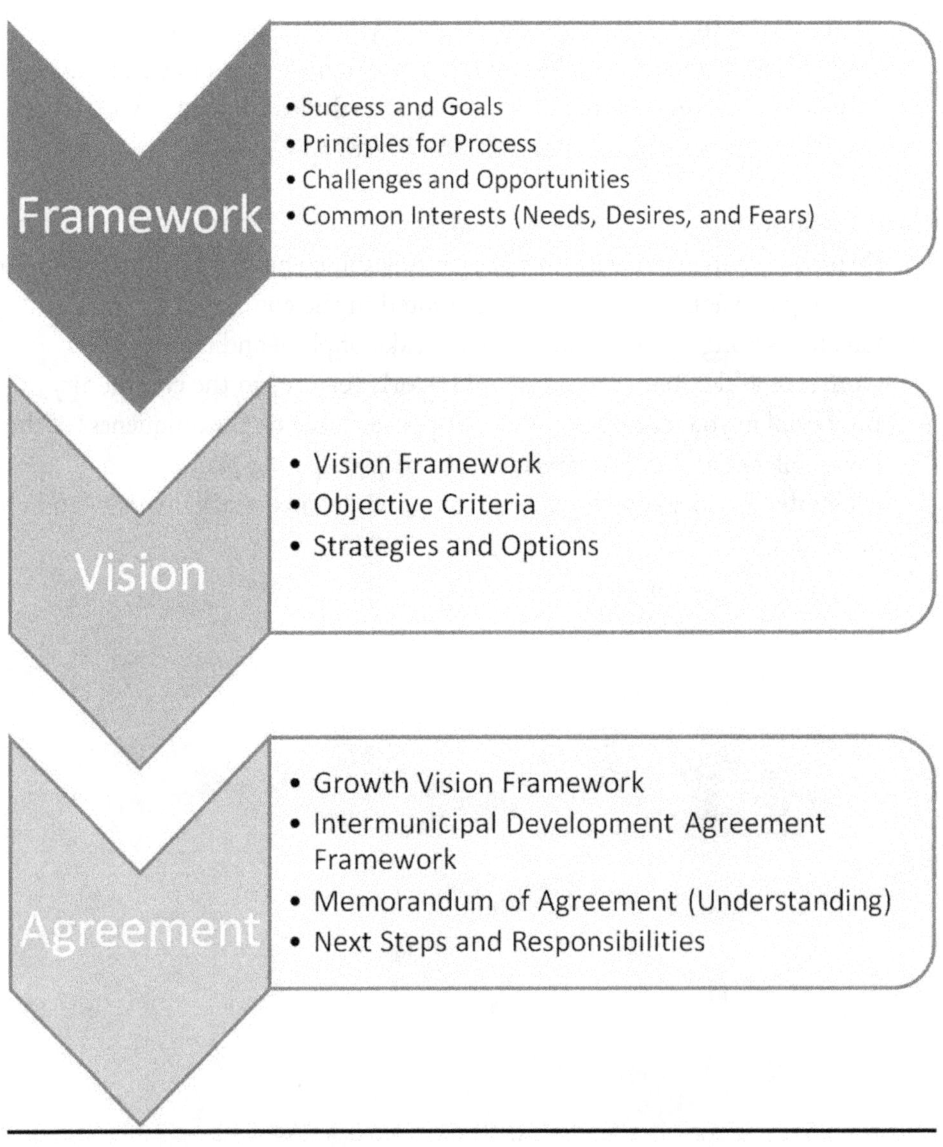
Framework
• Success and Goals
• Principles for Process
• Challenges and Opportunities
• Common Interests (Needs, Desires, and Fears)
Vision
• Vision Framework
• Objective Criteria
• Strategies and Options
Agreement
• Growth Vision Framework
• Intermunicipal Development Agreement Framework
• Memorandum of Agreement (Understanding)
• Next Steps and Responsibilities

Figure 8.1: Joint Planning Initiative Agreement Process

The developer was already well along in the process of approving an industrial development when the county approached them with an alternative. The county realized that they would run out of servable residential land within an estimated three to five years, and the Cambrian parcel was the last large parcel within the Urban Service Boundary. The county wanted to alter the plan to combine residential, commercial/ business, and recreational uses with a variety of industrial uses. The developer embraced the concept in exchange for a condensed review and approvals, and a vision of a complete and sustainable local community where residents could live, work, and play. The developer had county approval within a year.

Underlying Details

I lead the consulting team that helped facilitate this process. To build common, sustainable interests, and design the plan, tasks and timelines were agreed to, with the county helping to manage and expedite the process (known as the 'sustainable urban neighborhood process', or SUN). A memorandum of understanding (MOU) was signed by both parties to solidify the process, timing, and deliverables. The clock was ticking; we had twelve months to complete and approve the concept plan for 358 hectares (885 acres)!

Different attitudes toward development were soon replaced by principles of sustainability that had compelling economic, ecological, and social grounding. Both parties developed a shared vision and set of principles that became the foundation of the plan. Adjoining landowners were skeptical of the process at first and wondered why the area should be anything but industrial, because that was the major land use pattern west of the site. What would the mix of uses bring to the area?

Soon, via workshops and a four-day design charrette, the community came to support the proposal. The proposed development would provide numerous benefits to the community, including increased real estate values, convenient services, recreation, jobs, and improvements to the road network. The proposal presented a community that would house up to 7,200 residents in 2,600 units. Jobs would be close to home. Approximately 1.7 jobs per household would be provided within the community. Two schools and two places of worship were proposed to provide educational and spiritual needs of the community. A commercial service district would serve the industrial portion, while two local neighborhood service centers and a more major central town center would serve the balance of the residents. Basic services were to be located within a five-minute walk of most residents. Schools were also within a five-minute walk, supported by an interconnected network of trails and pathways along the Old Man Creek corridor and throughout neighborhoods. A bus transit network further helped movement patterns throughout the community and to other destinations.

Eight different neighborhoods evolved from the process to shape Cambrian Crossing, each with its own identity and mix of uses. The plan features a variety of single-family and multifamily options, inviting all demographics, from single to elderly, into the community. Higher densities are closest to the neighborhood centers, for convenience and supportive activities. An average density of 38 units/net residential hectare (15 units per net acre) provides for compact living that is mainly ground-oriented, important especially in suburban locations.

The resulting plan was designed as a complete, sustainable community. County staff brought the proposal forward to council, and Cambrian was approved within twelve months of initiation. Like any project of this size, Cambrian Crossing continues to face challenges, especially in servicing this property and associated road improvements.

Pearls of Wisdom

- Solidify commitments through joint process agreements.
- Provide roles and responsibilities for each team member.
- Act together and build momentum through victories, and through accomplishing milestones.
- Consider 'the other' in all your decisions.
- If the municipality is on your team, it makes approvals so much easier.

Planning Director Driven

Synopsis

My fourth experience brought me to the west coast of Vancouver Island where Canadian surfers chase their dreams. I was only there to turn around a failed development but in the process, discovered the merits of working closely with the director of planning to obtain mutually beneficial outcomes. It combined resort planning with local community needs and aspirations in Ucluelet, British Columbia.

This case study takes us to a project called *Oceanwest* that was first turned down by the local council. The project was re-invented and transformed into an award-winning plan that received unanimous council approval within the remarkably short time frame of six months. Normally, these processes take up to three to five years! The question is: How did this miracle happen?

Underlying Details

All the facts seemed against the project's future feasibility. The project had been turned down by unanimous vote of the local council. The prior developer had ignored the advice of the landowner—Weyerhaeuser Lands—as well as council, staff, and the community. The trust of the community was gone.

The director of planning invited me to help them out, as he was supportive of the development idea. I had to consider it carefully, as on first glance, the patient was dead on arrival. When I looked at the aerial photo of the 376-acre (152-hectare) property, my feelings changed instantly. The property looked spectacular. It was set out on the Ucluelet peninsula on the edge of the Pacific Ocean, with nothing between it and Japan. Enormous, brooding surf and a pristine coastline drew me to imagining its potential.

My first step was to meet with Charles Smith of Weyerhaeuser, the director of the project and landowner. Weyerhaeuser is an international forest resource company that owned the land for many years, originally for forest resource purposes. They intended to leave a legacy. This all showed promise, until Charles told me that they needed approval within six months, before the next council election. Despite the political history and timeline challenge, somehow, I held out hope for the project.

Rebuilding trust at all levels in the community was critical to success. I told Charles that we needed to create a local consulting team, with local contacts. Charles was an active contributor throughout our process—a key ingredient to our eventual success.

I built a local consulting team with ears, expertise, and boots on the ground. One sticky feature that had hampered previous plans was that the Wild Pacific Trail, the important trail network along the west coast, had not been adequately recognized in the past planning process. The community and council were not pleased.

In response, we at least *doubled* the Wild Pacific trail length by creating a series of trail loops within the property and retaining 80 percent of the trail along the waterfront. We also developed a policy that the first, more affordable lots, would be offered to local residents. These were among some of the concessions and community benefits that emerged from the discussions. Our ears were open, and our mouths were shut.

We did not know for sure until the public hearing if we were moving in the right direction. It was attended by nearly 300 people, or approximately 25 percent of the town's population. They recognized the process and the final development plan but, maybe most importantly, they recognized what the project would do for the community. The plan had value and substance. It was very different from the previous proposal, and the community amenity package that accompanied it would make a big difference for Ucluelet.

The public hearing had many speakers but it appeared at points to be a seesaw battle between those that supported the plan and those non-supporters. Finally, one of the last speakers points out, "we elect you councillors to make these difficult decisions." This statement was indeed correct. To our amazement, each councillor then stood up and addressed the audience one at a time. Each one stated the reasons why they *supported* the plan. It was approved unanimously by council that night!

The plan provides housing choice and affordability, protects environmental assets, and creates complementary tourism/recreation development. The intent of the rezoning application was to create a comprehensive development (CD) zone that permitted a variety of land uses that were sensitively clustered into the landscape.

Specifically, the plan:

- Protects valuable ecological and visually sensitive areas, as approximately 56 acres (22.5 ha) of the land is protected as open space, trails, and parks—including a 22-acre (8.9-hectare) central nature park that helps naturally connect Olsen Bay to the Pacific Ocean.
- Provides an alternative to rural sprawl housing and protects the natural resources of the site, while providing a variety of necessary cluster housing, including affordable housing in the form of small-lot and multiple-family housing, employee housing linked to the hotels, market town houses, as well as single-family housing.

- Expands hotel resort opportunities as part of economic diversification for the local economy, enhancing tourism, recreation, and associated employment in the area.
- Creates a necessary and logical extension to the community of Ucluelet that extends its form and character, as well as connects to the Wild Pacific Trail, other recreation facilities, and transportation links within the site.
- provides a unique cluster design that fits into the landscape and complements the rural character of the adjoining Ucluelet community.
- Introduces a customized development framework to minimize any impacts on the landscape, and reinforces the local rural character (e.g., tree retention and natural storm water management, where possible).

In addition to these strategies, Weyerhaeuser promised to make the following contributions to the Ucluelet community as part of a comprehensive community benefit package:

- Construct the Wild Pacific Trail at the time of development of the lands as part of 56 acres (22.5 hectares) of open space, park, and trail contributions.
- Provide 7 acres (2.8 hectares) of affordable housing (90 units at full development).
- Provide $25,000 each to the Westcoast Community Resource Society, the District of Ucluelet (for facilities associated with the new multipurpose field), bursaries for postsecondary forestry studies for Ucluelet students, and monies for the Ucluelet and Area Childcare Society.
- Contribute $20,000 for the highway rescue truck (which provides emergency rescue services for highway accidents) and $100,000 for the District of Ucluelet's Social Reserve Fund.
- Donate 10 acres (4 hectares) to the district for community uses.
- Restrict the marketing of any small lots less than 7,000 square feet (650 m^2) to Ucluelet residents for 60 days.

Pearls of Wisdom

- Pay attention to, and learn from, what happened to the last developer on the property.
- Build a local team that has roots in the community.
- Change strategies with the planning director's guidance.
- Build what you say you will and create a real legacy.

Common Interests Driven

Synopsis

My fifth experience was an experiment that took place in the City of Maple Ridge, east of Vancouver in 2019. A developer-sponsored process intended to improve an existing outdated plan in the northeast area of Maple Ridge. There were two views of the existing plan. The developer wanted to proceed with a standard plan of mainly single-family housing units, while the municipality wanted a greater mix of housing and more amenities for the community. I was brought in to facilitate the process – the cotton batten between two hard places.

To move to a new plan, we defined a process where the developer and the municipality would work closely together through a series of workshops to define the new plan. Then with a mutually supported plan, the municipality would hold open houses in the community to solicit feedback and then proceed to council for approvals.

The core of the challenge was to increase density and mix of housing in a suburban location. Additional parks and green space would also be required as part of this improved plan. The process itself was also seen by the developer as time-consuming, delaying his delivery of housing product into a marketplace that was hot at the time and could change with delays.

Participants were also not comfortable in a process they had not experienced before. The outcomes were not predictable at the beginning of the process, so both parties were anxious.

In addition, increased density in the form of townhomes and other forms of housing were not tested in the local market and any commercial or mixed-use additions were questionable. In parallel with this concern, the question arose: were new, more dense housing types and uses supported by adjoining neighbours who lived in single-family homes?

There were several civil engineers involved from both the developer side and the municipal side. Engineers are especially risk averse, as they use design standards (sometimes outdated) intended to protect the health, safety, and public welfare of the community. In essence, they could be responsible for modifying standards that could place the community at risk.

How was the result going to be different in this municipality? How were we going to modify behaviour and have municipal staff, developer, and community support the new and improved plan? Mission impossible, you say. Yes, in part, but I saw it as a prime opportunity. Plus, designing 'normal' is infinitely boring. It was time to get the creative juices flowing and to invigorate the conversation.

As the facilitator of this experimental process, I had to right the sails of the boat and put it on a course toward success. To do that, I had to do four things:

1. Excite the developer, municipality, and community participants about the project potential;
2. Draw in each professional, and understand their interests in the project;
3. Get each of the staff actively involved in the plan making process; and
4. Let staff make the big moves on paper so they feel ownership of the changes.

Underlying Details

I realized early that we were getting nowhere in the first two workshops. A train wreck was imminent! The train was rumbling down the tracks without brakes, heading for its demise. I needed to gain control of the situation, or better still, I needed to have the developer and municipality take active ownership of the process and make the intended changes to the plan.

I really didn't know what to do, as the audience (developer, consultants, and municipal staff) were not responding to my questions and challenges. I thought one last effort—getting them to draw and sketch the concepts—would break the ice. However, everyone was staying safely in their areas of expertise and not stretching to new ground. Status quo was the safe place to be.

There were two parties with conflicting positions at play here, and neither was gaining traction with their ideas. We had a choice to work together to develop a better plan, but it meant compromise, or did it? Could we build value and benefits for both parties – the developer and the municipality? As I discovered, there were common interests of building a great community that attracted a variety of home buyers looking for well-designed community with rich amenities including a connected network of parks and open spaces.

This was the first time this municipality had ever been through this process and it was an experiment to see if a developer-supported process could work to improve plans. If not, the alternative was to simply do the standard neighbourhood planning process.

The breakthrough came rather unexpectantly when I had both junior and senior city staff start drawing plan alternatives. I gave them pens and they started drawing concept plans that we had discussed earlier. They soon realized the trade-offs that would be needed regarding street layouts, the size and type of parks, location of housing density, and local neighbourhood commercial zoning. Before this exercise, they had been distant from the process; now, they were making a meal together with the development team.

The workshop concluded and the options were formally drawn up for public review and refinement. The public open houses further informed refinements to the plans with a healthy balance of townhomes and single-family compact housing integrated with a parks and open space network. A small mixed-use neighbourhood commercial corner finished the plan with good walking connections to the local elementary school. The street network was scaled to the neighbourhood with street tree planting and generous sidewalks. The plan was then approved by council without major issue.

Pearls of Wisdom

- Use a third party to be a neutral party in facilitating the process.
- Use measured criteria (e.g., principles and targets) to compare plan alternatives.
- Engage all staff members in some way and get them to draw some of the plan alternatives if possible.
- Create educational components of the process to inform staff and the development team of inspirational examples, technical challenges, and opportunities for the site.

Community Benefits Driven

Synopsis

My sixth experience brought me to the east coast. In Halifax, Nova Scotia the tallest building east of Montreal, and its surrounding parcels, was proposed as a major redevelopment project, the largest redevelopment at the time. A major contributor to the success of the Fenwick Tower redevelopment project was the comprehensive neighbourhood participation process and communication strategy that started in September 2009. It culminated in the Halifax Regional Municipality (HRM) unanimous council approval (17 councillors) in February 2011. As the project facilitator, I remember the Halifax vice-mayor's disbelief when only one person opposed the proposal at the public hearing. I know because she shared it with me afterwards. Considering the size of the redevelopment, she was completely surprised by this vote of confidence.

The consultation process provided valuable input to the form and character of the future redevelopment of the site, and also contributed valuable ideas for defining neighborhood needs and areas of improvement. It involved more than 10 local interest groups surrounding Dalhousie University. It is worthwhile to examine not only the content of the plans, but the principles, rationale for additional density, community benefits, and sustainability features. These elements informed the application by Templeton Properties to amend the Halifax Municipal Planning Strategy and Halifax Peninsula Land Use Bylaw. They also informed the detailed development agreement that followed the development application process. The community benefits package in particular was a major driver in the project's success.

Underlying Details

Fenwick Tower is a 33-storey residential building in Halifax's South End. Fenwick Tower, completed in 1971, is the highest building east of Montreal, at 321.5 feet (98 metres). The property was purchased by Dalhousie University to help serve part of their student housing needs. In 2009, Templeton Properties acquired the property with the intention of improving the residential tower and infilling the balance of the site with other buildings and associated amenities. The benefits given to the community through site redevelopment are important in measuring the 'net community gain' created by the development. The following is a list of items that evolved as a result of the comprehensive community dialogue.

Choice and diversity of housing

- Ten percent of new units will be affordable in accordance with CMHC standards.
- A combination of rental and ownership units will be provided.

- Various unit sizes, from bachelor to two bedrooms, will be provided.
- The unit orientation and improvements will expand the student emphasis to include young professionals.

Pedestrian-oriented redevelopment

- Fifty underground parking stalls will be dedicated for neighborhood parking use, taking some street parking off the streets in winter and providing a necessary local service.
- Bicycle parking will be expanded and provided at various points in the development.
- A car-sharing program will be considered in the redevelopment, with the provision of two car-share stalls, expanding the current nine dedicated locations in Halifax.
- The parking garage will be upgraded and expanded for safety, security, and accessibility, including access to South Street—dispersing the traffic and taking pressure off of Fenwick Street.

Improved streetscape, open space network, and community meeting space

- A through-block pedestrian mews will be provided that connects Fenwick Street and South Street, with appropriate lighting, seating, and a host of locally based retail shops and services focused along the mews for safety and vitality.
- The pedestrian mews and other rooftop spaces will be landscaped to bring plants, flowers, and small trees into the site.
- A number of public art pieces will be placed along the pedestrian mews to animate the space, adding local identity, history, and cultural richness to the experience.
- The streetscape along Fenwick Street will be improved by street trees, a new sidewalk, and six townhouses fronting on the street.

Cultural and social neighborhood meeting place

- A community meeting space will be available to neighborhood associations when necessary.
- Retail and office uses will favor local and appropriately scaled businesses (cafés, restaurants, professional offices, and other necessary services).
- The pedestrian mews will be an important 'third place' in the neighborhood to hold special gatherings, festivals, and displays.
- New commercial uses will be focused on providing necessary local services and providing for local businesses.
- Landscaping on-site will consider native plants that require less water and are hardier.

- A number of public art installations will be coordinated to enhance and reflect local identity and culture on-site.
- Roofs will be landscaped, providing amenity space for residents and positive overlooks from adjoining units.
- Site remediation and repair in terms of landscaping and amenity improvement will be embraced in redevelopment.
- Social and public meeting places will be part of the pedestrian mews design through the site—encouraging special events, festivals, and community activities throughout the year.
- An interior space will be open for neighborhood association meetings to further the idea of community capacity building and stewardship after the project is completed.

Pearls of Wisdom

- Real local community benefits are essential to obtaining approvals.
- Work with the community ringleaders in an open and transparent way (in this case, there was only one nay-sayer present at what would be deemed the public hearing).
- Communicate, communicate, and communicate.
- Engage, engage, and engage.
- Respond and incorporate reasonable suggestions.
- Disarm opposition by addressing their concerns directly.

Community Driven

Synopsis

Shawnigan Lake on Vancouver Island was the location of my seventh experience. Witnessing the power and determination of community-led initiatives can be somewhat daunting. Having the Area Director of the Regional District lead the charge is even more awesome to observe. Further, getting on the wave of support can make for a great express ride to approvals.

From a developer standpoint, even with community endorsement, there can be insurmountable technical challenges, such as community wastewater management, or potable water provision, that serve as continuing barriers to approvals. This was unfortunately the case with respect to the Shawnigan Lake Village Plan approved by the Cowichan Valley Regional District (CVRD) in 2020, after less than a year of community process and deliberations.

Underlying Details

Shawnigan Lake Village is located on Vancouver Island about 45 minutes' drive north of Victoria on the Island Highway. The distinguished Shawnigan Lake Private School is located on the edge of the lake. Many commuters to Victoria have found paradise on this beautiful lake.

The Shawnigan Lake Village Plan was initiated in the Spring of 2019, and council retained my design and planning team to complete the plan with the support of a local group lead by the Area Director. 'Keep Shawnigan' became the slogan for the project, and it was led by this enthusiastic group of citizens. Continuing issues of water pollution and an eroding community character were centrepieces of community discussion. They like small and local. They don't like big and slick.

Added to this conversation was the potential development of Shawnigan Lake Station, a development proposal headed by an established local family who had been part of the community for two generations. All these factors created an interesting, conflicting discussion. Keep Shawnigan Lake the way it is? Or change for the better for the sake of increasing housing needs and local services, not to mention more and better infrastructure improvements. There was also the complex and expensive problem of community wastewater management. Unfortunately, there were no government funds to support a major community wastewater management facility, and health regulations limit location and specifications, especially when a significant number of units are being considered.

At the same time, a rigorous process of dialogue and ideas resulted in an unanimously supported plan by the CVRD board of directors. This vote of confidence supported development and infill with the caveat that servicing had to be provided to support the increase in the intensity of development.

Pearls of Wisdom

- Leave the leadership to leadership if it is under good leadership.
- Help support the process without obstructing the well-intended process.
- Be careful to separate development facts from community interests.
- Without a sanitary sewer and water plan, there are no development approvals.

Council Driven

Synopsis

My eighth experience took me across the rocky mountains to the Town of Canmore, Alberta. There I discovered some of the sensitivities around affordable housing. I also realized that when a municipal council gets behind an effort and there are few options, they may take a leadership role in approving otherwise controversial plans.

In Canmore, Alberta, I was invited to be part of a consulting team to lead them through a hornet's nest of discussions about the Old Daycare Lands. There was a significant obstacle regarding an affordable housing initiative that would be on parklands that had been dedicated as public reserve. A community engagement process defined up to 11 alternatives, these were reduced to three, and then to one preferred concept.

In the end, council made the decision to go ahead with the affordable housing alternative on park lands with the proviso that they would significantly improve this largely derelict piece of land as park space with additional amenities. The affordable housing was built and improvements to the park are underway.

Underlying Details

The Daycare Lands in Canmore is an old park area that previously had a daycare facility on it that has since been removed. The five acres of land were rarely used, largely underutilized and were surrounded by various owned and rental housing. It was residual space ready for improvement as a park or otherwise.

Canmore, as a gateway to Banff National Park, faces a housing shortage and affordability crisis. Housing prices have skyrocketed with demand from across Alberta and elsewhere, as Canmore is seen as a prime recreation destination given that it sits at the foot of the Rocky Mountains and is easily accessible from Calgary, a convenient one hour drive away.

When the community was initially engaged with the proposed development, there was naturally push-back and hesitation when they heard that affordable rental housing was targeted for their local park. Alarm is a fair term for their response. Indeed, it was a park not a development parcel. However, after much discussion with the community and their leaders, it was determined that if the park was significantly improved as a result of the sensitive integration of additional affordable housing units along two edges, then they would consider the proposal. In the end, it took council's vote to approve the innovative affordable housing concept.

Pearls of Wisdom

- Solve a big challenge for council and the community (in this case park improvements for the community and affordable housing for council) to win support.
- Once council is behind you, who could be against you?
- Work with the neighbourhood to see if council's goals and neighbourhood goals can coincide with each other.
- Council has the final say, as they are deemed to represent the community.

First Nations Leadership Driven

Synopsis

My final experience took me to the Tlinget First Nations home territory that surrounds Atlin, British Columbia near the Yukon border. This country is as close to wilderness as anyone can imagine and is the home of the Taku River Tlinget peoples. Working with Jeff Cook of Beringia Consulting and the Tlinget First Nations, in 2004 and then again in 2013, we worked on sustainable land use planning. This work introduced me to the issues and challenges facing First Nations and gave me an inside look at what the potential of First Nations can be when conversation is through the lens of recognition and respect. With enlightened capacity-building and new leadership development, I believe there is a whole new world we can create with First Nations.

Underlying Details

As part of the consulting team, we developed a sustainable land use plan with the Taku River First Nation. This was a different and intensive process as we wanted to reflect *their* values, not our values, in the plan. Through small and large workshops, family meetings, fireside chats, community mapping, and sharing food, we discovered what the community needed and wanted.

We developed a leadership group and connected with the youth. We created talking rules for our meetings to develop their communication skills and we walked their beautiful lands, with the backdrop of Atlin Lake and the mountains providing a Swiss Alps-like setting. Magnificent and pristine are the words that come to mind. These river people fish salmon every year on the Taku River south of Atlin; the land and nature are sacred to them, and stewarding these, as well as preserving their rich culture and language, are core to their being.

The evolved land use plan was full of sketches and plans to reflect their values and goals and inspire their future. We tried to genuinely acknowledge and respect their culture at every meeting and to incorporate this within the planning documents. We worked with their leadership to develop further capacity in planning as a community, and integrated culture and language preservation when we could.

At the final meeting, the community created the name for the plan: *Many Eyes, One Vision*. The younger future leaders helped present the plan to their own members in a tearful ceremony. Leadership was born that day. We were so humbled by the experience and so grateful to be part of their future planning.

Pearls of Wisdom

- Develop heartfelt respect and acknowledgement for First Nations.
- Acknowledge their land and territory.
- Ask questions to understand protocols, culture, and traditions.
- Understand that each First Nations group is different.
- Speak only when you are asked and bring gifts if appropriate.
- Learn that First Nations richness of culture and traditions can enrich our own.

9. RE-VISIONS

> *Partnering is a key to primary greatness. Unless we are willing to work together, to sacrifice our pride of ownership of our ideas or our image, we will not meet the ever-growing demands of the marketplace.*
>
> *—Stephen R. Covey, Primary Greatness (2015)*

We end where we begin, and hopefully you have found 'new pathways' along the way. We often forget that we all have one common goal: To create great communities in British Columbia and across Canada. We can build commodity or community. Commodity is lifeless, soulless, and time sensitive as part of our consumer landscape. In contrast, community is vibrant, soulful, full of spirit, and timeless. It creates value and magical alchemy worth every bit of the process. Community is a partnership of will and execution. Why does it so often have to be a war of wills or resources, where the last man or women standing wins? Shocking, but true.

Over 2,000 years ago Sun Tzu believed that great generals never fight. Why? Because conflict is an unnecessary use of resources. Why do it if you don't have to create a confrontation. Both parties lose, and a sense of trust and integrity germane to letting parties do what they want to do is lost. Such simple logic, yet lost in battle.[72]

The Twenty-Eight Minute Meeting

Imagine a meeting where everything falls into place. You have a contact at city hall, and you make the call. The contact coincidentally is a friend and teaching colleague. There is an enduring trust between you. You request a meeting regarding a significant potential redevelopment of a shopping centre. He responds in one hour, proposing a meeting time the next week. The pinch is that you have only 30 minutes to convince senior staff of the proposal.

The next step is to send a comprehensive project brief that presents the site analysis, seven precedent project studies, and three concept alternatives. Choice is a key aspect of any discussion. Give a group a choice and they are engaged in the conversation. No choices tend to create a defensive response. Choices give people alternatives and then it is in their power to choose, and therefore become part of the project. They have their finger in the pie and become 'makers' of the proposal.

---

[72] Sun Tzu, *The Art of War*, 10.

The day of the meeting comes with some anticipation. The 'what ifs' come to mind and start spinning scenarios. Your group walks into the meeting and it is a warm hello with small talk to start the conversation and break the ice. Your vice-president provides an overview of the company and its intentions. The company has a good and trusted track record in the city. The Vice-President is down to earth in his delivery and brings with him seasoned experience in construction. You then quickly provide a brief overview of the development proposal, hitting the high points and the three options. There is silence which seems to go on forever, though it is actually only a brief few seconds.

The manager in charge of development applications simply says, "I like the second intermediate density option; it fits the site. What support do you need? We will help you through this process. We can proceed with this project when you are ready."

You almost fall off your chair in disbelief. Stop the timer—28 minutes! You shake hands and leave the meeting. The deal is done, though the work is just beginning.

This event happened to me not long ago in the City of Calgary, a city that normally has its own development process challenges, not unlike many municipalities throughout Canada.

In reviewing the scenario, we can see there is almost a predictable outcome based on specific facts, preparation, and relationships:

1. Proven relationships.
2. Right site and policy support.
3. Comprehensive review and study.
4. Proven and trusted developer.
5. Choices in development options.
6. Directed meeting with agenda.
7. Specific outcomes and directions.

Keep these elements in mind when you plan for your next meeting with the municipality or regional district. Staff will respect your preparation and the invitation to review an informed proposal. As I stated in this book's introduction, if you use the same old processes you will get the same old results. Be prepared and come with intent.

A Framework for Change Now

This book's proposed *Approvals+* approach is a more interactive and rigorous alternative to the hit and miss process we largely practice now. Nevertheless, this clinical, yet dynamically engaging and agile *Approvals+* process will hopefully inspire a re-examination and improvement of our current processes.

For seasoned professionals who largely know this process now and use a modified version, I commend them for their continued success. Hopefully, even given their knowledge and abilities, the ideas in this book will spawn improvement.

For less seasoned professionals who regard applications and approvals as just a 'check the box' process, and who have run into significant issues, these discussions will hopefully provide information to help them navigate approvals with more wisdom and better tools.

Perhaps this book is right now being read by someone who is only beginning to look at the applications and approvals process. In that case, this book's goal is to open your eyes to new pathways and show you the reasons certain things work, and other things don't.

Maybe most importantly, these examinations provide the groundwork for common understanding of where the approval process can be improved, and how to work together to do so. One thing is certain, applications and approvals processes will probably not get any simpler as more variables and standards, as well as regulations, enter the picture.

The challenge continues, as numerous municipalities are searching for efficiencies and ways to reduce time and resources. The Urban Development Institute has liaison committees to support those efforts.

I remember in 1991, almost 30 years ago, when the city of Vancouver planning department was going through a development review process and the then-current process was a labyrinth that covered almost a full office end wall! The stacks of policies and regulations have not shrunk but expanded, and the consulting teams for developers have expanded accordingly. From building envelope specialists, to arborists for tree assessments, to third-party economists to determine community amenity contributions … the list keeps growing. These additional costs are embedded in the development proforma and, by some arguments, are passed onto the consumer. And we wonder why we have an affordability crisis!

But these are complaints rather than solutions. It is so easy to be the critic rather than the opportunist who solves the problem. In essence, that is the spirit of the true developer. Let's really start working together, not only through committees and as advisors, but as citizens with a common goal—creating communities that sing!

Being the Change

I made a change 20 years ago that transformed my life and lifestyle. Leaving an exhausting and unhealthy commute to Vancouver, I combined consulting with teaching from my home studio. In so doing, I also built a virtual global consulting team and started to do what I wanted to do—to be an innovative creator and contributor to great community building.

There are so many municipalities and regional districts doing such great work across Canada. There are also many developers and builders making great efforts to execute complex plans. Then there are the neighbourhoods that are taking more interest in what happens in their communities. With directed and constructive energy, only good things come.

Langley City is thinking ahead, as are so many other communities. In 2019, they created a NEXUS strategy that framed a vision and direction for their community. They are now acting on it through official community plan and zoning bylaw updates that will further transform their community.

They are being proactive and visioning forward to a compact, self-sufficient, resilient community that welcomes Skytrain or a similar rapid transit system to their front door. They will be redesignating areas of the city in anticipation of residential density and height, yet will place transit in appropriate locations with transitions and connections to lower scale areas.

This kind of proactive process anticipates and invites the right development in the right place. The adjoining communities are aware well ahead of detailed plans, and sometimes are active supporters of what is being proposed. A supportive environment, a transparent process, and mutually beneficial results are collectively faster, cheaper, and value-added.

In closing, I want to leave you with 10 touchstones that summarize our discussions and will help you create gateways to approvals, rather than walls.

Ten Closing Touchstones

1. **Select the right property:** Find the right piece of land that matches your principles and goals.

2. **Do your due diligence:** Ensure that your diagnostics and due diligence are sound and ground-proofed.

3. **Expand relationships:** Meet early and often with the municipal or regional district staff and council, as well as trusted community members.

4. **Review policy and make no assumptions:** Do not assume policy can be changed. Review emerging policy through conversations with staff and council.

5. **Get to the power behind the who and why of approvals:** Find who holds the power, and who the influencers in the approvals process for your project are.

6. **Recruit a locally anchored team and a trusted third party:** Select a team with local knowledge and experience that will bring additional, practical insights to the process. A separate, objective third party coach is also important, so that local relationships do not cloud potential opportunities.

7. **Build value in every step:** Eliminate barriers to approvals, and you will build value in the property by eliminating risk factors and limitations.

8. **Expect the unexpected, and structure with anticipated agility:** Act on unexpected discoveries or changes with informed, humble confidence so they do not become crisis points, but management opportunities to build more value.

9. **Listen to your brain, not your heart—but trust your gut**: Avoid falling in love with a property (hard to do) if it has undeniable limitations and associated risk.

10. **Let go if necessary**: Pre-determine important management criteria and pre-set exit strategies that could still deem the project venture a success.

We have discovered both existing and new pathways on our journey. The existing pathways are full of barriers and opportunities, even those we cannot see. Depending on the project, we can choose the best route that matches our specific circumstances. We can think two steps ahead, and plan together.

Let's improve processes enroute and add value for everyone where possible. We will create awesome communities as a result. This exciting task lies ahead. Embrace it and do something that exceeds even your own expectations. In so doing, you will discover *new pathways* to success.

APPENDIX A

ACQUISITION COMPREHENSIVE CHECKLIST

CONTENTS

ACQUISITION COMPREHENSIVE CHECKLIST

Purpose and Scope

The purpose of this appendix is to provide a comprehensive checklist of items to review prior to property acquisition. It is a summary workbook of what are deemed to be the most important elements fundamental to an investment decision. In the final analysis, it is a tool to measure the level of risk associated with a property acquisition.

This checklist is a tool, not an end. The recommendations are intended to inform the senior management team and their partners as to the merits and detractors of a particular potential acquisition. It is not meant to structure or determine final acquisition decisions.

Checklist Guide

- Every item is critical to measure the viability and risk associated with a given property.
- Ensure that you fill out every line. If the line is not applicable, place a N/A and ensure that it is not applicable.
- Be careful with your prejudices and presumptions. Back up your answers with verifiable information or evidence that supports the response (provide references and websites).
- Obtain two or three sources of information to ensure that the information reflects the real and projected trend lines (e.g., market data triangulation).
- Add reference information and proof to this checklist document as attachments (e.g., market information, maps, and appraisals).
- Ensure that all individuals involved with the evaluation are documented, and the sources of information, phone numbers, emails, and website references are cited for further scrutiny and due diligence.
- Check your sources and measure three times before you come to the best answer.
- Note in yellow highlight those areas that need more investigation.
- Finally, obtain the most information possible, as you want to find whether the property fits the criteria for acquisition (e.g., risk profile, location, size, and uses) or not.

A. SUMMARY OF FINDINGS

1. **Date(s) of review:**_____ first: _____ second: _____ final: _____
2. **Name of project (locator and identifier):**_____
3. **Contact(s) and email/phone numbers:**_____
4. **Location and development potential description:**_____
5. **Price, terms, project summary, and recommendations:**_____
6. **Risk analysis summary and gap analysis** (Why is this proposition the best option? What information or partner is still missing? What requirements do we need to make for the deal to work for us?) _____
7. **Project analysis status:**

	Underway	Complete
b. Land use (current and potential)	☐	☐
c. Market (macro analysis and local analysis)	☐	☐
d. Legal (liens, rights-of ways, access, property ownership)	☐	☐
e. Finance (partners, outstanding obligations, financial status)	☐	☐
f. Corporate partners covenant (reputation, track record)	☐	☐
g. Environmental (noise, riparian areas, contamination)	☐	☐
h. Geotechnical (soils, hazards, extraordinary costs)	☐	☐
i. Climate Change (flood levels, grade change, fill requirements)	☐	☐
j. Transportation (access, capacity, improvements)	☐	☐
k. Water (off-site and on-site)	☐	☐
l. Sanitary Sewer (off-site and on-site)	☐	☐
m. Stormwater (off-site and on-site)	☐	☐
n. First Nations (rights, interests, archeological findings)	☐	☐
o. Pro forma cash flow (back of envelope, detailed)	☐	☐
p. Valuations: Current and past appraisals and comparables	☐	☐

B. BASIS DATA

1. **Owner:**____
2. **Size of property (ha/acres):**________________________________
3. **Current use of land:**_____________________________________
   ____
4. **Current income and leases?**________________________________
   ____
5. **Current taxation on lands and assumed assessments?**________________
   ____
6. **Legal description of the land:**______________________________
   ____
7. **Special information about owner:**____________________________
8. **Price and terms:**____
   ____
9. **Source of lead and real estate broker fees:**_____________________
10. **Could joint owners or family affect the sale?**____________________
11. **Is it urgent to tie up the land quickly (option or otherwise)?**__________
    ____
12. **If the owner is a public agency what is the procedure for sale?**__________
    ____
    ____
13. **Will the owner want to control what we develop or put on the land?**______
    ____
14. **Does the owner want to be a partner in the project and under what conditions?**
    ____
    ____
15. **Will the owner allow access to the property?**_____________________
16. **Will the seller indemnify purchaser or certify no contamination or toxic waste?**____
    ____
17. **Are there First Nations claims (or interests) on the lands?**_____________
    ____
18. **Should a separate entity (new company) take title to the land?**__________
    ____
19. **Planning designation and zoning:**____________________________
20. **Subdivision, development permit, building permit status:**_____________
    ____
    ____
21. **Notes:**____
22. **Special conditions:**______________________________________

C. EXISTING LIENS AND OTHER RESTRICTIONS

1. **First lien:**____

2. **Second lien:**____

3. **Other liens:**____

4. **Can liens be assumed or removed?**________________________________

5. **Existing restrictions:**____

   Use restrictions:____

   Building restrictions (riparian setbacks, highway setbacks, contamination, conservation areas):________________________________

   Architectural restrictions (height, form, massing, character):____________

   Lot size restrictions:____

   Other restrictions (rights-of-way, easements, floodplain, hazards, future highway expansion plans or public works etc.):________________________

   Can these restrictions be removed or changed and under what conditions (explain each restriction and removal or alteration potential)**?**

6. **Any other agreements affecting the land or buildings** (long term leases etc.):

D. PHYSICAL ANALYSIS

1. **Site visit(s) date(s):**____________________
2. **Elevation(s) and views from land** (north, south, east, west):____________________
3. **Topographical and aerial mapping** (historical digital mapping available and accurate):____________________
4. **Survey for property and adjoining lands** (noting parcels, exact dimensions, areas, easements and rights-of-ways, power lines etc.):____________________
5. **Adjoining land uses and patterns** (smells, noises, compatible use, sun, shadow, railway tracks, heavy industry, truck routes, high water table, fire hazard, air traffic and proximity, power lines):____________________
6. **Roads and streets conditions and improvement requirements** (existing, access, capacity, rights-of-ways, and future plans):____________________
7. **Do mineral rights go with the land and implications?**____________________
8. **Site drainage issues** (too flat, too steep and debris flow issues off-site):__________
9. **Contamination report and possibilities verified** (smells, adjoining landfills, evidence of dumping):____________________
10. **Servicing available on site** (water, sanitary sewer, stormwater, and other utilities):____________________

    Potable water (capacity and upgrades/costs):____________________

    Sanitary sewer (capacity and upgrades/costs):____________________

Stormwater (capacity and upgrades/costs):

Other utilities (gas, fiber optic, electrical capacities, upgrades, and costs):

11. **If servicing is not available on site, then what are the requirements** (costs, distances and off-site improvements required)**?**

12. **Are archeological studies available and are there any signs of First Nations activities or history** (talk to the local people)?

13. **Is there any environmental mapping available for the property** (check planning policy documentation and any previous adjoining applications for information)**?**

    Water courses and setbacks:

    Wetlands and setbacks:

    Hazard areas and setbacks:

    Rare plant community and wildlife preservation areas:

14. **Is there any information on soils and associated reports and implications?**

15. **Is the area affected by heritage conservation policies** (check planning policies for landscapes and buildings)?

16. **Earthquake implications:**

17. **Climate change implications** (minimum flood levels and building requirements)**:**

E. GOVERNMENT POLICY AND REGULATIONS

1. **Primary approval agencies** (planning and subdivision):________________
2. **Overall regional growth management plan** (e.g., regional growth strategy and associated policies for growth and locations):________________
3. **Current land use** (conforming or non-forming to current policy):__________
4. **Official plan designation:**________________
5. **Current zoning** (uses, details of setbacks, height, FSR/FAR):__________
6. **Are there other current or anticipated policies that apply (**e.g., green building, sustainability checklist, etc.)?________________
7. **What is the possibility of official plan changes and rezoning to a more desirable use** (political support, community support and staff support)?
8. **What is the proposed highest and best use** (most appropriate use for the land from the jurisdiction's perspective; talk to the planning department)?_______
9. **On-site and off-site amenity package requirements** (detail please):_______
10. **Engineering on-site and off-site improvements** (additional road widening and dedications, servicing upgrades, and other infrastructure):________________
11. **Costs of applications from official plan to rezoning and others:**__________
12. **Other applicable fees and dedications** (school, park and other):__________

13. **Project approvals and projected timeframe** (6 months; 12 months; 24 months):
    a. Municipal approval requirements:
        i. OCP Amendment: Y/N______________________
        ii. Zoning amendment: Y/N______________________
        iii. Development permit: Y/N______________________
        iv. Building permit: Y/N______________________
        v. Plan of subdivision: Y/N______________________
    b. Other special permissions (if any): Y/N______________________
    c. Provincial approvals:
        i. Transportation (roads/streets): Y/N______________________
        ii. Environment: Y/N (soil contamination/site profile; wildlife/plants/trees) ______________________
        iii. Archeological survey (First Nations and other): Y/N ______________
        iv. Other (specify): Y/N______________________
    d. Federal Approvals:
        i. Fisheries and oceans (water lot use; water course setbacks/ wetlands): Y/N______________________
        ii. Other (specify): Y/N______________________
    e. Other Approvals: Y/N (CN or CP Rail Crossings)______________
14. **Off-site and on-site infrastructure status and approvals:**
    a. Water: ______________________
    b. Sanitary sewer:______________________
    c. Stormwater:______________________
    d. Electricity/gas:______________________
    e. Other utilities:______________________
15. **Notes on approvals and support/process requirements:**______________
    ____
    ____

F. MARKET ANALYSIS

1. **Regional (macro) analysis:**
   - Regional/provincial growth:
   - Employment projections:
2. **Regional housing supply and demand analysis:**
   - Supply trends
   - Demand trends
   - Housing prices in specific segments
   - Niche markets
3. **Local market trends and demands:**
   - Supply trends
   - Demand trends
   - Housing prices in specific segments
   - Niche markets
   - Competition and sales patterns
4. **Market positioning:**
   - Target markets
   - Competitive advantages
   - Site location and merits
   - Proximity to facilities and amenities
   - Projected absorption rates
5. **Product offering:**
   - Product types
   - Unique type and site development qualities
   - Marketing strategies

G. PRO FORMA ANALYSIS

1. **Revenue/costing assumptions and sources of information** (state source, date and comparables):____

   ____

2. **Revenue projections** (escalation rates)?____________________________

   Residential units/sizes/ projected revenue/square foot

   ____

   Commercial revenue/cap rates comparable in market

   ____

   Other source of revenue (recreation amenity etc.)

   ____

3. **Costs**____

   Hard costs:

   Land (appraised value or cost?)

   Construction estimate: Need for detailed architectural construction, engineering sewer, water, stormwater, cut and fill, clear and grub, landscape architecture, site grading, streets construction, parks and recreation improvements, wetlands and stream restoration, storm drainage etc.)

   Soft costs: (a minimum 30% and up to 60% of hard costs)

   Permit fees (list all of them including amenity contribution fees)

   - Consultants Marketing
   - Finance
   - Development management fee
   - Contingency

4. **Profit**____

   Simple returns: (target of 15% to 20% minimum)

   Return on cost; Return on revenue

   (Optional: Return on equity)

   Dynamic Returns

   - Internal rate of return (IRR)
   - Net present value (NPV)

H. VALUATIONS

1. **What evaluations for value have there been on the property?**

2. **Appraisal(s) on property and assumptions?**

3. **Current comparables:**

4. **Highest and best use (most appropriate use) projected evaluation:**

   Land use scenario 1:

   Land use scenario 2:

   Land use scenario 3:

5. **Proposed best purchase price potential:**

I. ATTACHMENTS

This section should at least include:

- Location mapping including regional, local and site.
- Site survey, if available.
- Site aerial photography.
- Official community plan designation mapping and context.
- Zoning bylaw mapping and context.
- Market information and value proposition.
- Valuations (costing, pro forma and appraisals).

APPENDIX B

BUILDING AGREEMENT THROUGH A CONSENSUAL PROCESS

1. *Initiate* collective action by making a suggestion (*a clear proposal*—any participant).
2. If you (other stakeholder) don't agree with the recommendation made, respond by offering a specific *amendment.* Quickly name the concern behind your amendment. More importantly, identify how the change you propose to the original proposal will clearly address that concern and make the proposal stronger in implementation.

   (Don't just defer to particular individuals, small group dictatorship, or majority rule. And avoid 'plops'—suggestions that land on the floor and go nowhere because others fail to respond.)

3. (All participants) Save your breath when it comes to telling people why you *don't* agree. Tell them instead why you think your amendment will be an improvement. And for participants who like a proposal, don't use up the airtime in cheerleading. Focus instead on listening to, and helping to resolve, others' concerns. *Park* impatience—and use *inquiry* skills to deepen understanding.
4. (Facilitator) After a proposal has been discussed, *check* for unanimous support. Ask if there is anyone who *cannot* support the proposal (rather than asking who likes it). Give time to those who have concerns rather than to those already convinced of the proposal's value.
5. *Repeat* the procedures if necessary, i.e., use the expression of concerns to identify possible improvements. Then begin the initiation cycle by incorporating those changes and presenting a revised proposal. Ask again if there is anyone who cannot support the proposal.
6. If you don't agree with the improved plan and cannot propose specific revisions, offer *an alternative proposal.* (This step only happens here—not as step #2.)
7. (Facilitator) Conduct a *straw vote* to make visible how the group is split. To the group: Indicate which proposal—A or B—is, in your view, the strongest proposal. If different groups are attracted to different proposals (i.e., there is not just one lone advocate of a contrary proposal), consider allowing each group *caucus* time. Ask them to use this time to prepare a presentation to identify the *relative* strengths of their approach. Arrange for *one spokesperson from each group* to address the entire team (following the caucus time).

8. (Facilitator and participants) Look for possible ways to merge proposals without diluting strength. (If it is not yet possible to integrate the suggestions into one proposal, ask people to consider the distinct proposals in light of the additional information presented, and to identify their *proposal preference*.)
9. Working with the proposal that is supported by the largest number of people in the room, ask again for people who are *not* willing to support it to identify specific concerns. *Call* for help from all to use that information to improve the proposal.
10. *Remind people what consensus is.* It is an agreement that all people involved in negotiating the agreement can uphold—an acknowledgement by each person that s/he 'can live with' the proposal. It can range from ecstatic embrace of a proposal to grudging acceptance. It does not mean the evaporation of all reservations, but it *is* an agreement to *not* sabotage actions that are congruent with the stated proposal. It is a compromise that results from consideration of all participants' interests.

    If, through repeated cycles of these procedures, agreement is still not reached, refocus discussion to a new question: *What might help the group reach agreement?* Taking a short break, reviewing the proposal with other stakeholders, confirming information, or undertaking further research might be useful next steps that will lead quickly to consensus in a follow-up meeting. Considering *consequences* (short-term, long-term, and for various groups of people) may also help individuals break through to a new understanding with one another and an agreement with 'sticking power'. Considering *while staying together as a group* the consequences of *no* agreement and taking *no* united action can also be very helpful at this stage.

Adopted from Holland, Sylvia and von Hausen, Michael, *Public Process Playbook.* [73]

[73] Holland, Sylvia, and Michael von Hausen, *Public Process Playbook*, Vancouver: SFU 2007, 83

ACKNOWLEDGEMENTS

I would like to thank all those organizations and individuals who helped me refine my countless drafts, and who helped ensure the accuracy in the content of this book. Their care and support through this process is appreciated beyond words. My good friend and teaching colleague, Dave Witty, has always been there as a mentor and close friend. He was one of the first people to say I should pursue this book, and he reviewed early drafts.

I would also like to acknowledge the contributions of specific individuals to the content and review of this book including Mike Harcourt, Ken Cameron, Gordon Harris, Susan Haid, Judy Oberlander, Andy Yan, Deana Grinnell, David Bouskill, Bob Ransford, Michael Geller, Pamela Shaw, Jeff Cook, Mark Holland, Hugh Carter, Gordon Price, Gerry Mulholland, Aeron Cheng, David Eger, David Gordon, and Gary Pooni.

Many thanks as well to Ann McMullin, Chief Executive Officer, Urban Development Institute Pacific Region, for her strong support for the FortisBC School of Development as it continues to grow and mature. Yvonne Lo and Jeff Fisher have also been great supporters of the FortisBC School of Development, and also contributed to this book with their continuous encouragement and support. Further, I would like to thank FortisBC for their continuing, rock-solid support for UDI's FortisBC School of Development.

A big thank you goes to the City Program at Simon Fraser University, and to Andy Yan, Director; Joshua Randall, Program Coordinator; and Ryan Noakes, Program Assistant for their continuing innovation, direction, and contributions during these challenging times. My editor and book designer at Tellwell have both remained steadfast and committed throughout the book-making process. They provided the clarity and composition expertise that have given it a professional look and tone. Thanks to my publisher, Tellwell, for their timely response and ongoing commitment.

Finally, to my daughter, Athena, who continues to share her professional planner wisdom with me and the world, and my wife, Laura, who has given me endless wisdom and support throughout our life-long partnership. And lastly, thanks go to my grandson Jackson, who constantly sheds new light and inspiration on things that may appear obvious, but are brilliant in their own right.

BIBLIOGRAPHY

Auerbach, Herb. *Placemakers: A Brief History of Real Estate Development.* Vancouver, BC: Figure 1 Publishing, 2016.

Beasley, Larry. *Vancouverism.* Vancouver, BC: UBC Press, 2019.

Beaton, William R. *Real Estate Investment.* New Jersey: Prentice-Hall, 1977.

Berridge, Joe. *Perfect City: An Urban Fixer's Global Search for Magic in the Modern Metropolis.* Toronto: Sutherland House, 2018.

Blanchard, Ken. *Leading at a Higher Level.* New Jersey: Prentice Hall, 2007.

Carnegie, Dale. *How to Win Friends & Influence People.* New York: Gallery Books, 1981.

Caro, Robert A. *The Power Broker: Robert Moses and the Fall of New York.* New York: Vintage Books, 1975.

Daniels, P.S. and Stephen G. Hyslop. *Almanac of World History.* Washington: National Geographic, 1994.

Covey, Stephen. *The Seven Habits of Highly Successful People: Powerful Lessons in Personal Change.* New York: Simon & Shuster, 1989.

———. *The Third Alternative: Solving Life's Most Difficult Problems.* New York: Simon & Shuster, 2011.

———. *Great Quotes on Leadership and Life.* Naperville: Sourcebooks, 2013.

———. *Primary Greatness: The 12 Levers of Success.* New York: Simon & Shuster, 2015.

Duany, Andrés, Elizabeth Plater-Zyberk, and Jeff Speck. *Suburban Nation: The Rise of Sprawl and the Decline of the American Dream.* New York: North Point Press, 2000.

Duany, Andrés, Jeff Speck, and Mike Lydon. *The Smart Growth Manual.* New York: McGraw-Hill, 2010.

Eppli, Mark J. and Charles C. Chu. *Valuing the New Urbanism: The Impact of the New Urbanism on Prices of Single-Family Homes.* Washington, D.C.: ULI, 1999.

Ewing, Reid, MaryBeth DeAnna, Christine C. Heflin, and Douglas R. Porter. *Best Development Practices: Doing the Right Thing and Making Money at the Same Time.* Chicago: American Planning Association Planners Press, 1996.

Fisher, Roger, and William Ury. *Getting to Yes: Negotiating Agreement Without Giving In.* New York: Penguin Books, 1983.

Florida, Richard. *Who's Your City? How the Creative Economy Is Making Where You Live the Most Important Decision of Your Life.* Toronto: Random House Canada, 2008.

Gardner, David. *Closing Shot.* Toronto, ReNew Canada: March/April 2020, p.42.

Gladwell, Malcolm. *The Tipping Point: How Little Things Make a Difference.* New York: Little, Brown & Company, 2000.

———. *Blink: The Power of Thinking Without Thinking.* New York: Little, Brown & Company, 2005.

———. *Outliers: The Story of Success.* New York: Little, Brown & Company, 2008.

———. *Talking to Strangers: What We Should Know About the People We Don't Know.* New York: Little, Brown & Company, 2019.

Glaeser, Edward. *Triumph of the City: How Our Greatest Invention Makes Us Richer, Smarter, Greener, Healthier, and Happier.* New York: Penguin Books, 2011.

Goldenberg, Susan. *Men of Property: The Canadian Developers Who Are Buying America.* Toronto: Personal Library, 1981.

Goldman, Daniel. *Social Intelligence: The New Science of Human Relationships.* New York: Bantam Dell, 2006.

Haden, Bruce, Mark Holland, and Bruce Irvine. *Urban Magnets: How Activity Subcultures Can Be a Catalyst for Rejuvenating Cities.* Vancouver, BC: Page Two Books, 2020.

Harcourt, Mike, Ken Cameron, and Sean Rossiter. *City Making in Paradise: Nine Decisions that Saved Vancouver.* Vancouver, BC: Douglas & McIntyre, 2007.

Harris, Gordon, and Richard Littlemore. *Building Community: Defining, Designing, Developing UniverCity.* Seattle: Ecotone, 2018.

Hoggan, James. *Do the Right Thing: PR Tips for a Sceptical Public.* Herndon: Capital Books, 2009.

Hodge, Gerald, David Gordon and Pamela Shaw. *Planning Canadian Communities: An Introduction to the Principles, Practice, and Participants.* 7th ed. Toronto: Nelson, 2020.

Holland, Sylvia, and Michael von Hausen. *Public Process Playbook.* Vancouver, BC: Simon Fraser University, 2007.

Housing Vancouver Strategy: Annual Progress Report and Data Book 2019. City of Vancouver, Housing Vancouver, 2019.

Jacobs, Jane. *The Death and Life of Great American Cities.* New York: Random House, 1961.

———. *The Economy of Cities.* New York: Random House, 1969.

———. *Cities and the Wealth of Nations.* New York: Random House, 1984.

———. *Dark Age Ahead.* New York: Random House, 2004.

Jahren, Hope. *The Story of More: How We Got to Climate Change and Where Do We Go from Here.* Toronto: Vintage Canada, 2020.

Jarvis, Frederick D. *Site Planning and Community Design.* Washington: Home Builder Press, 1993.

Jensen, David. *How to Win at the Zoning Table.* Washington: National Association of Home Builders, 1984.

Joseph, Bob and Cynthia F. Joseph. *Indigenous Relations: Insights, Tips & Suggestions to Make Reconciliation a Reality.* Vancouver: Indigenous Press/Page Two Books, 2019.

Kunstler, James Howard. *The Geography of Nowhere: The Rise and Decline of America's Man-Made Landscape.* New York: Touchstone, 1993.

———. *The Long Emergency: Surviving the Converging Catastrophes of the Twenty-First Century.* New York: Atlantic Monthly, 2005.

———. *Living in the Long Emergency: Global Crisis, the Failure of the Futurists, and the Early Adapters Who Are Showing Us the Way Forward.* Dallas: BenBella, 2020.

Lencioni, Patrick. *The Five Dysfunctions of a Team: A Leadership Fable*. San Francisco: Jossey-Bass, 2002.

Lemire, Robert A. *Creative Land Development*. Boston: Houghton Mifflin, 1979.

Maxwell, John C. *The 21 Indispensable Qualities of a Leader.* Nashville: Thomas Nelson, 1999.

Ministry of Municipal Affairs and Housing. *Development Approvals Process Re*view. Victoria: Province of British Columbia, 2019.

Ministry of Municipal Affairs and Housing. *Homes for B.C.: A 30-Point for Housing Affordability in British Columbia.* Victoria: Province of British Columbia, February 2018.

Montgomery, Charles. *Happy City*. Toronto: Anchor Canada, 2014.

National Association of Home Builders. *Financing Land Acquisition and Development.* Washington: National Association of Home Builders of the United States, 1987.

Punter, John. *The Vancouver Achievement: Urban Planning and Design*. Vancouver, BC: UBC Press, 2003.

Peiser, Richard B. and Anne B. Frej. *Professional Real Estate Development: The ULI Guide to the Business.* Second Edition. Washington, DC: ULI, 2003.

Rybczynski, Witold. *The Last Harvest: From Cornfield to New Town*. New York: Scribner, 2008.

Rocky Mountain Institute. *Green Development: Integrating Ecology and Real Estate.* New York: John Wiley & Sons, 1998.

Rollo, Paul. *The Tools of Real Estate Investment Analysis.* Vancouver: Simon Fraser University, 2009.

Saul, John Ralston. *The Comeback.* Toronto: Penguin, 2014.

School of Architecture and Landscape Architecture. *Imagining an Affordable Vancouver for 2060.* Vancouver: University of British Columbia, 2020.

Sipe, James W. and Don M. Frick. *Seven Pillars of Servant Leadership: Practicing the Wisdom of Leading by Serving.* New York: Paulist Press, 2009.

Schmitz, Adrienne, and Deborah L. Brett. *Real Estate Market Analysis: A Case Study Approach*. Washington, D.C.: ULI, 2001.

Sturgeon, Amanda. *Creating Biophilic Buildings.* Seattle: Ecotone Publishing, 2017.

Relationships London: School of Life, 2016.

Value in Urban Design London: Commission for Architecture and the Built Environment; Department of Environment, Transport and the Regions, 2001.

Tzu, Sun. *The Art of War.* Translated by Thomas Cleary. Boston: Shambhala, 1991.

Von Hausen, Michael A. *Real Estate Economics in Urban Design: The Role of Civic Economics in Place-Making.* Vancouver, BC: Simon Fraser University, 2004.

———. *Dynamic Urban Design: A Handbook for Creating Sustainable Communities Worldwide.* Bloomington: iUniverse, 2013.

———. *Small is Big: Making the Next Great Small to Mid-Size Downtowns.* Nanaimo: Vancouver Island University, 2018.

Vancouver Social Indicators Profile 2019. City of Vancouver Social Policy and Projects, Vancouver: 2019.

Urban Development Institute, Pacific Region. *State of the Market Quarterly Market Research Report*. Vancouver: May 2020.

Ury, William. *Getting Past No: Negotiating Your Way from Confrontation to Cooperation*. New York: Bantam Books, 1993.

———. *The Power of a Positive No: How to Say No and Still Say Yes*. New York: Bantam Books, 2007.

Whitehead, Jim. *Real Estate Development*. Vancouver: Sauder School of Business, UBC, 2008.

Wickman, Gino. *Traction: Get a Grip on Your Business*. Dallas: BenBella, 2011.

GLOSSARY OF TERMS

Affordable housing. Accessible, adequate housing available at a cost that does not compromise the attainment and satisfaction of an individual's other basic needs. Occupant needs can be cost-effectively met by quality design if identified early in the process. Affordable housing in a general sense can be partially satisfied by providing a diversity of housing types and tenures. In the strict sense of the word, affordable housing can be defined as not exceeding 30 percent of the household income (Canada Mortgage and Housing Corporation).

Amenities. Community amenities improve the livability of an area, and can include parks, libraries, community or recreation centres, community performing arts centres, streetscape improvements, greenways, daycare space, or community space.

Area Plan (also normally referred to as a 'neighbourhood plan', but may be more general in content). These types of plans provide further details on a specific area as a subset of the official community plan, and include land uses, specific policies, objectives, and sometimes development permit guidelines. These areas have a specific vision developed with the community that includes particular housing types, densities, and environmentally sensitive areas, as well as cycling and pedestrian networks among other amenities.

BC Building Code. The BC Building Code is a provincially regulated document that contains regulations regarding the health and safety aspects of building construction. The Code specifies minimum standards of building requirements including structural integrity, fire safety, plumbing, heating, ventilation, energy efficiency, and many other aspects of building construction. It is the responsibility of the property owner/builder to ensure that the building construction is in compliance with the Code.

Building Efficiency. The ratio of useable or leasable building area to gross building area expressed as a percentage. For example, the average efficiency of an office building is 85 to 90 percent. That is, the common area and other space that is not leasable takes up 10 to 15 percent in this case.

Built form. Buildings and structures that represent the three-dimensional man-made components of urban design.

Capitalization Rate. The ratio of net operating income to sales price of comparable income producing properties. Dividing the net operating income by the capitalization rate yields an estimated property value.

Cash Flow. Annual or monthly net income received from an income-producing property by taking the gross revenue, then subtracting operating costs and mortgage payments (see also Discounted Cash Flow).

Cash on Cash or Return on Equity. Net operating income—subtract mortgage payments and divide by equity investment.

Cluster Development. A rural development concept that groups houses or buildings together to conserve open space and natural resources.

Coach house. A self-contained dwelling unit located by the back lane, normally above a garage or carport and not to exceed a maximum area (for example, 60 m^2 (645 square feet).

Community. A group of people living in a particular locality who share government and often have a common cultural and historical heritage. Normally, a community can consist of several smaller neighborhoods and represent a sector of the city or larger community.

Community amenity contribution (CAC). CACs are a contribution made by a developer when City Council approves specific types of rezoning applications. The CAC is either a flat rate per square metre or a negotiated amount based on the increase in land value (percentage of land lift) as a result of rezoning. The CAC is used to fund amenity improvements in the area.

Comprehensive development zone (CD). A land use area that requires additional consideration and sensitivity to the future use and development of land or buildings within this area.

Concept. A general notion or idea that creates the basis for further detailed design.

Connections. The linkages within the community that bring together and move pedestrians, bicycles, vehicles, etc., from one area to another.

Council. The governing body of the city or municipality. In regional districts in British Columbia, the approving council are the board of directors. The approving authority in rural areas is the Ministry of Transportation and Infrastructure for subdivision.

Current Dollar Analysis. Financial analysis that takes into account inflation on revenue and costs over many years.

Discounted Cash Flow. Annual cash flows are forecast and then discounted or present valued for use in determining net present value and internal rate of return. This technique is useful to compare different investments over the short, medium and long terms.

Density. The number of dwelling units on a site expressed in dwelling units per acre or units per hectare. Density can also be expressed by floor area ratio (FAR) or in some jurisdictions floor space ratio (FSR). FAR means the quotient of the gross floor area of a building divided by the gross site area. FAR is one of the ways to control the size or density of a building in relation to the size of the parcel of land it occupies. See the examples below. The building may also be regulated by building setbacks (i.e., front yard, side yard, and rear yard), building height, site or lot coverage or landscaping, parking, etc., depending on different land use districts or zones. *See also Floor area ratio.*

FAR demonstration: A lot area of 30.48 m (100 feet) by 32.81 m (107.6 feet) has a gross site area of 1,000 m^2 (10,764 square feet). Development potential based on FAR:

FAR 1 = 1,000 m^2 (10,764 sq. ft) x 1 floor = 1,000 m^2 (10,764 sq. ft) of gross floor area

FAR 2 = 1,000 m^2 (10,764 sq. ft) x 2 floors = 2,000 m^2 (21,528 sq. ft) of gross floor area

FAR 3 = 1,000 m^2 (10,764 sq. ft) x 3 floors = 3,000 m^2 (32,292 sq. ft) of gross floor area

Density Bonus. Density Bonus is an optional financial contribution made by a developer when City Council approves additional density at the time of rezoning. The amount of the financial contribution is specified in the Zoning Bylaw. The financial contribution is a portion of the increase in land value as a result of rezoning.

Design charrette. An intensive series of meetings, workshops, and presentations with multiple stakeholders and experts to advance innovative ideas.

Development cost charges (DCC). DCCs are fees on all new development paid either per housing unit or per square metre of new development. DCC rates are set citywide by Council and Provincial legislation controls what DCCs can be spent on. Currently, DCCs can be spent on streets, water and sewer utilities, new parks, greenways, and storm drainage infrastructure.

Development permit. A document authorizing a development, issued by the approving officer pursuant to the zoning bylaw or any previous bylaw or other legislation authorizing development within the city, and which includes the plans and conditions of approval. The Development Permit controls the form and character of a proposed new building and ensures it meets the standards and requirements of the particular zone. Those areas within a Development Permit Area have special requirements and guidelines that direct the form and character of development.

District. An area identified by a distinguishing feature such as land use, heritage, cultural, and/or any other significant characteristic.

Effective Gross Income. Gross operating income less vacancy.

Enhancement. The augmentation of an area, street, or open space in quality, value, beauty, or effectiveness.

Equity. The investor's money that must be invested in the project. Equity is determined by total project cost minus financing.

Financing (Construction): Financing for the interim construction period.

Financing (Long Term or Take-Out Financing). Financing for longer term once the income property is sufficiently leased.

Floor area ratio (FAR) or floor space ratio (FSR). The quotient of the gross floor area of a building divided by the gross site area. FAR is the ratio of the building to the lot area. For example, if the building area covers 100 percent of the site with one floor, that equals 1.0 FAR. Alternatively, if the building area covers half the site with two floors, it is still 1.0 FAR. The calculation is total square feet (m^2) of building (area of building) divided by the area of the site. In some jurisdictions FAR is referred to as floor space ratio (FSR). *See also Density.*

Greenfrastructure: A description of infrastructure elements that can be designed where possible to mimic natural systems such as rainwater, natural planting, wastewater, and potable water systems.

Heritage Overlay District. The Downtown Heritage Overlay District is intended to create a specific area that recognizes the importance of significant buildings and landscapes that should be further considered for conservation, enhancement, and recognition within an area. The extent of conservation, enhancement, and recognition will be determined by further regulations and design guidelines with a specific plan, as well as further work in identifying the specific significance of individual buildings and landscapes.

Landmark. A building or structure, such as a bridge, memorial, or public art, and/or landscape that has a special historical, architectural, or cultural significance.

Landscaping (soft and hard). The modification and enhancement of a site through the use of any or all of the following elements: vegetation such as trees, shrubs, hedges, grass, and ground cover (soft landscaping); nonvegetative material such as brick, stone, concrete, tile, wood, or other material (hard landscaping); architectural elements consisting of sculptures and the like.

Land Use Designations. These designations within the official community plan (OCP) determine the type of property use for a particular area. Each OCP designation normally has a number of zones that can be applied through rezoning or may be pre-zoned in the development or update of the OCP.

Legal suite. A self-contained unit in a single dwelling that has a separate entrance and parking in the back lane or otherwise accepted by the municipality.

Mixed-use development. The development of land, a building, or a structure with two or more different uses in a compact form, such as residential, office, and retail.

Mode. A method of travel. Examples include walking, cycling, transit, and vehicular.

Mass/massing. The arrangement of the bulk of a building on a site and its visual impact in relation to adjacent buildings.

Multi-dwelling (family) residential. These land use areas are intended to serve the community by providing intensification of residential to increase populations that support amenities and transportation modes. Multi-dwelling areas shall be sensitively integrated and designed. Where policy directs, multi-dwelling residential may be designed in conjunction with other uses, such as commercial.

Neighbourhood. An area that is primarily residential and/or primarily residential or mixed use. Each neighborhood is planned to be primarily residential with considerations for supporting land uses, movement systems, public realm and design, and amenities that would achieve complete and integrated neighborhoods.

Net community gain. The community or neighborhood is better off after development than before development. This difference should be measured by the increase in community services, safety, traffic, noise, real estate values, and other values that can determine the extent of the improvements to the quality of life.

Net Operating Income (NOI). Gross income minus operating costs.

Official Community Plan. The Official Community Plan (OCP) is an overall plan that directs land use and growth over a 20 to 30-year period enabled through the Provincial government's Local Government Act (LGA) in British Columbia. It contains land use designations, objectives, policies and development guidelines that direct growth.

Open space. An area or place that is open and accessible to all citizens, regardless of gender, race, ethnicity, age, or socioeconomic level. Also refers to the public realm (streets, sidewalks, etc.), parks, urban plazas, and so on.

Pedestrian-oriented or pedestrian-friendly. An environment designed to make movement (on foot or by wheelchair) attractive and comfortable for various ages and abilities (i.e., visually and hearing-impaired, mobility-impaired, developmentally challenged, situationally impaired). Considerations include separation of pedestrian and vehicular circulation, building scale and street walls, street furniture, clear directional and informational signage, safety, visibility, shade, lighting, surface materials, trees, sidewalk width, prevailing wind direction (canopies), intersection treatment, curb cuts, ramps, and landscaping.

Parking courts. A variation of a parking lot that is divided into smaller units, well landscaped, and designed to be pedestrian-friendly with walkways, sitting areas, lighting, and shelter.

Pedestrian scale/human scale. The scale (height or proportions) and comfort level that the street level and lower stories of a building provide for the pedestrian as they walk alongside the building(s).

Promenade. A formally designed pedestrian-priority walkway that is normally wider - 4 to 6 metres (13-20 feet) that includes urban features such as benches, garbage receptacles, pedestrian-scale lighting, etc. and could, if wide enough, include separate pedestrian and bicycle lanes.

Public realm. The area of space in the urban environment that is around the built form accessible to the public. The public realm consists of three different domains: public domain (all publicly owned streets, sidewalks, rights-of-way, parks, and other publicly accessible open spaces, and public and civic buildings and facilities); semiprivate domain (the space between a building facade and a public sidewalk, as well as any private spaces that may be accessible to the public, such as enclosed atriums or gallerias, etc.; semiprivate space ties together the public realm connections—streets, sidewalks, etc.—and built form in a comprehensive and connected public realm); and private domain (private space or buildings that are visually incorporated into the public realm and allow(s) for limited access to the public).

Quality. Character with respect to fineness or grade of excellence.

Redevelopment. Rebuilding of an urban residential, commercial, or other land use area that is in decline or in need of a new vision and policy direction.

Rezoning. The process of changing the existing land use and density on a specific property to another zone. The rezoning process requires public notifications of nearby property owners, a Public Hearing, and approval by City Council.

Riparian Areas. These areas are vegetated areas adjoining a water course that helps to maintain water quality, drainage, and fish habitat.

Setback. An area measured as a distance from a public right-of-way or private lot line, restricting building development in this area.

Shall. Where "shall" is used in a policy, the policy is considered mandatory. However, where actual quantities or numerical standards are contained within a mandatory policy (for example, density policies), the quantities and standards may be deviated from provided that the deviation is necessary to address unique circumstances that will otherwise render compliance impractical or impossible, and the intent of the policy is still achieved.

Should. Where "should" is used in a policy, the intent is that the policy is to be complied with. However, the policy may be deviated from in a specific situation where the deviation is necessary to address unique circumstances that will otherwise render compliance impractical or impossible or to allow an acceptable alternative means to achieve the intent of the policy.

Sidewalk. Walkway principally used for pedestrians and located to the side of a thoroughfare within a road right-of-way.

Single-dwelling residential. Primarily single-dwelling areas. These areas are intended to serve the traditional single-family dwelling needs of the community and city while providing an opportunity for sensitively integrated infill development. It is the intent of these areas to support intensification for the purposes of enhancing the single-dwelling areas while not impacting the quality of a primarily single-dwelling residential area.

Smart Growth. Land use, development practices, and the efficient use of tax dollars to enhance the quality of life, preserve the natural environment, save money over time by limiting costly urban sprawl, and create more livable and vibrant neighborhoods.

Streetscape. All the elements that make up the physical environment of a street and define its character, including paving, trees, lighting, building type and style, setbacks, pedestrian amenities, and street furniture.

Subdivision. Subdivision is the process of changing the legal size or shape of a piece of land called a Lot. Subdivision includes both dividing a Lot into two or more smaller parcels or consolidating a number of smaller lots into a large lot.

Suburban retrofit. An emerging trend in urban design that redevelops existing suburban development that is aging, can infill additional density, and incorporate various other land uses.

Sustainable development. Land development that aims to meet human needs while conserving the environment so that these needs can be met not only in the present but also in the future. The three areas of sustainable development are environmental sustainability, economic sustainability, and social sustainability, together representing a more holistic approach.

Transfer of Development Credits (TDC). A tool to retain valued land in its current state that enables the permitted density (units per acre/ha) of the entire parcel to be transferred to a smaller portion to conserve farmland, natural features, and wildlife habitat. Called Transfer of Development Rights (TDR) in Canada.

Transit. All components of providing transit to residents, workers, and tourists (i.e., type of transit, routes, schedules, etc.).

Transit oriented development (TOD). A classification of higher density mixed used development that is located within walking distance of high-volume rapid transit stops.

Yard. That portion of a site that is not covered by a building.

Zone. An area of the city designated for particular uses contained in the Zoning Bylaw. For example, C-4 is the primary zone in an area that has an emphasis on commercial uses. It specifies the permitted and discretionary uses, density, yards, and associated setbacks, and building coverage.

Zoning Bylaw. It regulates the present use of land. Zoning is a tool to implement the City's policies and land use designations within the official community plan. The zoning bylaw establishes procedures to process and decide upon land use amendment and development applications and divides the city into land use districts or zones. It sets out the rules that affect how each piece of land in the city may be used and developed. It also includes the actual zoning maps. The zoning bylaw specifies land use, setbacks, coverage, density, and discretionary uses for each zoned area.

ABOUT THE AUTHOR

Michael is a teacher, trainer, facilitator, and professional community builder. He developed and facilitates the Urban Development Institute's FortisBC School of Development and has been part of the program for the past 20 years. Michael worked for the City of Vancouver for nearly 10 years and has been in the development and finance industries for 30 years. He is currently working on large developments in the Lower Mainland of British Columbia, Vancouver Island, Edmonton, and Calgary. He helps lead planning, design, and development teams to create outstanding communities that are unique, valuable, and resilient.

Michael works and teaches around the world, but focuses his practice in western Canada. He is president of MVH Urban Planning & Design Inc., a global consulting firm that has received numerous local, national, and international awards for innovative development, planning, and design work, including the 2019 Canadian Institute of Planners Award of Excellence for the Cowichan Bay Vitalization Strategy. The firm has practiced urban design and development planning in Canada, the United States, Russia, China, and Mexico.

Michael is also adjunct professor at Simon Fraser University and Vancouver Island University. He has taught across Canada in Vancouver, Calgary, Edmonton, and Ottawa, at the University of British Columbia, Queens University (Ontario), and at the University of Colorado.

He can be reached at vhausen@telus.net, or view his website at www.mvhinc.com.

OTHER PUBLICATIONS BY THE AUTHOR

Other publications available by the author in this series include the following:

Small Is Big: Making the Next Great Small and Mid-Size Downtowns. Vancouver Island University Press, Nanaimo, 2018. (for purchase through VIU Bookstore) or 2019 edition through Amazon.com or Tellwell.com.

Dynamic Urban Design: A Handbook for Creating Sustainable Communities Worldwide. iUniverse, Bloomington, Indiana, 2013. (for bulk purchase through iUniverse or singularly through Amazon.com).

Eco-Plan: Community Ecological Planning and Sustainable Design. Simon Fraser University, Vancouver, 2011.

Urban Design and Planning Graphics Resource Book: Effective Visual Communications for Informed Decision-Making. Simon Fraser University, Vancouver, 2011.

100 Timeless Urban Design Principles. Simon Fraser University, Vancouver, 2008.

Real Estate Economics in Urban Design: The Role of Civic Economics in Place-Making. Simon Fraser University, Vancouver, 2004.

Leading Edges: Alternative Development Standards in British Columbia Municipalities. Real Estate Foundation of British Columbia, Vancouver, 2002.

These publications are available through Amazon, iUniverse, or Vancouver Island University as noted or:

Michael A. von Hausen FCIP, RPP, CSLA, MLAUD, LEED®AP
President, MVH Urban Planning & Design Inc.
Telephone: (604) 536-3990; Fax: (604) 536-3995
E-mail: vhausen@telus.net / Website: www.mvhinc.com

CPSIA information can be obtained
at www.ICGtesting.com
Printed in the USA
BVHW011421100422
633499BV00003B/9